I0092749

WALDEN-ish

A WOMAN'S ADAPTATION OF
HENRY DAVID THOREAU'S "WALDEN"

HENRY DAVID THOREAU
& KRIMSEY LILLETH

Walden-ish
Henry David Thoreau
Krimsey Lilleth

Book design by Emily Ruf
Letter to Thoreau by Krimsey Lilleth (using excerpts
from letter to Thoreau by William Ellery Channing)
Photograph on Dedication page by Moni Bieser

Originally written by Henry D. Thoreau in 1854.
Adapted in 2024 by Krimsey Lilleth.

Published by DabbleRouser

Second U.S. Edition, 2024

Print ISBN: 979-8-9889485-4-4
Ebook ISBN: 979-8-9889485-1-3

Printed in the U.S.A.

Dedicated to Ken Kifer.
Walden scholar, writer, bicyclist, teacher.
Killed by a drunk driver while bicycling
near his home near Scottsboro, Alabama.

"I fully believe that people are designed to be a part of Nature and that our turning away has created major problems for us.... The situation, although bad, is far from hopeless. Nonetheless, we cannot afford to ignore our own personal contributions to the problem and wait for politicians to find the bravery to force us to do what we will not do ourselves. It is up to us to begin making changes in our lives. Changes in our diet, our transportation, our personal economy, and our lifestyle can not only contribute our bit towards solving world problems but they can also enrich our lives."

—Ken Kifer

"I wish to be translated to the future, and look at my work as if it were a structure on the plain, to observe what portions have crumbled under the influence of the elements."

—Henry David Thoreau
Jan. 1, 1852 (journal entry)

CONTENTS

PREFACE

W*alden-ish* is an adaptation of Henry David Thoreau's 1854 treasured book, *Walden; or Life in the Woods*. His original version is one of America's most celebrated books. And like any great book, it's more than a book—it's a symbol of a different way of engaging with the world. To me, it's almost a spiritual text, one that profoundly changed how I think about my place in this world and how I move throughout my day-to-day life.

Though *Walden* was a literary masterpiece—one cited by Gandhi, MLK Jr, and Tolstoy—I was lucky enough to avoid being assigned the book to read in high school. As I worked through it at thirty-two years old, I wondered why anyone would think that a teenager would get much out of it. *Walden* was a book meant to be read carefully, once one has found themselves at a place in life where things don't really make much sense anymore. When you take a moment to breathe, look around, and wonder, "What is everyone actually doing?" That moment can only come once you've had a chance to get caught up in life, notice what's happening, and then feel confused about what you're even doing on Earth. Often, this chain of events is prompted by a big personal "failure," loss, or disappointment of some kind. It can happen at any age, but doesn't happen before prom, for most.

I chose *Walden* off a bookstore shelf in 2020 because I thought it would be an adventure story about a guy in the woods, roughing it in the wild against all odds. It was hilariously the opposite of that. Instead, Thoreau spent most of his days swimming in Walden Pond, listening to the birds, smelling flowers, and pondering life's oddities. He visited town regularly, sometimes to eat with friends, and sometimes to drop off his laundry at his mom's. I chuckled to myself frequently while reading–sometimes at Thoreau's quirky thoughts, and more often because of the weird synchronicities that made me put the book down, look around, and wonder if I was being filmed. This book was published in 1854, but it may as well have been yesterday. Our biggest human struggles have always been consistent. We've been wrestling with the same existential questions for all of recorded history, and likely longer.

Thoreau's take on things reset my compass. His words were the ones I needed to hear most when I felt lost in the hum of society's chaos, wondering what really mattered to me. So many others were going through the same things in 2020. But when I brought the book up to friends, most replied with some variation of "*Walden*?...oh yeah, I think I read that in high school. About a guy living in the woods?" There was no chance they'd be picking that book up again. Their teen interpretation of it had seared a permanent "STUPID/BORING" stamp on it forever. They'd been exposed too young.

However profound the takeaways, getting through the book was still a struggle for me. I had to work for those nuggets. Beyond Thoreau's complicated syntax and jumbled (yet admittedly poetic) sentence structures, he was also using the standard language of the times, which was over-the-top masculine and patriarchal. He only spoke of "townsmen," "mankind," and "brothers." Innocent enough, sure, but still a jagged reminder that the book wasn't written for me. I would change that with my edits, of course. As I dug deeper into Thoreau's life and writings to strengthen my knowledge of his viewpoints and style, I found things in his journal that...weren't very nice. He had a clear distaste for women's society—and thus logically following—most women. Though he loved and respected a few special women (mostly family members and the wives of close friends), he generally poked fun at women's intelligence, morals, and motives.

> "She can entertain a large thought with hospitality, and is not prevented by any intellectuality in it, as women commonly are. In short, she is a genius, as a woman seldom is..." (November 13, 1851, journal entry)

Oh, yikes. Though his journal was more explicit with opinions, his true thoughts still crept through the pages of *Walden*:

> "...But before the owner gave me a deed of [the house], his wife—every man has such a wife—changed her mind and wished to keep it."

> "The society of young women is the most unprofitable I have ever tried. They are so light and flighty that you can never be sure whether they are there or not there."

His pokey comments felt like jabs to the heart, as if I was the friend who didn't get invited to the birthday party because I wasn't cool or smart enough. Or maybe because I was missing a penis. I felt betrayed by Thoreau, an otherwise kind and thoughtful man, who somehow couldn't extend his compassion to the women in his society. Would he have considered me worthy of conversation, or capable of understanding his writings? Why did he have such a hard time offering his townswomen grace and understanding, when they were not allowed to be educated, vote, work outside of the home, or even have radical thoughts to themselves? Though Thoreau was typically a fighter for the oppressed (he was a well-known abolitionist, conservationist, and generally compassionate man who even mourned the loss of trees cut down in his village), he wasn't able to apply that same empathetic attitude to the women around him. He was a man of the times, and struggled to separate his townswomen from their conditioning–innocent victims trapped in systems of oppression, doing their best to survive in a world created by men, for men.

But also contained in *Walden*, there were passages that nudged me along. "There is more day to dawn...It is never too late to give up our prejudices." I imagined Thoreau tossing about and mourning from his grave, wishing he'd been able to see what he sees now–removed from the first-person perspective, and perhaps realizing that his own romantic rejections could have played a part in his attitudes toward women. I couldn't help but to forgive him. And now, editing *Walden* wasn't just for me anymore, it was for him, too.

The revision work became increasingly more involved as the project progressed. For three years, this book was my life. I pulled in excerpts from his journal, and added my own words where appropriate. I visited Walden Pond and explored the town of Concord, sitting at Thoreau's grave for advice. I modernized complicated and outdated prose, neutered unnecessarily gendered language, restructured sentences and paragraphs for digestibility, softened some crassness, and edited miscellaneous items to add to the general flow and inclusiveness of the text (get in-depth info about these editing details and philosophies at krimdom.com/waldenishprocess). I hope that my adaptation amplifies the intended messages for you, and makes Thoreau's thoughts a joy to read.

This work was truly a labor of love, and I consider it to be the most important work I've ever done–making a timeless, powerful book accessible to all. Now more than ever, our society can benefit from the messages of natural simplicity, harmony, and beauty found in this classic work of American literature.

As you read this book, I hope you are able to feel the personal nature of the messages within, and know that it is no accident. This book was written for you.

Krimsey

Mood Music:

New York, March 5, 1875

My dear Thorean,

The hand-writing of your letter is so miserable that I am not sure I have made it out. If I have, it seems to me you are the same old sixpence you used to be, rather rusty, but a genuine piece.

I see nothing for you in this earth but that field of Emerson's which I once christened "Briars"; go out upon that, build yourself a hut, and begin the grand process of devouring yourself alive. I see no alternative, no other hope for you. Eat yourself up; you will eat nobody else, nor anything else.

Ever yours, my dear Thorean

ECONOMY, PART I

When I wrote the following pages, or rather the bulk of them, I lived alone in the woods, a mile from any neighbor, in a house which I had built myself on the shore of Walden Pond in Concord, Massachusetts. I earned my living by the labor of my hands only. I lived there for two years and two months, visiting town at times. At present, I am a sojourner in civilized life again.

I would not obtrude my affairs so much upon my readers if very particular inquiries had not been made by my townspeople concerning my mode of life, which some would call impertinent, though they do not appear to me at all impertinent. Instead, considering the current state of things in the world, this mode feels very natural and utterly pertinent to me.

Some have asked what I got to eat; if I did not feel lonesome; if I was not afraid; and the like. Others have been curious to learn what portion of my income I devoted to charitable purposes; and some, who have large families, wonder how many poor children I maintained. I will therefore ask those of my readers who feel no particular interest in me to pardon me if I undertake to answer some of these questions in this book.

In most books, the *I*, or first person, is omitted; in this it will be retained. We commonly do not remember that it is, after all, always the first person that is speaking. I would not talk so much about myself if there were anybody else whom I knew as well. Unfortunately, I am confined to this theme by the narrowness of my experience. Moreover, the use of "I" requires every writer to give a simple and sincere account of their own life, and not merely what they have heard of others'.

Perhaps these pages are more appropriately addressed to poor students, but as for the rest of my readers, I hope that they will accept such portions that apply to them. I trust that none will stretch the seams in putting on the coat, for it may do good service to whom it fits.

I have traveled a good deal in Concord, and everywhere—in shops, offices, and fields—the inhabitants have appeared to me to be doing penance in a thousand remarkable ways. I have heard of what some kind choose to do in order to discipline the spirit through punishment, like looking into the face of the sun; or hanging suspended with their heads downward over flames; or dwelling, chained for life, at the foot of a tree; or standing on one leg on the tops of pillars...even these forms of conscious penance are hardly more incredible and astonishing than the scenes which I daily witness. The twelve labours bestowed upon Hercules by Hera were trifling in comparison with those which my neighbors have undertaken; for they were only twelve, and had an end; but I could never see that these townspeople slew or captured any monster or finished any labor. They have no friend to help burn the root of the hydra's head with a hot iron, so as soon as one head is crushed, two spring up.

I see young people, my townspeople, whose misfortune it is to have inherited farms, barns, cattle, and farming tools; for these are more easily acquired than got rid of. Better if they had been born in the open pasture and suckled by a wolf, that they might have seen with clearer eyes what field they were called to labor in. Who made them serfs of the soil? Why should they tend their sixty acres, when one is condemned to eat only their small peck of crop? Why should they begin digging their graves as soon as they are born? How many a poor immortal soul have I met nearly crushed and smothered under the load of farm ownership, creeping down the road of life, pushing before it a barn seventy-five feet by forty, its Augean stables never cleansed, and one hundred acres of land, tillage, mowing, pasture, and wood-lot! The portionless, who struggle with no such unnecessary inherited encumbrances, find it labor enough to cultivate a few cubic feet of earth for their own use. Do we labor excessively under mistake?

It is said that Deucalion and Pyrrha survived the great flood, and then in their grief, created a new race of humans by throwing stones over their heads behind them. We possess such a propensity for blind obedience to a blundering oracle. The better part of the human is soon plowed into the soil for compost. By a seeming fate, commonly called necessity, they are employed, as it says in an old book, laying up tangible treasures which moth and rust will corrupt, and thieves break through and steal. It is a fool's life, as often found at the end of it, if not before. What will you gain, if you own the whole world but destroy yourself?

Most people, even in this comparatively free country, through mere ignorance and mistake, are so occupied with the factitious cares and superfluously coarse labors of life that its finer fruits cannot be plucked by them. Their fingers, from excessive toil, are too clumsy and tremble too much for that. The laborer has no leisure for true integrity day by day; their labor would be depreciated in the market. They have only time to be machines. Rats might well be outdone by the impossible race we've created for ourselves. How can one remember well their ignorance—which their growth requires—who has so often to use their knowledge? We should feed and clothe each other gratuitously, and look up from the quest more than periodically to avoid breeding alienation and violence, on account of nothing of much importance. The finest qualities of our nature, like the bloom on fruits, can be preserved only by the most delicate handling. Yet we do not treat ourselves, nor one another, thus tenderly.

Some of you, we all know, are poor. You find it hard to live, and are sometimes, as it were, gasping for breath. I have no doubt that some of you who read this book are unable to pay for all the dinners which you have already eaten, or for the coats and shoes which are fast wearing or are already worn out, and you have come to this page to spend borrowed or stolen time, robbing your creditors of an hour. It is very evident what unfair and cruel lives many of you live, for my sight has been sharpened by experience; always on the limits, trying to get into business and trying to get out of debt, a very ancient slough; always promising to pay, promising to pay, tomorrow, and dying today, insolvent; seeking to gain favor; lying, flattering, voting, contracting yourselves into a nutshell of civility or dilating into an atmosphere of thin and vaporous generosity, that you may persuade your neighbor to let you make their shoes, or their hat, or their coat, or their carriage, or import their groceries for them; making yourselves sick, that you may lay up something against a sick day, something tangibly monetary to be tucked away in an old chest, or in a stocking behind the plastering, or, more safely, in the brick bank; no matter where, no matter how much or how little.

Look at the herd driver on the highway, wending to market by day or night; does any divinity stir within them? Their highest duty is to fodder and water their horses! See how they cower and sneak, how vaguely all the day they fear, not being immortal nor divine, but the prisoner of their own opinion of themselves, a fame won by their own deeds. Public opinion is a weak tyrant compared with our own private opinion. What a person thinks of themselves determines, or rather indicates, their fate. Think, also, of the workers weaving toilet cushions against the last day! As if you could kill time without injuring eternity.

The mass of people lead lives of quiet desperation. A silent, resigned mourning fuels a hidden rage, one that always erupts as violence against ourselves and others, whether subtle and slow-leaking, or abrupt and loud. What a pity, the lives lost to this phenomenon. From the desperate city you go into the desperate country, and have to console yourself with the bravery of minks and muskrats. An unconscious despair is concealed even under what are called the games and amusements of humankind. There is no play in them, for this comes only after work, and their durations are bounded. It is a desperate reach for some form of fleeting satisfaction before the next work day begins. But it is a characteristic of wisdom not to do desperate things.

It appears as if most people have deliberately chosen the common mode of living because they preferred it to any other. Yet truly, it seems that they think there is no choice left. But alert and healthy natures remember that the sun rises clear. It is never too late to give up our prejudices. No way of thinking or doing, however ancient, can be trusted without proof. What everybody echoes or in silence passes by as true to-day may turn out to be falsehood to-morrow, mere smoke of opinion, which some had trusted for a cloud that would sprinkle fertilizing rain on their dying fields. Ancient people did not know enough once, perchance, to fetch fresh fuel to keep the fire a-going; new people put a little dry wood under a pot, and are whirled round the globe with the speed of winds.

Age is no better qualified for an instructor as youth, for it has not profited so much as it has lost. One may almost doubt if the wisest person has learned any thing of absolute value by living, unless they do so with wide eyes and rambunctious spirit, and understand that these lessons cannot apply to others. Practically, the majority of the elderly have no important advice to give the young, for the young are freest of all; the world is boundless. Best let them be, and learn for themselves; they have much to teach us. Our authorities do not like to contemplate their miserable past failures and shortcomings; it is much easier to control and scold. Many have some faith left which promises to contradict that experience, and that they are only less young than they once were.

"There is still time!" We chant until our last breath. Here is my life, an experiment to a great extent so far untried by me; but it does not avail me that they have tried it, and not enjoyed it fully. If I have any experience which I think valuable, I am sure to reflect that this my Mentors said nothing about; it is only mine.

Old ideas for the dead, and new ideas for the living. One farmer says to me, "You cannot live on vegetable food solely, for it furnishes nothing to make bones with," talking while they walk behind their oxen, which, with their vegetable-made bones, jerk them and their lumbering plough along in spite of every obstacle.

The whole ground of human life seems to have been prescribed by its predecessors, both the heights and the valleys, and all things to care for and about. According to Evelyn, "the wise Solomon prescribed ordinances for the very spacing of trees; and the Roman officials have decided how often you may go into your neighbor's land to gather the acorns which fall on it without trespass, and what share belongs to that neighbor." Hippocrates has even left directions how we should cut our nails; that is, even with the ends of the fingers, neither shorter nor longer. Undoubtedly the very tedium and ennui which presume to have exhausted the variety and the joys of life are as old as the first humans. But humankind's capacities have never been measured; nor are we to judge what one can do by any precedents, for so little has been tried. Whatever have been thy failures hitherto, "be not afflicted, my child, for who shall assign to thee what thou hast left undone?"

It is easy to get trapped inside one's mind, but the same sun which ripens my beans likely illuminates at once a system of earths like ours. If I had remembered this, it would have prevented some mistakes. What distant and different beings in the various mansions of the universe are contemplating the same thought at the same moment! Or what creatures within our very habitats, crawling between blades of grass and flying above our roofs? Nature and human life are as various as the number of stars twinkling in the night sky. Who shall say what prospect life offers to another? Could a greater miracle take place than for us to look through each other's eyes for an instant? There, we find all the ages of the world in an hour; ay, in all the worlds of all the ages. History, Poetry, Mythology! I know of no detailed reading of another's experience so startling and informing as experiencing the world through another's eyes.

The greater part of what my neighbors call good I believe in my soul to be bad, and if I repent of anything, it is very likely to be my good behavior. What demon possessed me that I behaved so well for so long? You may say the wisest thing you can, old one—you who have lived seventy years, not without notable honor of a kind—but I hear an irresistible voice which invites me away from all that. "Society everywhere is in conspiracy against the humanity of every one of its members," a quote from Emerson. One generation abandons the enterprises of another like stranded vessels. It is our duty to re-assimilate, always in a freer way than the last, if we should be of stable, noble mind.

I think that we may safely trust the unknown a good deal more than we do. Nature is as well adapted to our weakness as to our strength. The incessant anxiety and strain of some is a well-nigh incurable form of disease. We are made to exaggerate the importance of what work we do; and yet how much is not done by us! Or, what if we had been taken sick?

How vigilant we are! Determined not to live by faith if we can avoid it; all the day long on the alert, and only at night we unwillingly say our prayers and commit ourselves to uncertainties of the subconscious. So thoroughly and sincerely we are compelled to hold our lived lives so sacred, and deny the possibility of change. This is the only way, we say; but there are as many ways as there can be drawn radii from one center. All change is a miracle to contemplate; but it is a miracle which is taking place every instant. Confucius said, "To know that we know what we know, and that we do not know what we do not know, that is true knowledge." When one has reduced a fact of the imagination to be a fact to their knowledge, they have joined the masses in living this way, believing that they understand.

Let us consider for a moment what most of the trouble and anxiety which I have referred to is about, and how much it is necessary that we be troubled about it. It would be some advantage to live a primitive and frontier life, though in the midst of an "advanced" civilization, if only to learn what are the gross necessaries of life and what methods have been taken to obtain them; or even to look over the old day-books of the merchants, to see what it was that people most commonly bought at the stores, what they stored, that is, what are the grossest groceries. For the improvements of ages have had but little influence on the essential laws of humankind's existence; as our skeletons, probably, are not to be distinguished much from those of our ancestors. At times, it may even be that the improvements presented to us are merely distractions, to convert us to profits. Methinks it is wise and prudent to sift carefully through prescribed "improvements" in search of what is truly beautiful, necessary, and pure. A wise and skeptical lens focuses away from the rabbit hole of shallow distraction, which knows no end and picks away at time otherwise ripe for tangible joy and discovery.

All that one obtains by their own exertions has become so important to our accepted mode of human life that few, if any, ever attempt to do without it. To many creatures there is but one necessary of life, Food. To the bison of the prairie, it is a few inches of palatable grass, with water to drink; unless she seeks the shelter of the Forest or the Mountain's shadow. None of the brute creation requires more than Food and Shelter. Are we not brute at heart? Perhaps, once we were. The necessaries of life for a human in this climate may, accurately enough, be distributed under the several heads of Food, Shelter, Clothing, and Fuel; for not 'til we have secured these are we prepared to entertain the true problems of life with freedom and a prospect of success. Humankind has invented, not only houses, but clothes and cooked food; and possibly from the accidental discovery of the warmth of fire, and the consequent use of it, at first a luxury, arose the present necessity to sit by it. We observe cats and dogs acquiring the same second nature. By proper Shelter and Clothing we legitimately retain our own internal heat in environments otherwise unsuitable to our survival; but with an excess of these, or of Fuel, that is, with an external heat greater than our own internal, may not cookery properly be said to begin?

Darwin, the naturalist, says of the inhabitants of Tierra del Fuego, that while his own party, who were well clothed and sitting close to a fire, were far from too warm, the naked indigenous, who were farther off, were observed, to his great surprise, "to be streaming with perspiration at undergoing such a roasting." So, we are told, the New Hollander goes naked with impunity, while the European shivers in their clothes. Is it impossible to combine the hardiness of these indigenous people with the so-called intellectualness of the so-called civilized?

The grand necessity, then, for our bodies, is to keep warm, to keep the vital heat in us. What pains we accordingly take, not only with our Food, and Clothing, and Shelter, but with our beds, which are our additional night-clothes, taking from the nests and breasts of birds to prepare this shelter within a shelter, as the mole has its bed of grass and leaves at the end of its burrow. The summer, in some climates, makes it possible to have a sort of Elysian life.

> "To the eutopian Elysian plains of the after-life...where life is easiest... No snow is there, nor heavy storm, nor ever rain, but ever does Ocean send up blasts of the shrill-blowing West Wind that they may give cooling..." —Homer

Fuel, except to cook Food, is then unnecessary; the sun is the fire, and many of the fruits are sufficiently ripened by its flames, while Food generally is more various, and more easily obtained, and Clothing and Sh   elter are wholly or half unnecessary. At the present day, and in this country, as I find by my own experience, a few implements, a knife, an axe, a spade, a wheelbarrow, etc., and for the studious, lamplight, stationery, and access to a few books, rank next to necessaries, and can all be obtained at a trifling cost. Yet some, maybe not so wisely, go to the other side of the globe, to barbarous and unhealthy regions, and devote themselves to trade for ten or twenty years, in order that they may simply return to live—that is, to keep always comfortably warm—and die in New England at last. The luxuriously rich are not simply kept comfortably warm, but unnaturally hot; they are cooked, of course à la mode. The pursuit of comfort is a never- ending buying game, all merchandisers perpetually devising new ways for you to be yet even more comfortable, and though it was never considered before, upon hearing of the newest cushions or stoves, all of society now requires the latest and greatest model to survive.

Most of the luxuries, and many of the so-called comforts of life, are not only not indispensable, but positive hindrances to the elevation of humankind. With respect to luxuries and comforts, the wisest have always lived a more simple and meagre life than the poor. The ancient philosophers, Chinese, Hindoo, Persian, and Greek, were a class than which none has been poorer in outward riches, none so rich in inward. We know not much about them; it is remarkable that we know so much of them as we do. The same is true of the more modern reformers and benefactors of their race. None can be an impartial or wise observer of human life from the vantage ground of what we should call voluntary poverty. There are nowadays professors of philosophy, but not philosophers. Yet it is admirable to profess because it was once admirable to live. To be a philosopher is not merely to have subtle thoughts, nor even to found a school, but so to love wisdom as to live according to its dictates, a life of simplicity, independence, magnanimity, and trust. It is to solve some of the problems of life, not only theoretically, but practically. The success of great scholars and thinkers is commonly a courtier- like success, not royal, not observable. They live merely by conformity, practically as their parents did, and are in no sense the founders of a noble race of humans. Why do people degenerate ever? What makes families disband? What is the nature of the luxury which enervates and destroys nations? Are we sure that there is none of it in our own lives? The philosopher is in advance of their age even in the outward form of their life. They are not fed, sheltered, clothed, and warmed like their contemporaries.

When one is warmed by the several modes which I have described, what do they want next? Surely not more warmth of the same kind, but more and richer food, larger and more splendid houses, finer and more abundant clothing, more numerous incessant and hotter fires, and the like. When they have obtained those things which are necessary to life, there is another alternative than to obtain the superfluities; and that is, to adventure in life now. The soil, it appears, is suited to the seed, for it has sent its radicle downward, and it may now send its shoot upward also with confidence. Why has humankind rooted itself thus firmly in the earth, if not that they may rise in the same proportion into the heavens above? For the nobler plants are valued for the fruit they bear at last in the air and light, away from the ground.

I do not mean to prescribe rules to strong and valiant natures, who will mind their own affairs whether in heaven or hell, and perchance build more magnificently and spend more lavishly than the richest, without ever impoverishing themselves—if, indeed, there are any such, as has been dreamed. Nor do I prescribe rules to those who find their encouragement and inspiration in precisely the present condition of things and cherish it with the fondness and enthusiasm of lovers. To some extent, I reckon myself in this number. I do not speak to those who are well employed, in whatever circumstances, and only they know whether they are well employed or not... But mainly I speak to the mass of people who are discontented, and idly complaining of the hardness of their lot or of the times, when they might improve them. There are some who complain most energetically and inconsolably of any, because they are, as they say, doing their duty. I also have in my mind the seemingly wealthy, but most terribly impoverished class of all, who have accumulated valuable rubbish, but know not how to use it, or get rid of it, and thus have forged their own golden or silver shackles.

ECONOMY, PART II

If I should tell how I desired to spend my life in years past, it would probably surprise those of my readers who are somewhat acquainted with its actual history. I will only hint at some of the enterprises which I have cherished.

In any weather, at any hour of the day or night, I have been anxious to improve the nick of time, and notch it on my stick too; to stand on the meeting of two eternities, the past and future, which is precisely the present moment; to toe that line. You will pardon some obscurities, for there are more secrets in my trade than in most, and yet not voluntarily kept, but inseparable from its very nature. I would gladly tell all that I know about it, and never paint "No Admittance" on my gate.

How many mornings, summer and winter, before yet any neighbor was stirring about their business, have I been about mine! No doubt, many of my townspeople have met me returning from this enterprise, farmers starting for Boston in the twilight, or woodchoppers going to their work. It is true, I never assisted the sun materially in her rising, but, doubt not, it was of most importance only to be present at it. How could a naturalist miss the morning roll call?

So many autumn, ay, and winter days, spent outside the town, trying to hear what was in the wind, to hear and carry it expressly! I fully sunk all my capital in it, and lost my own breath into the bargain, running in the face of it. At other times watching from the observatory of some cliff or tree, to telegraph any new arrival; or waiting at evening on the hill-tops for the sky to fall, that I might catch something valuable, though I never caught much.

For a long time I was an unpaid, solo reporter to a hand-written journal, of no very wide circulation, whose editor has never yet seen fit to print the bulk of my contributions. In it, I described the weather daily, in sometimes only a few words, as it affects our feelings. That which was so important at the time cannot be unimportant to remember.

For many years I was a self-appointed inspector of snowstorms and rainstorms, and did my duty faithfully. I was a surveyor—if not of highways, then of forest paths and all across-lot routes—keeping rights-of-way open, and keeping ravines bridged and passable at all seasons, where the public heel had testified to their utility.

I have looked after the wild stock of the town, which give a faithful herdsperson a good deal of trouble by leaping fences; and I have had an eye to the unfrequented nooks and corners of the farm; though I did not always know whether Jonas or Mary worked in a particular field to-day; that was none of my business. I have watered the red huckleberry, the sand cherry and the nettle tree, the red pine and the black ash, the white grape and the yellow violet, which might have withered in dry seasons.

In short, I went on thus for a long time, I may say it without boasting, faithfully minding my business, 'til it became more and more evident that my towns-people would not after all admit me into the list of town officers, nor make my place a sinecure with a moderate allowance. My accounts, which I can swear to have kept faithfully, have never been audited, but have also not been accepted by any government or businesses, and even less paid and settled. However, I have not set my heart on that.

Not long since, a strolling crafter went to sell baskets at the house of a well-known lawyer in my neighborhood. "Do you wish to buy any baskets?" they asked. "No, we do not want any," was the reply. "What!" exclaimed the artist as they went out the gate, "do you mean to starve us?" Having seen their neighbors so well off—that the lawyer had only to weave arguments, and by some magic, wealth and standing followed—they had said to themselves "I will go into business; I will weave baskets; it is a thing which I can do." Thinking that when they had made the baskets, they would have done their part, and then it would be the wealthy person's duty to buy them. They had not discovered that it was necessary for them to make it worth the other's while to buy them, or at least make them think that it was so, or to make something else which it would be worth their while to buy. I too had woven a kind of basket of a delicate texture, but I had not made it worth any one's while to buy them. Yet in my case, I did not think it worth my while to weave them, and instead of studying how to make it worth others' while to buy my baskets, I studied rather how to avoid the necessity of selling them. The life which people praise and regard as successful is but one kind. Why should we exaggerate any one kind at the expense of the others?

Finding that my fellow-citizens were not likely to offer me any room in the courthouse or position of artist's regard, I turned my face more exclusively than ever to the woods, where I was better known. I was determined to go into business at once, and not wait to acquire the usual capital, using such slender means as I had already got. My purpose in going to Walden Pond was not to live cheaply nor to live dearly there, but to transact some private business with the fewest obstacles; to learn common sense and business sense, and not be drowned in the shallow and ever-expanding floodplains of typical enterprise.

I have always endeavored to acquire strict business habits; they are indispensable. If your trade is with the eastern hemisphere, then some small counting house on the coast, in some Salem harbor, will be fixture enough. You will export such articles as the country affords, purely native products, much ice and pine timber and a little granite, always in native ships. These will be good ventures. To oversee all the details yourself in person; to be at once pilot and captain, and owner and underwriter; to buy and sell and keep the accounts; to read every letter received, and write or read every letter sent; to superintend the discharge of imports night and day; to be upon many parts of the coast almost at the same time; to be your own telegraph, unweariedly sweeping the horizon; to keep up a steady dispatch of commodities, for the supply of such a distant and exorbitant market; to keep yourself informed of the state of the markets, prospects of war and peace everywhere, and anticipate the tendencies of trade and civilization,—taking advantage of the results of all exploring expeditions, using new passages and all improvements in navigation;—charts to be studied, the position of reefs and new lights and buoys to be ascertained, and ever, and ever, the logarithmic tables to be corrected, for by the error of some calculator the vessel often splits upon a rock that should have reached a friendly pier. There is the untold fate of La Perouse, whose wrecked ships still sleep silently, somewhere; there is universal science to be kept pace with, studying the lives of all great discoverers and navigators, great adventurers and merchants, from the explorer Hanno and the ancient thalassocratic Phœnicians, down to our day; an account of stock to be taken from time to time, to know how you stand. It is a labor to task the faculties of a person, such problems of profit and loss, of interest, of allowances and deductions, and gauging of all kinds in it, as it demands a universal knowledge. The poet's practice is no different.

I have thought that Walden Pond would be a good place for my business, and not solely on account of the nearby railroad and the opportunity for ice trade; it also offers advantages which it may not be good policy to divulge; it is a good port and a good foundation for this private business. No marshes to be filled; though you must everywhere build on piles of your own driving.

As this business was to be entered into without the usual capital, it may not be easy to conjecture where those means, that will still be indispensable to every such undertaking, were to be obtained. As for clothing, to come at once to the practical part of the question, perhaps we are led more often by the love of novelty in procuring it, and a regard for the opinions of others, than by a true utility. Let one who has work to do recollect that the object of clothing is, first, to retain the vital heat, and secondly, in this state of society, to cover nakedness, and they may judge how much of any necessary or important work may be accomplished without adding to their wardrobe. Royals and celebrities who wear an article but once, though made by some tailor or dressmaker to their majesties, cannot know the comfort of wearing an article that truly fits. They are no better than wooden horses to hang the clean clothes on. Every day our garments become more assimilated to ourselves, receiving the impress of the wearer's character, until we hesitate to lay them aside, without solemnity. No one ever stood the lower in my estimation for having a patch in their clothes; yet I am sure that there is greater anxiety, commonly, to have fashionable, or at least clean and unpatched clothes, than to have a sound conscience. I sometimes try my acquaintances by such tests as this—who could wear a patch, or two extra seams only, over the knee? Most behave as if they believed that their prospects for life would be ruined if they should do it. It would be easier for them to hobble to town with a broken leg than with a broken pantaloon. Often if an accident happens to a person's legs, they can be mended; but if a similar accident happens to the legs of their pantaloons, there is no help for it; for they consider, not what is truly respectable, but what is respected. We know but few people, and a great many coats and breeches. Dress a scarecrow in your best and last suit, you standing shiftlessly shiftless by, who would not soonest salute the scarecrow? I have heard of a dog that barked at every stranger who approached their master's premises with clothes on, but was easily quieted by a naked thief. It is an interesting question how long one would retain their relative rank if they were divested of their clothes. Could you, in such a case, tell surely which ones within a group of people belonged to the most respected class? When the legendary Madam Pfeiffer, in her adventurous travels round the world, from east to west, had got so near home as Asiatic Russia, she says that she felt the necessity of wearing more than a traveling dress when she went to meet the authorities, for she "was now in a civilized country, where people are judged of by their clothes." Even in our democratic New England towns, the accidental possession of wealth and its manifestation in dress and carriage alone, obtain for the possessor almost universal respect. But they harvest a respect so heathen, that the admirers need to have a missionary sent to them. Besides, clothes introduced sewing, a kind of work which you may call endless; the need for novel clothing is eternal, work never done; old garments cast aside in favor of new.

A person who has found something worthwhile to do will not need to get new clothing to do it in; for them, the old will do, that which has lain dusty in the attic for an indeterminate period. Old shoes will serve a hero longer than they have served a royal. Only they who go to soirées and legislative halls must have new shoes and coats, coats to change as often as the person changes in them. But if my jacket and trousers, my hat and shoes, are fit to worship God in, they will do; will they not? Does anyone actually see their old clothes—their old coat—truly worn out, resolved into its primitive elements, so that it was no longer a deed of charity to bestow it on some poor child? So ragged that the child perchance might reject it, and bestow it on some poorer still, or shall we say richer, who could do with less? I say, beware of all enterprises that require new clothes, and not rather a new wearer of clothes. If you have any enterprise before you, try it in your old clothes. All people want something to do, or rather, something to be. Perhaps we should never procure a new suit, however ragged or dirty the old, until we have so conducted, so enterprised or sailed in some way, that we feel like new people in the old, and that to retain it would be unnatural. Our molting season, like that of the fowls, must be a crisis in our lives. The loon retires to solitary ponds to spend it. Thus, also the snake casts its slough, and the caterpillar its wormy coat, by an internal industry and expansion; for clothes are but our outermost cuticle and mortal coil. Otherwise, we shall be found sailing under false colors, and be inevitably dismissed at last by our own opinion, as well as that of humankind.

When it comes to clothing, a sound investment lasts many years, while articles poorly made float away with the spring breeze, so long as the wearer is not persuaded by the critiques of the fashionable. Off to buy a new one! It is desirable that a person be clad so simply that they know where all items can be found in the dark, and that they live in all respects so compactly and preparedly, that, if an enemy take the town, they can, like the old philosopher, walk out the gate empty-handed without anxiety. A few solid garments should do it.

When I ask for a garment of a particular form, as we all must do, my tailor tells me gravely, "They do not make them so now," not emphasizing the "They" at all, as if one did not just quote an authority as powerful and impersonal as the Fates, who assign individual destinies to mortals at birth. I find it difficult to get made what I want, simply because the tailor cannot believe that I mean what I say, that I am so rash. When I hear this oracular sentence, I am for a moment absorbed in thought, emphasizing to myself each word separately that I may come at the meaning of it, that I may find out by what degree of consanguinity "They" are related to me, and what authority "They" may have in an affair which affects me so nearly. Finally, I am inclined to answer the tailor with equal mystery, and without any more emphasis of the "They,"—"It is true, they did not make them so recently, but they do now." Of what use is this measuring of me if the tailor does not measure my character, but only the breadth of my shoulders, as it were a peg to hang the coat on? We worship not any god, nor mythology, but Fashion. Fashion spins and weaves and cuts with full authority. The head monkey in Paris puts on a traveler's cap, and all the monkeys in America do the same. I sometimes despair of getting anything quite simple and honest done in this world by the help of humans. They would have to be passed through a powerful press first, to squeeze their old notions out of them, so that they would not soon get upon their legs again, and then there would be someone in the company with a maggot in their head, hatched from an egg deposited there nobody knows when, for not even fire kills these things, and you would have lost your efforts.

I made myself a pair of clay-colored corduroy pants, but most of my friends are disturbed by my wearing of them. But, I like them, and the minks do not mind them, either.

On the whole, I think that it cannot be maintained that everyday dressing has risen to the dignity of an art. At present, people makeshift to wear what they can get. Like shipwrecked sailors, they put on what they can find on the beach, and at a little distance, whether of space or time, laugh at each other's masquerade. Every generation laughs at the old fashions, but follows religiously the new. We are amused at beholding the costume of Henry VIII., or Queen Elizabeth, as much as if it was that of the king and queen of the petting zoo.

The childish and brute taste for new patterns keeps droves of people shaking and squinting through kaleidoscopes that they may discover the particular figure which this generation requires today, and will forfeit lifeforce for. The manufacturers have learned that this taste is merely whimsical. Of two patterns which differ only by a few threads more or less of a particular color, the one will be sold readily, the other lie on the shelf, though it frequently happens that after the lapse of a season the latter becomes the most fashionable. Comparatively, tattooing is not the hideous and barbaric custom which it has been called. Because the printing is skin-deep and unalterable, it is perhaps the most noble of all fashions: permanent.

I cannot believe that our factory system is the best mode by which people may get clothing. As far as I have heard or observed, the principal object is, not that humankind may be well and honestly clad, or that Nature be revered, or that workers be gainfully employed; but, unquestionably, that corporations may be enriched. Not just with regards to clothing, but to any peddling of a trinket, gadget, whoot-a-ma-who, or snake oil.

But who whips up the eternal need for more things, for more tools, more fuels, more conveniences? It is not the makers—not the evil, monstrous corporations—but the buyers. It is the buyers who clog up the breath of the earth and set rubbish adrift in the sea, for we have nowhere left to stash the evidence of our excessive consumerism. The gluttonous corporations are we.

I see many devil's needles zigzagging along the brook—some green, some blue—both with black and perhaps velvety wings. They are confined to the brook. How lavishly they paint it! How cheap was the paint!

Just after sunrise one morning, I saw my acquaintance, Hayden, walking with his team, slowly dragging a heavy stone behind them, all sweating as they drudged. Honest, peaceful industry; A reproach to all sluggards and idlers. The day went by, and that evening as I passed a rich man's yard, I saw the stone again, lying by a whimsical structure intended to adorn this Lord Timothy Dexter's mansion, and the dignity forthwish departed from Hayden's labor, in my eyes. How much of the industry of the poor, traced to the end, is found thus to be subserving some rich person's foolish enterprise!

As for a Shelter, I will not deny that this is now a necessary of life, though there are instances of others having done without it for long periods in colder countries than this. Samuel Laing, a railway administrator and writer, says that "the Native Laplander in their skin dress, and in a skin bag which they put over their head and shoulders, will sleep night after night on the snow—in a degree of cold which would extinguish the life of one exposed to it in any tailored clothing." He had seen them asleep thus. Yet he adds, "They are not hardier than other people." But, probably, humans did not live long on the earth without discovering the convenience which there is in a house, the domestic comforts, which phrase may have originally signified the satisfactions of the house more than of the family within the house. In our climate, in the summer, a house was formerly almost solely a covering at night. To the Indigenous People, a wigwam was the symbol of a day's march, and a row of them cut or painted on the bark of a tree signified that so many nights they had camped there. Humans were not made so large-limbed and robust so that they may narrow their world, and wall in a space such as fitted them. Humans were at first bare and out of doors as they expanded their reach of the globe; but though this was pleasant enough in serene and warm weather by daylight, the rainy season and the winter, to say nothing of the torrid sun, would perhaps have nipped their race in the bud if they had not made haste to clothe themselves with the shelter of a house. Adam and Eve, according to the fable, wore the house before other clothes. Humankind wanted a home, a place of warmth, or comfort, even before they desired the warmth of the affections.

Every child goes outside and begins the world again, to some extent, and loves to stay outdoors, even in wet and cold. They play house, as well as horse, having an instinct for it. Who does not remember the interest with which their younger self looked at shelving rocks, or any approach to a cave? It was the natural yearning of that portion of our most primitive ancestor which still survived in us. From the cave we have advanced to roofs of palm leaves, of bark and boughs, of linen woven and stretched, of grass and straw, of boards and shingles, of stones and tiles. At last, we know not what it is to live in the open air, and our lives are domestic in more senses than we think. From the hearth to the field is a great distance. Birds do not sing in caves, nor do doves cherish their innocence in dovecots. It would be well perhaps if we were to spend more of our days and nights without any obstruction between us and the celestial bodies, for the poet did not speak so much from under a roof, or the saint dwell there so long, lest they forget the beauty that led them to salvation. She reigns, despite our ignorance of her happenings.

However, if one designs to construct a dwelling house, it behooves them to exercise a little shrewdness, lest after all they find themselves in a workhouse, a labyrinth without a clue, a museum, an almshouse, a prison, or a splendid mausoleum instead. Consider first how slight a shelter is absolutely necessary. I have seen Penobscot Natives in this town living in tents of thin cotton cloth, while the snow was nearly a foot deep around them, and I thought that they would be glad to have it deeper to keep out the wind. Formerly, when contemplating how to get my living honestly, with freedom left for my proper pursuits, it became a question which vexed me more than it does now, for unfortunately I have become somewhat callous. Now, I see a large box by the railroad, six feet long by three wide, in which the laborers lock up their tools at night, and wonder if every person who was hard pushed might get such a one for a dollar, and, having bored a few auger holes in it, to admit the air at least, get into it when it rained and at night, and hook down the lid, and so have freedom in their love, and in their soul be free. This does not appear the worst, nor by any means a despicable alternative to capitalist servitude, at least for some. You could sit up as late as you pleased, and, whenever you got up, go abroad without any landlord or house-lord dogging you for rent. Many a worker is harassed to death to pay the rent of a larger and more luxurious box who would not have frozen to death in such a box as this. I am far from jesting. Economy is a subject which admits of being treated with levity, but it cannot so be disposed of. A comfortable house for a rude and hardy race, that lived mostly out of doors, was once made here almost entirely of such materials as Nature furnished ready in their hands. Gookin, who was superintendent of the Natives subject to the Massachusetts Colony, writing in 1674, says, "The best of their houses are covered very neatly, tight and warm, with barks of trees, slipped from their bodies at those seasons when the sap is up, and made into great flakes, with pressure of weighty timber, when they are green. The meaner sort are covered with mats which they make of a kind of bulrush, and are also indifferently tight and warm, but not so good as the former.... Some I have seen, sixty or a hundred feet long and thirty feet broad. I have often lodged in their wigwams and found them as warm as the best English houses." He adds that they were commonly carpeted and lined within with well-wrought embroidered mats, and were furnished with various utensils. The Indigenous had advanced so far as to regulate the effect of the wind by a mat suspended over the hole in the roof and moved by a string. Such a lodge was in the first instance constructed in a day or two at most, and taken down and put up in a few hours; and every family owned one, or its apartment in one.

In the primitive colony, every family owns a shelter as good as the best, and it is sufficient for their coarser and simpler wants; but I think that I speak within bounds when I say that, though the birds of the air have their nests, and the foxes their holes, and the Natives their wigwams, in modern civilized society not more than one half the families own a shelter. In the large towns and cities, where civilization especially prevails, the number of those who own a shelter is a very small fraction of the whole. The rest pay an annual tax for this structural garment—becoming dependent on it summer and winter—which would buy a village of wigwams, but now helps to keep them poor for as long as they live. I do not mean to insist here on the disadvantage of renting compared with owning, but it is evident that the Native owns their shelter because it costs so little, while others in the city rent commonly because they cannot afford to own it. Nor can they, in the long run, any better afford to rent it. But by merely paying this rent, the poor urbanized person secures an abode which is a palace compared with the Native's. An annual rent they can barely afford entitles them to spacious apartments, clean paint and wallpaper, fireplaces, plastering, Venetian blinds, copper pumps, wine cellars, and many other things. If it is asserted that civilization is a real advance in the condition of humankind—and I think that it is, though only the wise improve their advantages—it must be shown that it has produced better dwellings without making them more costly. And the cost of a thing is the amount of what I will call "life" which is required to be exchanged for it, immediately or in the long run. An average house in this neighborhood costs perhaps ten to fifteen years of the laborer's life, even if they have not acquired dependents, so that they must have commonly spent more than half of their life before their wigwam will be earned. If we suppose them to pay a rent instead, this is but a doubtful choice of evils. Would the Natives have been wise to exchange their wigwam for a "palace" on these terms?

It may be guessed that I reduce almost the whole advantage of holding this superfluous property as a fund in store against the future, so far as the individual is concerned, mainly to the defraying of funeral expenses. But perhaps one should not be required to bury oneself. Nevertheless, this discussion on dwelling places points to an important distinction between the civilized person and the feral one. The life of a civilized person has become an institution, in which the life of the individual is to a great extent absorbed, in order to preserve and perfect that of the race. But I wish to show at what a sacrifice this advantage is at present obtained, and to suggest that we may possibly so live as to secure all the advantage without suffering any of the disadvantage.

When I consider my neighbors, the farmers of Concord, who are at least as well off as people in other places, I find that for the most part they have been toiling twenty, thirty, or forty years, that they may become the real owners of their farms, which commonly they have inherited with encumbrances, or else bought with borrowed money—which ultimately costs them triple the value of their property. The encumbrances sometimes even outweigh the value of the farm, so that the farm itself becomes one great encumbrance, and still one is eager to inherit it, being well acquainted with it and knowing nothing more. Upon querying the assessors, I am surprised to learn that they cannot at once name a dozen in the town who own their farms free and clear. The person who has actually paid for their farm is so rare that every neighbor can point to them. I doubt if there are three such people in Concord. What has been said of the merchants—that a very large majority, even ninety-seven in a hundred are sure to fail—is equally true of the farmers. With regard to the merchants, however, one of them says pertinently that a great part of their failures are not genuine monetary failures, but merely failures to fulfil their engagements with integrity. It is the moral character that breaks down. But this puts an infinitely worse face on the matter and suggests that even the three who succeed in business probably failed in saving their souls.

They are perchance bankrupt in a worse sense than they who fail honestly. Bankruptcy and denial are the springboards from which much of our civilization vaults and turns its somersets. Yet the Middlesex Cattle Show goes off here with conspicuous success hooplah annually, as if all the joints of the agricultural machine were smooth and agreeable.

The farmer is endeavoring to solve the problem of a livelihood by a formula more complicated than the problem itself. To get their shoestrings, they deal in herds of cattle. With perfect skill they have set their trap with a hair spring to catch comfort and independence, and then, as they turned away, got their own leg into it. This is the reason they are poor; and for a similar reason we are all poor, though surrounded by a thousand luxuries. As Chapman sings,—

"The false society of humans—
—questing for earthly greatness
All heavenly comforts evaporates into thin air."

And when the farmer has finally got their house, they may not be the richer but the poorer for it, and it be the house that has got them. As I understand it in Greek mythology, it was a valid objection presented by Momus against the house which the Minerva originally made for show, that she "had not made it movable, by which means a bad neighborhood might be avoided;" and it may still be urged, for our houses are such unwieldy property that we are often imprisoned rather than housed in them. And the bad neighborhood to be avoided is our own scurvy selves. I know one or two families, at least, in this town, who for nearly a generation have been wishing to sell their houses in the outskirts and move into the village, but have not been able to accomplish it, and only death will set them free.

While civilization has been improving our houses, it has not equally improved the people who are to inhabit them. It has created palaces, but it was not so easy to create nobility. And if the civilized person's pursuits are no worthier than the brute's, if they are employed the greater part of their life in obtaining gross necessaries and comforts merely, why should they have a better dwelling than the former?

But how do the poor minority fare? Perhaps it will be found, that just in proportion as some have been placed in outward opinion above the brute, others have been degraded below them. The luxury of one class is counterbalanced by the extreme poverty of another. On the one side is the palace, on the other are the homeless shelters and "silent poor." The myriads who built the pyramids to be the tombs of the Pharaohs were fed on garlic, and were perhaps not decently buried themselves. The mason who finishes the cornice of the palace returns at night perchance to a hut not even as good as a wigwam. It is a mistake to suppose that, in a country where the usual evidence of civilization exists, a very large body of the inhabitants may live comfortably. To know this I should not need to look farther than to the shanties which everywhere border our railroads, that most recent improvement in civilization; where I see in my daily walks human beings living in sties, and all winter with an open door, for the sake of light, without any visible, often imaginable, wood pile, and the forms of both old and young are permanently contracted by the long habit of shrinking from cold and misery, and the development of all their limbs and faculties is stunted. It is by their hands that the works which distinguish this generation are accomplished. Such too, to a greater or less extent, is the condition of the operatives of every denomination in England, which is the great work-house of the world. Or I could refer you to Ireland, which is marked as one of the enlightened spots on the map. Contrast the physical condition of the Irish with that of the Native North American, or the South Sea Islander, or any other race, before they and their surrounding ecosystem was degraded by contact with the civilized human. I have no doubt that those people's rulers are as wise as the average person. Their condition only proves what squalidness may consist within a civilization. I hardly need refer now to the laborers in our Southern States who produce the staple exports of this country and are themselves a staple production of the South. But I will confine myself to those who are said to be in moderate circumstances, rather than include those who are not granted even the most basic of human rights.

Most people appear never to have considered what a house is, and are therefore needlessly poor all their lives because they think that they must have such a one as their neighbors have. As if one were to wear any sort of coat which the tailor might cut out for them, but leave off the palmleaf hat or patch of woodchuck skin, complain of hard times because they could not afford to buy themselves a crown! It is possible to invent a house still more convenient and luxurious than the richest already have. Shall we always study to obtain more of these things, and not sometimes to be content with less? Shall the respectable citizen thus gravely teach, by precept and example, the necessity of the young adult having a certain number of superfluous shoes, and umbrellas, and empty guest chambers for empty guests, before they die? Why should not our furniture be as simple as the Native's? When I think of those whom we have apotheosized as messengers from heaven, bearers of divine gifts to humankind, I do not see in my mind any entourage at their heels, any car-load of fashionable furniture. At present our houses are cluttered and defiled with crap, and a good housekeeper would sweep out the greater part into a dust hole as part of their morning work. Morning work! By the beard of the prophet, what should be person's morning work be in this world? I had three pieces of limestone on my desk, but I was terrified to find that they required to be dusted daily, when the furniture of my mind was all undusted still, and I threw them out the window in disgust. How, then, could I have a furnished house? I would rather sit in the open air, for no dust gathers on the grass.

It is the luxurious and dissipated who set the fashions which the herd so diligently follow. I think that in the railroad car we are inclined to spend more on luxury than on safety and convenience, and it has still become no better than a modern drawing room, with its sofas, and ottomans, and sun-shades, and a hundred other decorative things, which we are taking west with us as necessities. I would rather sit on a pumpkin and have it all to myself than be crowded on a velvet cushion. I would rather ride on earth in an ox cart with a free circulation, than go to heaven in the fancy car of an excursion train and breathe of influenza all the way.

The very simplicity and nakedness of primitive humans' lives imply that they need not require much other than to pass through—no necessity for luxuries in a temporary living space. When they were refreshed with food and sleep, they contemplated their journeys again. They dwelt in no more than mere tents, and were found either threading the valleys, or crossing the plains, or climbing the mountain tops. But lo! Humans now have become the tools of their tools. One who independently plucked the fruits when they were hungry has become a farmer; and they who stood under a tree for shelter, a housekeeper. We now no longer camp as for a night, but have settled down on chosen earth and forgotten heaven. We have adopted Christianity merely as an improved method of agriculture. We have built for this world a family mansion, and for the next a family tomb. The best works of art are the expressions of humankind's struggle to free themselves from this condition, but the effect of our art being hung on walls is merely to make this low state comfortable and that higher state to be forgotten. There is actually no place in a utopian village for a work of fine art, if any had come down to us, for we have no proper pedestal for it. There is not a nail to hang a picture on, nor a shelf to receive the bust of a hero or a saint. When I consider how our houses are built and paid for, or not paid for, and their internal economy managed and sustained, I wonder that the floor does not give way under the visitor while they are admiring the gewgaws upon the mantelpiece. Might we instead let them through into the cellar, to some solid and honest earthy foundation. I cannot but perceive that this so called rich and refined life is a thing jumped at, and I do not get on in the enjoyment of the fine arts which adorn it, my attention being wholly occupied with the jump. The first question which I am tempted to put to the proprietor of such great impropriety is, Who bolsters you? Are you one of the ninety-seven who fail, or of the three who succeed? Answer me these questions, and then perhaps I may look at your bawbles and find them ornamental. The cart before the horse is neither beautiful nor useful. Before we can adorn our houses with beautiful objects the walls must be stripped, and our lives must be stripped, and beautiful housekeeping and beautiful living be laid for a foundation: now, a taste for the beautiful is most cultivated out of doors, where there is no house and no housekeeper. And if we wish to decorate our homes, wildflowers may provide the furnishing.

Old Johnson, in his Wonder-Working Providence, speaking of the first settlers of this town, with whom he was contemporary but perhaps problematically agenda-driven, and some would call his work nothing short of an apologia..., he nonetheless still accounts of the history: "All of the first settlers of this town burrowed themselves in the earth for their first shelter under some hillside." No one did "provide them houses," he says , "till the earth, by the Lord's blessing, brought forth bread to feed them." The first year's crop was so light that "they were forced to cut their bread very thin for a long season." The secretary of the Province of New Netherland, writing in Dutch in 1650, states more particularly for those that might wish to come here, that "those in New Netherland, and especially in New England, who have no means to build farmhouses at first according to their wishes, dig a square pit in the ground, cellar fashion, six or seven feet deep, as long and as broad as they think proper, case the earth inside with wood all round the wall, and line the wood with the bark of trees or something else to prevent the caving in of the earth; floor this cellar with plank, and wainscot it overhead for a ceiling, raise a roof of spars clear up, and cover the spars with bark or green sods, so that they can live dry and warm in these houses with their entire families for two, three, and four years," it being understood that partitions are run through those cellars which are adapted to the size of the family. The wealthy and principal leaders of this town, in the beginning of the colonies, commenced their first dwelling houses in this simple fashion for two reasons; firstly, in order not to waste time in building, and not to want food the next season; secondly, in order not to discourage poor laboring people whom they brought over in numbers from England. Over the course of three or four years, when the country became adapted to agriculture, they built themselves handsome houses, spending on them magnitudes more, while the poor continued to live in modest dwellings.

In this course which our ancestors took, there was a show of prudence at least, as if their principle were to satisfy the more pressing wants first. But are the more pressing wants satisfied now? When I think of acquiring for myself one of our luxurious dwellings, I am deterred, for the country is not yet adapted to human culture, and we are still forced to cut our spiritual bread far thinner than our ancestors did their wheaten. Not that all architectural ornament is to be neglected even in the rudest periods; but let our houses first be lined with this beauty where they meet our lives, like the tenement of the shellfish, and not overlaid with it. But, alas! I have been inside one or two of them, and know what they are lined with.

Though since we are not so primitive that we might possibly want to live in a cave today, it behooves us to accept the advantages which the invention and industry of mankind offer. In such a neighborhood as this, boards, shingles, lime, and bricks are cheaper and more easily obtained than suitable caves, or whole logs, or bark in sufficient quantities, or even well-tempered clay or flat stones. I speak understandingly on this subject, for I have made myself acquainted with it both theoretically and practically. With a little more wit we might use these materials so as to become richer than the richest now are, and make our civilization a blessing. The civilized human is just a more experienced and wiser brute.

But now, to make haste to my own experiment.

ECONOMY, PART III

Near the end of March, 1845, I borrowed an axe and went down to the woods by Walden Pond, nearest to where I intended to build my house, and began to cut down some tall, arrowy white pines, still in their youth, for timber. It is difficult to begin without borrowing, but perhaps it is the most generous course thus to permit your fellows to have an interest in your enterprise. The owner of the axe, as they released their hold on it, said that it was the apple of their eye; but I returned it sharper than I received it. It was a pleasant hillside where I worked, covered with pine woods, through which I looked out on the pond and a small open field in the woods where pines and hickories were springing up. The ice in the pond was not yet dissolved, though there were some open spaces, and it was all dark colored and saturated with water. There were some slight flurries of snow during the days that I worked there; but for the most part when I came out on to the railroad, on my way home, its yellow sand heap stretched away gleaming in the hazy atmosphere, and the rails shone in the spring sun, and I heard the lark and pewee and other birds already come to commence another year with us. They were pleasant spring days, in which the winter of one's discontent was thawing as well as the earth, and the life that had lain torpid began to stretch itself.

One day, when my axe head had come off and I had cut a green hickory for a new handle, driving it with a stone, and had placed the whole to soak in a pond hole in order to swell the wood, I saw a striped snake run into the water, and she lay on the bottom, apparently without inconvenience, as long as I stayed there, at least for a quarter of an hour; perhaps because she had not yet fairly come out of the torpid state. It appeared to me that for a like reason, people remain in their present low and primitive condition; but if they should feel the influence of the spring of springs arousing them, they would of necessity rise to a higher and more ethereal life. I had previously seen the snakes in frosty mornings in my path with portions of their bodies still numb and inflexible, waiting for the sun to thaw them. On the 1st of April it rained and melted the ice, and in the early part of the day, which was very foggy, I heard a stray goose groping about over the pond and cackling as if lost, or like the spirit of the fog.

So I went on for some days cutting and hewing timber, and also studs and rafters, all with my narrow axe, not having many communicable or scholar-like thoughts, singing to myself silly tunes. I shaped the main timbers six inches square, most of the studs on two sides only, and the rafters and floor timbers on one side, leaving the rest of the bark on, so that they were just as straight and much stronger than sawed ones. Each stick was carefully mortised or tenoned by its stump, for I had borrowed other tools by this time. My days in the woods were not very long ones; yet I usually carried my dinner of bread and jam, and read the newspaper in which it was wrapped, at noon, sitting amid the green pine boughs which I had cut off, and to my bread was imparted some of their fragrance, for my hands were covered with a thick coat of pitch. Before I had finished, I was more the friend than the foe of the pine tree, though I had cut down some of them, having become better acquainted with them. Sometimes a rambler in the wood was attracted by the sound of my axe, and we chatted pleasantly over the chips which I had made.

By the middle of April, for I made no haste in my work, but rather made the most of it, my house was framed and ready for the raising. I had already bought the shanty of James Collins, an Irishman who worked on the Fitchburg Railroad, for boards. James Collins' shanty was considered an uncommonly fine one. When I called to see it, he was not at home. I walked about the outside, at first unobserved from within, the window was so deep and high. It was of small dimensions, with a peaked cottage roof, and not much else to be seen, the dirt being raised five feet all around as if it were a compost heap. The roof was the soundest part, though a good deal warped and made brittle by the sun. Doorsill there was none, but a perennial passage for the hens under the door board. Ms. Collins came to the door and asked me to view it from the inside. The hens were driven in by my approach. It was dark, and had a dirt floor for the most part, dank, clammy, and aguish, only here a board and there a board which would not bear removal. She lighted a lamp to show me the inside of the roof and the walls, and also that the board floor extended under the bed, warning me not to step into the cellar, a sort of dust hole two feet deep. In her own words, they were "good boards overhead, good boards all around, and a good window." Only the cat had passed out this window lately, ay, tossed out. There was a stove, a bed, and a place to sit, a silk parasol, a golden looking-glass, and a coffee mill nailed to an oak sapling, all told. The bargain was soon concluded, for James had in the meanwhile returned. I to pay four dollars and twenty-five cents to-night, he to vacate at five tomorrow morning, selling to nobody else meanwhile: I to take possession at six. At six the next morning, I passed him and his family on the road. One large bundle held their all—bed, coffee-mill, looking-glass, hens,— all but the cat, she took to the woods and became a wild cat, and, as I learned afterward, trod in a trap set for woodchucks, and so became a dead cat at last.

I took down this dwelling the same morning, drawing the nails, and removed it to the pond side by small cartloads, spreading the boards on the grass there to bleach and warp back again in the sun. One early thrush gave me a note or two as I drove along the woodland path. I was informed treacherously by a young Patrick that neighbor Seeley, in the intervals of my carting, transferred the still tolerable, straight, and drivable nails, staples, and spikes to his pocket, and then stood by when I came back to pass the time of day, casually commenting that there was "a dearth of work." He was there to represent spectatordom, and help make this seemingly insignificant event a proper one, as though this dismantling of Collin's shanty were as significant as the Trojan War.

I dug my cellar in the side of a hill sloping to the south, where a woodchuck had formerly dug his burrow, down through sumac and blackberry roots, and the lowest stain of vegetation, six feet square by seven deep, to a fine sand where potatoes would not freeze in any winter. The sides were left shelving, and not stoned; but the sun having never shone on them, the sand still keeps its place. It was but two hours' work. I took particular pleasure in this breaking of ground, for in almost all latitudes, people dig into the earth for an equable temperature. Under the most splendid house in the city is still to be found the cellar where they store their roots crops to keep them cool, and long after the superstructure has disappeared, people shall still see its dent in the earth. The house is still but a sort of porch at the entrance of a burrow.

In the beginning of May, I set up the frame of my house with the help of some of my closest acquaintances, more to enjoy the gift of neighborliness rather than from any labor necessity. No one was ever more honored in the character of their frame raisers than I. They are destined, I trust, to assist at the raising of loftier structures one day. I began to occupy my house on the 4th of July, as soon as it was boarded and roofed, for the boards were carefully feather-edged and lapped, so that it was perfectly impervious to rain; but before boarding I laid the foundation of a chimney at one end, bringing two cartloads of stones up the hill from the pond in my arms. I built the chimney after my hoeing in the fall, before a fire became necessary for warmth, doing my cooking meanwhile out of doors on the ground, early in the morning: which mode I still think is in some respects more convenient and agreeable than the usual one. When it stormed before my bread was baked, I fixed a few boards over the fire, and sat under them to watch my loaf, and passed some pleasant hours in that way. In those days, when my hands were much employed,

I read but little, but the scraps of paper which lay on the ground, as my holder, or tablecloth, afforded me as much entertainment, and in fact answered the same purpose as the Iliad.

It would be worth the while to build still more deliberately than I did, considering, for instance, what foundation a door, a window, a cellar, a garret, have in the nature of humankind, and perchance never raising any superstructure until we found a better reason for it than our temporal necessities even. There is some of the same fitness in a person's building their own house that there is in a bird's building its own nest. Who knows but if people constructed their dwellings with their own hands, and provided food for themselves and families simply and honestly enough, the poetic faculty would be universally developed, as birds universally sing when they are so engaged? But alas! we do like cowbirds and cuckoos, which lay their eggs in nests which other birds have built, and cheer no traveler with their chattering and unmusical notes. Shall we forever resign the pleasure of construction to the carpenter? I never in all my walks came across a person engaged in so simple and natural an occupation as building their house. Where is this division of labor to end? And what object does it finally serve? No doubt another may also think for me; but it is not desirable that they should do so to the exclusion of my thinking for myself.

True, I have heard of at least one architect in this country possessed with the idea of architectural ornaments having a core of truth, and therefore a necessity. But a sentimental reformer in architecture, he began at the cornice, not at the foundation. It was only how to put a core of truth within the ornaments, that every sugar plum in fact might have an almond

or caraway seed in it,—though I hold that almonds
are most wholesome without the sugar,—and not
how the inhabitant, the indweller, might build truly
within and without, and let the ornaments take care of
themselves in due time. What reasonable person ever
supposed that ornaments were something outward
and in the skin merely,—that the tortoise got his spotted shell, or the shellfish its mother-o'-pearl tints,
by such a contract as the inhabitants of the Trinity
Church on Broadway? We have no more impact on
the style of our houses than a tortoise with that of its
shell: nor need the soldier be so idle as to try to paint
the precise color of their virtue on their shield. The
enemy will find it out. What of architectural beauty
I now see, I know has gradually grown from within
outward, out of the necessities and character of the
indweller, who is the only builder—out of some unconscious truthfulness, and nobleness, without ever a
thought for the appearance. And whatever additional
beauty is destined to be produced will be preceded by
a similar unconscious beauty of life. The most interesting dwellings in this country, as the painter knows,
are the most unpretending, humble log huts and cot-
tages of the poor commonly; it is the life of the inhabitants whose shells they are, and not any peculiarity in
their surfaces merely, which makes them picturesque;
and equally interesting will be the citizen's suburban
box, when their life shall be as simple and as agreeable
to the imagination, and there is as little straining in the
style of their dwelling. A great proportion of architectural ornaments are literally hollow, and a September
hurricane would strip them off, like borrowed pea-
cock plumes, without injury to the substantials. They
can do without architecture who have no olives nor
wines in the cellar. What if an equal ado were made

about the ornaments of style in literature, and the architects of our bibles spent as much time about their cornices as the architects of our churches do?

Much it concerns a person, truthfully, how a few sticks are slanted over them or under them, and what colors are daubed upon their box. If the tenant has no spirt in life, they build their own coffin,—the architecture of the grave, and "carpenter" is but another name for "coffin-maker."

One says, in their despair or indifference to life, to take up a handful of the earth at your feet, and paint your house that color. Are they thinking of their last and narrow house? Toss up a shiny penny for it as well. What an abundance of leisure they must have! Why do you even bother to take up a handful of dirt? Better to let your house be colored of your own complexion; let it turn pale or blush for you; a useful and functioning coat of paint. Simplicity—an enterprise to improve the style of cottage architecture!

Before winter I built a chimney, and shingled the sides of my house, which were already impervious to rain, with imperfect and sappy shingles made of the first slice of the log, whose edges I was obliged to straighten with a plane.

I have thus a tight shingled and plastered house, ten feet wide by fifteen long, and eight-feet posts, with an attic and a closet, a large window on each side, two trap doors, one door at the end, and a brick fireplace opposite. The exact cost of my house, paying the usual price for such materials as I used, but not counting the work, all of which was done by myself, was as follows; and I give the details because very few are able to tell exactly what their houses cost, and fewer still, if any, the separate cost of the various materials which compose them.

Cost of House:

Boards:	$8.03 (mostly shanty.)
Rubbish shingles for roof sides:	4.00
Laths:	1.25
Two second-hand windows:	2.43
One thousand old bricks:	4.00
Two casks of lime:	2.40 (That was high.)
Hair: (More than I needed.)	0.31
Mantle-tree iron:	0.15
Nails:	3.90
Hinges and screws:	0.14
Latch:	0.10
Chalk:	0.01
Transportation:	1.40
(I carried a good part.)	
In all:	$28.12½[a]

These are all the materials excepting the timber stones and sand, which I claimed by squatter's right. I have also a small wood-shed adjoining, made chiefly of the stuff which was left after building the house.

I have intended to build me a house which will surpass any on the main street in Concord in grandeur and luxury, or at least, it will please me as much and will cost me no more than my present one.

I thus found that the student who wishes for a shelter can obtain one for a lifetime at an expense not greater than the rent which they now pay annually. If I seem to boast more than is becoming, my excuse is that I brag for humanity rather than for myself; and my shortcomings and inconsistencies do not affect

---

a. According to the Consumer Price Index, this amount would equate to roughly $907 in 2022.

the truth of my statement. I am resolved that I will not, through humility, become the devil's attorney. I will endeavor to speak a good word for the truth.

At Cambridge College, the cost of a student's room to rent is thirty dollars each year, which is just slightly more than the total end cost of my own, though the corporation had the advantage of building thirty-two side by side and under one roof, and the occupant suffers the inconvenience of many and noisy neighbors, and perhaps even a residence in the second story. Those conveniences which the student requires at Cambridge or elsewhere cost them or somebody else ten times as great a sacrifice of life as they would with proper management on both sides. Those things for which the most money is demanded are never the things which the student most wants. Tuition, for instance, is an important item on the university bill, while the far more valuable education which they get by associating with the most cultivated of their contemporaries is not charged. The mode of founding a college is, commonly, to get up a subscription of dollars and cents, and then following blindly the principles of a division of labor to its extreme, a principle which should never be followed but with circumspection,—to call in a contractor to lay the foundations, while the students that are to inhabit these teaching halls and dwellings stand idly by. They are said to be fitting themselves for it; and for these oversights successive generations have to pay. I think that it would be better than this for the students, even to lay the foundation themselves. The student who secures their leisure and retirement by systematically shirking any labor necessary obtains but an ignoble and unprofitable leisure, defrauding themselves of the experience which alone can make leisure fruitful. "But," says one, "you do not mean that the students should go to work with their hands instead of their heads?" I do not mean that exactly, but I mean something which one might think a good deal like that; I mean that they should not play life, or study it merely, while the community supports them at this game. But instead, to earnestly live it from beginning to end. How could youths better learn to live than by at once trying the experiment of living? Methinks this would exercise their minds as much as mathematics. If I wished a child to know something about the arts and sciences, for instance, I would not pursue the common course, which is merely to send them into the care of some professor, where everything is professed and practiced except for the sacred art of life. Where one can learn to survey the world through a telescope or a microscope, and never see with their natural eye; to study chemistry, and not learn how their bread is made; to discover new moons of Neptune, and not to understand to what degree they are a satellite in this universe themselves; or to be unconsciously devoured by the monsters that swarm all around them, while deeply contemplating the monsters in a drop of blood. Which would have advanced the most at the end of a month? The young woman who had made her own jackknife from the ore which she had dug and smelted, reading as much as would be necessary for this, or the one who had attended the lectures on metallurgy at the Institute and had received a Rodgers' penknife from her mother as a graduation gift? Which would be most likely to cut her fingers?...

To my astonishment I was informed on leaving college that I had studied navigation! Why, if I had taken one turn down the harbor, I should have known more about it. In the same regard, poor students study political economy, while the economy of living (which is synonymous with philosophy) is not sincerely professed in our colleges. The consequence is, that while they are paying to hear lectures on free-trade and capitalism, they run to their parents in debt irretrievably.

As with our colleges, and so with a hundred "modern improvements"; there is an illusion about them; there is not always a positive advance. The devil goes on exacting compound interest for his early share and numerous succeeding investments in them. Our inventions are often merely pretty toys, which distract our attention from better things. They are but improved means to an unimproved end, an end which it was already but too easy to arrive at; as railroads lead to Boston or New York. We are in great haste to construct a magnetic telegraph from Maine to Texas; but Maine and Texas, it may be, have nothing important to communicate. As the man who was earnest to be introduced to a distinguished deaf woman, but when he was presented, and one end of her ear trumpet was put into his hand, had nothing to say. As if the main object were to talk fast and not to talk sensibly. We are eager to tunnel telegraph cables under the Atlantic and bring the old world some weeks faster to the new; but perchance the first news that will leak through into the broad, flapping American ear will be that the Prince Albert has the whooping cough. After all, the horse who trots a mile in a minute does not carry the most important messages. I doubt if the famous race horse, Flying Childers, ever carried a peck of corn to mill. One says to me, "I wonder that you do not lay up money; you love to travel; you might take the cars and go to Fitchburg to-day and see the country." But I have learned that the swiftest traveler is one that goes afoot. I say to my friend, Suppose we race to see who will get there first. The distance is thirty miles; the fare ninety cents. That is almost a day's wages. I remember when wages were sixty cents a day for laborers on this very road. Well, I start now on foot, and get there before night; I have traveled at that rate by the week together. You will in the meanwhile have earned your fare, and arrive there some time tomorrow, or possibly this evening, if you are lucky enough to get a job in season. Instead of going to Fitchburg and enjoying the journey along the way, you will be working here the greater part of the day. And so, if the railroad reached round the world, I think that I should keep ahead of you, in time and in experiences accumulated, while seeing the country all on my own terms.

Such is the universal law, which no one can ever outwit, and with regard to the railroad—we may say it is as broad as it is long. To make a railroad round the world available to all humankind is equivalent to grading the whole surface of the planet. People have an indistinct notion that if they keep up this activity long enough, they will finally ride somewhere, in next to no time, and for nothing; but though a large crowd rushes to the depot, and the conductor shouts "All aboard!" when the smoke is blown away and the vapor condensed, it will be observed that a few are actually riding, and the rest have been run over. And it will be called, and will be, "A melancholy accident." No doubt they can ride at last, all who shall have earned their fare. That is, if they survive so long, but they will probably have lost their elasticity and desire to travel by that time. This spending of the best part of one's life earning money in order to enjoy a questionable liberty during the least valuable part of it, reminds me of the Englishman who went to India to make a fortune first, in order that he might return to England and live the life of a poet. He should have gone up to the attic at once. "What!" exclaim a million Irish speaking up from all the shantiest shanties in the land, "is not this railroad which we have built a good thing?" Yes, I answer, comparatively good, that is, you might have done worse; but I wish, as you are loved brothers of mine, that you could have spent your time better than digging in this dirt.

ECONOMY, PART IV

Before I finished my house, wishing to earn ten or twelve dollars by some honest and agreeable method in order to meet my unusual expenses, I planted about two and a half acres of Emerson's light and sandy soil chiefly with beans, but also a small part with potatoes, corn, peas, and turnips. The whole lot contains eleven acres, mostly growing up to pines and hickories, and was sold the preceding season for eight dollars and eight cents an acre. One farmer said that it was "good for nothing but to raise cheeping squirrels on." I put no manure whatever on this land, not being the owner, but merely a squatter, and not expecting to cultivate so much again. I did not quite hoe it all once; I got out several rows of stumps in ploughing, which supplied me with fuel for a long time, and left small circles of nutritious compost, easily distinguishable through the summer by the greater luxuriance of the beans there. The dead and for the most part unmerchantable wood behind my house, and the driftwood from the pond, have supplied the remainder of my fuel. I was obliged to hire a team for the ploughing, though I held the plough myself. The seed corn was given me. This never costs anything to speak of, unless you plant more than enough. I got twelve bushels of beans, and eighteen bushels of potatoes, some peas, and sweet corn. The yellow corn and turnips were too late to come to anything. My whole income from the farm was $23.44.

Deducting the outgoings:	$14.72½
There was left:	8.71½,

In addition, I consumed produce estimated at a total value of $4.50. All things considered, that is, considering the value of one's soul, I believe that that was doing better than any farmer in Concord did that year. The next year I did better still, for I spaded up all the land which I required, about a third of an acre, and I learned from the experience of both years, not being in the least influenced by many traditionally celebrated agricultural practices. If one would live simply and eat only the crop which they raised, and raise no more than they ate, and not exchange it for an insufficient quantity of more luxurious and expensive things, they would need to cultivate only a few rods of ground, and that it would be cheaper to spade up that than to use oxen to plough it, and to allow natural cover plants to add nutrients to the soil, rather than to manure it, and they could do all his necessary farm work as it were with their left hand at odd hours in the summer; and thus would not be tied to an ox, or horse, or cow, or pig at present. I desire to speak impartially on this point, and as one not interested in the success or failure of the present economical and social arrangements. I was more independent than any farmer in Concord, for I was not anchored to a house or farm, but could follow the bent of my mind, which is a very crooked and unpredictable one, every moment. And if my house had been burned or my crops had failed, I should have been nearly as well off as before, not balancing my future well-being on the required success of any particular endeavor.

I am inclined to think that we are not so much the keepers of herds, as herds are the keepers of us. The former are so much freer. Humans and oxen exchange work; but if we consider necessary work only, the oxen will be seen to have greatly the advantage. The farmer does some of their part of the exchange work in their six weeks of haying for oxen feed, and it is no child's play. Certainly no nation that lived simply in all respects, that is, no nation of philosophers, would commit so great a blunder as to use the labor of animals. True, there never was and is not likely soon to be a nation of philosophers, nor am I certain it is desirable that there should be. However, I should never have broken a horse or bull and taken it to board for any work it might do for me, for fear I should become a horse-man or a herds-man merely. Granted, I recognize that some public works and monuments would not have been constructed without this animal aid, and let us share the glory of such with the ox and horse. But does it not follow that they could have accomplished works yet more worthy of themselves in that case? When we begin to do, not merely artistic, but luxurious and idle work, with the assistance of animals or machinery, it is inevitable that a few do all the exchange work with the oxen and machinery, or, in other words, become the slaves of the strongest. A person thus not only works for the animal within them, but, for a symbol of this, they work for the animal outside of them. Though we have many substantial houses of brick or stone, the prosperity of the farmer is still measured by the degree to which the barn overshadows the house. This town is said to have the largest houses for oxen, cows, and horses hereabouts, and it is not behindhand in its public buildings; but there are very few halls for free worship or free speech in this county that won't swat away, or smash, an open and fair discourse on slavery. It should not be by their architecture, but by their power of abstract thought, that nations should seek to commemorate themselves. How much more admirable the written word of Bhagvat-Geeta than all the ruins of the East!

Towers and temples are the luxury of royals. A simple and independent mind does not toil at the orders of any prince. Genius is not a retainer to any emperor, nor is its material silver, or gold, or marble, except to a trifling extent. To what end, pray, is so much stone hammered? In beautiful Arcadia, when I was there, I did not see any hammering stone. The leaders of most nations are possessed with an insane ambition to perpetuate the memory of themselves by the amount of hammered stone they leave. What if equal pains were taken to smooth and polish their manners or intellectual growth? One piece of good sense would be more memorable than a monument as high as the moon. I love better to see stones in their nature place. The grandeur of Thebes was a vulgar grandeur. The religions and civilizations which are most barbaric and heathenish build splendid temples; but what you might call "spirituality" or "universal oneness" does not. It harmonizes with Earth. Most of the stone a nation hammers goes toward its tomb only. It buries itself alive. As for the Pyramids, there is nothing to wonder at in them so much as the fact that so many people could be found degraded enough to spend their lives constructing a tomb for some ambitious booby. As for the religion and love of art of the builders, it is much the same all the world over, whether the building be an Egyptian temple or a United States Bank, it costs more than it comes to. The mainspring is vanity, assisted by the love of bread and butter. As for our high towers and monuments, there was a crazy fellow once in this town who undertook to dig through to China, and he got so far that, as he said, he heard the Chinese pots and kettles rattle; but I think that I shall not go out of my way to admire the hole which he made. Many are concerned about the monuments of the West and the East,—to know who built them. For my part, I should like to know who in those days did not build them,—who were above such trifling. But to proceed with my statistics.

By surveying, carpentry, and day-labor of various other kinds in the village in the meanwhile, for I have as many trades as fingers, I had earned $13.34. The expense of food for eight months, namely, from July 4th to March 1st,—not counting potatoes, a little green corn, and some peas, which I had raised.

Rice:	$1.73½
Molasses:	1.73 (Cheapest form of the saccharine.)
Rye meal:	1.04¾
Corn meal:	0.99¾ (Cheaper than rye.)
Pork:	0.22
Flour:	0.88 (Costs more than cornmeal, both money and trouble.)
Sugar:	0.80
Lard:	0.65

Apples:	0.25
Dried apple:	0.22
Sweet potatoes:	0.10
One pumpkin:	0.06
One watermelon:	0.02
Salt:	0.03

Yes, I did eat $8.74, all told;[b] but I do not thus unblushingly publish my guilt, for I know that most of my readers are equally guilty with myself, and that their deeds would look no better in print. The next year I sometimes caught a mess of fish for my dinner, and once I went so far as to slaughter a woodchuck which ravaged my bean-field, and devour him, partly for experiment's sake; but though it afforded me a momentary enjoyment, notwithstanding a musky flavor, I saw that the sustained habit would not make that a good practice.

So the total pecuniary outgoings, excepting for washing and mending done out of the house, for their bills have not yet been received, though my mother may never get around to sending one—were:

Outgoing:	
House:	$28.12½
Farming expenses for one year:	14.72½
Food eight months:	8.74
Clothing, etc., eight months:	8.40¾
Oil, household utensils, etc.:	2.00
——————	
In all:	$61.99¾[c]

---

b. According to the Consumer Price Index, this amount would equate to roughly $282 in 2022.

c. According to the Consumer Price Index, this amount would equate to roughly $2,000 in 2022.

I address myself now to those of my readers who have a living to get.

Incoming:

Farm produce sales:	$23.44
Earned by day-labor:	13.34
————————	
In all:	$36.78,[d]

which subtracted from the sum of the outgoes leaves a balance of $25.21¾ on the side not in my favor,— this being very nearly the exact amount with which I started. But I have traded it for leisure and independence and health, and a comfortable house for me as long as I choose to occupy it.

These statistics, however accidental and therefore uninstructive they may appear, still have a certain completeness, and a certain value. Nothing was given me of which I have not rendered some account. It appears from the above estimate, that my food alone cost me in money about twenty-seven cents a week. It was, for nearly two years after this, rye and corn meal without yeast, potatoes, rice, a very little salt pork, molasses, and salt, and my drinking water. It was fit that I should live on rice, mainly, as it aligns so well the philosophy of India. To meet the objections of some trivial quibblers, I may as well state, that if I dined out occasionally, as I always had done, and I trust shall have opportunities to do again, it was frequently to the detriment of my preferred domestic arrangements.

I learned from my two years' experience that it would cost incredibly little trouble to obtain one's necessary food, even in this latitude; if one would

---

d. According to the Consumer Price Index, this amount would equate to roughly $1,186 in 2022.

use as simple a diet as the herbivorous animals of the forest, and yet still retain health and strength. I have made a satisfactory dinner, satisfactory on several accounts, simply off a dish of purslane weeds (Portulaca oleracea) which I gathered in my cornfield, boiled and salted. And pray what more can a reasonable person desire, in peaceful times, in ordinary noons, than a sufficient number of ears of green sweet-corn boiled, with the addition of salt? Even the little variety which I used was a yielding to the demands of appetite, and not of health. Yet people have come to such a pass that they frequently starve, not for want of necessaries, but for want of luxuries.

The reader will perceive that I am treating the subject rather from an economic than a dietetic point of view, and one will not venture to put my suggestions to the test if one has a well- stocked pantry. With economic fortune comes greater access to healthy, hearty foods of the earth—nutritious fruits, vegetables, greens, and nuts. But alas, I am alive on the most basic of provisions. Though food is important, health also requires relaxation, an aimless life at times, which most choose to sacrifice for goods. This is life in the present, as the animals have;—and we are animals, after all, though it may be inconvenient to consider.

Bread I at first made of pure corn meal and salt,— they were genuine hoecakes,—which I baked with my fire out of doors on a shingle or the end of a stick of timber sawed off, leftover from building my house; but it got smoked and had a piny flavor. I tried flour also; but have at last found a mixture of rye and corn meal most convenient and agreeable. In cold weather it was no little amusement to bake several small loaves of this in succession, tending and turning them as carefully as fowl watching their hatching eggs. They were a real cereal fruit which I ripened, and they had to my senses a fragrance like that of other noble fruits, which I kept in as long as possible by wrapping them in cloths. I made a study of the ancient and indispensable art of bread-making, consulting such authorities as offered, going back to the primitive days and first invention of the unleavened kind, when from the wildness of gathered berries and hunted game humans first reached the mildness and refinement of this diet. I traveled gradually in my studies through that accidental souring of the dough which, it is supposed, taught the leavening process, and through the various fermentations thereafter, 'til I came to "good, sweet, wholesome bread," the staff of life. Yeast, which some deem the soul of bread, the spiritus which fills its cellular tissue, which is religiously preserved like the vestal fire. It is some precious bottle-full, I suppose, first brought over in the Mayflower. It did the business for America, and its influence is still rising, swelling, spreading, in yeasty billows over the land,—this ingredient I regularly and faithfully procured from the village, 'til at length one morning I forgot the rules, and accidentally scalded my yeast; by which accident I discovered that even this yeast was not indispensable,—for my discoveries were not by the synthetic but analytic process,—and I have gladly omitted it since, though most experienced bread makers earnestly assure me that wholesome bread without yeast is impossible, and some people prophesied a speedy decay of my vital life forces. Yet I find it not to be an essential ingredient, and after going without it for a year, I am still in the land of the living; and I am glad to escape the trivialness of carrying a bottle-full of yeast in my pocket, which would sometimes pop and discharge its contents to my discomfiture. It is simpler and more respectable to omit it. Humans are animals who more than any other can adapt themselves to all climates and circumstances. Neither did I put any sal soda, or other acid or alkali, into my bread. It would seem that I made it according to the recipe which Marcus Porcius Cato gave about two centuries before Jesus Christ.

"Panem depsticium sic facito. Manus mortariumque bene lavato. Farinam in mortarium indito, aquæ paulatim addito, subigitoque pulchre. Ubi bene subegeris, defingito, coquitoque sub testu." Which I take to mean—"Make kneaded bread thus. Wash your hands and trough well. Put the meal into the trough, add water gradually, and knead it thoroughly. When you have kneaded it well, mould it, and bake it under a cover."

That is, in a baking-kettle. Not a word about leaven.

Every New Englander might easily raise all their own breadstuffs in this land of rye and corn, and not depend on distant and fluctuating markets for them. Yet so far are we from simplicity and independence that, in Concord, fresh and sweet meal is rarely sold in the shops, and hominy and corn in a still coarser form are hardly used by any. For the most part, the farmer gives to their cattle and hogs the grain of their own producing, and buys flour, which is at least no more wholesome, at a greater cost, at the store. I saw that I could easily raise my bushel or two of rye and corn, for the former will grow on the poorest land, and the latter does not require the best, and I grind them in a hand-mill, and so do without rice and pork; and if I must have some concentrated sweet, I found by experiment that I could make a very good molasses either of pumpkins or beets, and I knew that I needed only to tap a few maples to obtain it more easily still.

As the Forepeople sang,—"we can make liquor to

sweeten our lips, Of pumpkins and parsnips and wal-
nut-tree chips."

Finally, as for salt, that grossest of groceries, to
obtain this might be a fit occasion for a visit to the
seashore, or, if I did without it altogether, I should
probably drink the less water. I do not learn that the
Natives ever troubled themselves to go after it.

Thus I could avoid all trade and barter, so far as
my food was concerned, and having a shelter already,
it would only remain to get clothing and fuel. The
pantaloons which I now wear were woven in a farmer's family,—thank Heaven there is so much virtue
still in us; for I think the fall from the farmer to the
corporate operative as great and memorable as that
from the wild human to the domesticated farmer.
And in this new country, any need for fuel is an encumbrance, other than my freely gathered fallen
wood. As for a habitat, if I were not permitted still to
squat, I might purchase one acre at the same price for
which the land I cultivated was sold—namely, eight
dollars and eight cents. But as it was, I considered that
I enhanced the value of the land by squatting on it.

There is a certain class of unbelievers who sometimes ask me such questions as, if I think that I can
live on vegetable food alone;—I am accustomed
to answer such, that I can live on grass and bark. If
they cannot understand that, they cannot understand
much that I have to say. I heard that a young man
tried for a fortnight to live on hard, raw corn on the
ear, using his teeth for all mortar. The squirrel tribe
tried the same, but succeeded. For my part, I am glad
to hear of experiments of this kind being tried. How
else might we understand what we are capable of?

My furniture, part of which I made myself,
consisted of a bed, a table, a desk, three chairs, a

looking-glass three inches in diameter, a pair of fire tongs and andirons for holding the firewood, a kettle, a skillet, and a frying-pan, a dipper, a wash- bowl, two knives and forks, three plates, one cup, one spoon, a jug for oil, a jug for molasses, and a lamp. None is so poor that they actually need sit on a pumpkin. That is shiftlessness. There is a plenty of such chairs as I like best in the village garrets to be had for taking them away. Furniture! Thank God, I can sit and I can stand without the aid of a furniture warehouse. What person would not be ashamed to see their collection of furniture packed in a cart and going up country exposed to the light of heaven and the eyes of humans? I could never tell from inspecting such a load whether it belonged to a so-called rich person or a poor one; the owner always seemed poverty-stricken. Indeed, the more you have of such things the poorer you are. Each load looks as if it contained the contents of a dozen shanties; and if one shanty is poor, this is a dozen times as poor. Pray, for what do we move ever but to get rid of our furniture, our exuviæ; and finally at last to go from this world to another newly furnished, and leave our things here to be burned? It is the same as if all these traps were buckled to a person's belt, and they could not move over the rough country without dragging them,—dragging their traps. He was a lucky fox that left his tail in the trap. The muskrat will gnaw her leg off to be free. No wonder people have lost their elasticity. How often they are at a dead set! "Excuse me, if I may be so bold, what do you mean by a dead set?" If you are a seer, whenever you meet someone, you will see all that they own, ay, and much that they pretend to disown, behind them. Even to their kitchen furniture and all the trumpery which they save and will not burn, and they will appear to be harnessed to it and making what headway they can. I think that the person is at a dead set who has got themselves through a knot hole or gateway, but their sledge load of furniture cannot follow them through. I cannot but feel compassion when I hear some trig, compact- looking person, seemingly free, all girded and ready, speak of their "furniture," as whether it is insured or not. "But what shall I do with my furniture?" My gay butterfly is entangled in a spider's web then. Even those who seem for a long while not to have any, if you inquire more narrowly you will find they have some stored in somebody's barn. I look upon England today as an old gentleman who is traveling with a great deal of baggage, trumpery which has accumulated from long housekeeping, which he has not the courage to burn; great trunk, little trunk, bandbox, and bundle. Throw away the first three at least. It would be beyond the powers of a healthy person nowadays to take up their bed and walk, and I should certainly advise a sick one to lay down their bed and run. If I have got to drag my trap, I will take care that it be a light one and do not nip me in a vital part. But perchance it would be wisest never to put one's paw into it.

I would observe, by the way, that it costs me nothing for curtains, for I have no gazers to shut out but the sun and moon, and I am obliged that they should look in. The moon will not sour milk nor taint meat of mine, nor will the sun injure my furniture or fade my carpet, and if the sun is sometimes too warm a friend, I find it still better economy to retreat behind some curtain which nature has provided, than to add a single item to the details of housekeeping. A lady once offered me a mat, but as I had no room to spare within the house, nor time to spare within or without to shake it,

I declined it, preferring to wipe my feet on the sod before my door. It is best to avoid the beginnings of evil.

Not long ago I was present at the auction of a deacon's things. As usual, a great proportion was trumpery which had begun to accumulate in their parents' age. Among the rest was a dried tapeworm. And now, after lying half a century in their garret and other dust holes, these things were not burned; instead of a bonfire, or purifying destruction of them, there was an auction. The neighbors eagerly collected to view them, bought them all, and carefully transported them to their garrets and dust holes, to lie there 'til their estates are settled, too. "The evil that we do lives long after us."

The customs of some ancient nations might, perchance, be profitably imitated by us, for they go through the ceremony of casting their slough, debts, and grudges annually. Would it not be well if we were to celebrate such a "Busk," as has been the custom of many tribes? When a community celebrates the Busk, they collect all their worn out clothes and other despicable things, sweep and cleanse their houses, squares, and the whole town of their filth, which with all the remaining grain and other old provisions they cast together into one common heap, and consume it with fire. After having taken medicine, and fasted for three days, all the fire in the town is extinguished. During this fast they abstain from the gratification of every appetite and passion whatsoever. A general amnesty is proclaimed; all malefactors may return to their town. On the fourth morning, the high priest, by rubbing dry wood together, produces new fire in the public square, from whence every habitation in the town is supplied with the new and pure flame. They then feast on the new corn and fruits, and dance and sing for three days, and the four following days they receive visits and rejoice with their friends from neighboring towns who have in like manner purified and prepared themselves.

For more than five years I maintained myself thus solely by the labor of my hands, and I found, that by working about six weeks in a year, I could meet all the expenses of living. The whole of my winters, as well as most of my summers, I had free and clear for study. I have thoroughly tried school-keeping for the schools of others, and found that my expenses were in proportion, or rather out of proportion, to my income, for I was obliged to dress and train, to say, think, and believe accordingly, and I lost my time into the bargain. As I did not teach for the good of my fellows, but simply for a livelihood, this was a failure. I have tried trade; but I found that it would take ten years to get under way in that, and that then I should probably be on my way to the devil. I was actually afraid that I might, by that time, be doing what is called a "good business." When formerly I was looking about to see what I could do for a living, some sad experience in conforming to the wishes of friends being fresh in my mind to tax my ingenuity, I thought often and seriously of picking huckleberries; that surely I could do, and its small profits might suffice,—for my greatest skill has been to want but little,—so little capital it required, so little distraction from my wonted moods, I foolishly thought. While my acquaintances went unhesitatingly into trade or the professions, I contemplated this occupation as most like theirs; ranging the hills all summer to pick the berries which came in my way, and thereafter carelessly dispose of them; so, to keep the flocks of Admetus.

As Apollo said, "Blessed be your flocks, Admetus," smiling. "They shall prosper even though I leave them."

I also dreamed that I might gather the wild herbs, or carry evergreens to such villagers that loved to be reminded of the woods, or even to the city, by hay-cart loads. But I have since learned that trade curses everything it handles; and though you trade in messages from heaven, the whole curse of trade attaches to the business.

As I preferred some things to others, and especially valued my freedom, as I could fare hard and yet be happy, I did not wish to spend my time in earning rich carpets or other fine furniture, or delicate cookery, or a house in the Grecian or the Gothic style just yet. If there are any to whom it is no interruption to acquire these things, and who know how to use them when acquired, I relinquish to them the pursuit. Some are "industrious," and appear to love labor for its own sake, or perhaps because it keeps them out of worse mischief; to such I have at present nothing to say. Those who would not know what to do with more leisure than they now enjoy, I might advise to work twice as hard as they do,—work 'til they pay for themselves, and get their free papers. For myself I found that the occupation of a day-laborer was the most independent of any, especially as it required only thirty or forty days in a year to support one. The laborer's day ends with the going down of the sun, and they are then free to devote themselves to their chosen pursuit, independent of their labor; but their employer, who speculates from month to month, has no respite from one end of the year to the other.

In short, I am convinced, both by faith and experience, that to maintain one's self on this earth is not a hardship but a joyful pastime, if we will live simply and wisely; as the pursuits of the simpler nations are still the sports of the more artificial. It is not necessary that one should earn their living by the sweat of their brow, unless they sweat easier than I do.

One young woman of my acquaintance, who has inherited some acres, told me that she thought she should live as I did, if she had the means. I would not have any one adopt my mode of living on any account; before she has fairly learned it, I may have found out another for myself, and I desire that there may be as many different persons in the world as possible; but I would have each one be very careful to find out and pursue their own way, and not their father's or mother's or neighbor's instead. The youth may build or plant or sail; let her not be hindered from doing that which she tells me she would like to do. We may not always arrive at our port within a calculable period, but we preserve the true course, which is only mappable once the journey is complete.

Undoubtedly, in this case, what is true for one is truer still for a thousand, just as a large house is not proportionally more expensive than a small one, since one roof may cover, and one cellar underlie, and one wall separate several apartments. But for my part, I preferred the solitary dwelling. Moreover, it will commonly be cheaper to build the whole yourself than to convince another of the advantage of the common wall; and when you have done this, the common partition, to be much cheaper, must be a thin one, and that other may prove a bad neighbor, and also not keep their side in repair. The only cooperation which is commonly possible is exceedingly partial and superficial; and what little true cooperation there is, is often a harmony inaudible to humankind. If one has faith, they will cooperate with equal faith everywhere; if one has not faith, they will continue to live like the rest of the world, whatever company they are joined to. To cooperate, in the highest as well as the lowest sense, means to get our living together, and humankind has much trouble with this. One who goes alone can start to-day; but one who travels with another must wait 'til that other is ready, and it may be a long time before they get off.

But all this is very selfish, I have heard some of my townspeople say. I confess that I have hitherto indulged very little in philanthropic enterprises. I have made some sacrifices for a sense of duty, and have sacrificed the pleasures gained from duty as well. There are those who have used all their arts to persuade me to undertake the supporting of some poor family in the town; and if I had nothing to do, for the devil finds employment for the idle, I might try my hand at some such activity as that. However, when I have thought to indulge myself in this respect, and under obligation maintain certain poor persons in all respects as comfortably as I maintain myself—and have even ventured so far as to make them the offer—they have one and all unhesitatingly preferred to remain poor. While my townspeople are devoted in so many ways to the good of their fellows, I trust that at least one person may be spared to other and less humane pursuits. You must have a genius for charity as well as for anything else to not get wrung dry. As for Doing-Good, that is one of the professions which are full. Moreover, I have tried it fairly, and, strange as it may seem, am satisfied that it does not agree with my constitution. Probably I should not consciously and deliberately forsake my particular calling so that I may do the good which society demands of me, which is to save the universe from annihilation; and I believe that a like but infinitely greater steadfastness elsewhere is all that now preserves it. But I would not stand between any one and their genius; and to they who do this work, which I decline, with his whole heart and soul and life, I would say, Persevere, even if the world calls it doing evil, as it is most likely they will.

I am far from supposing that my case is a peculiar one; no doubt many of my readers would make a similar defense. In regards to doing something good,—I do not hesitate to say that I should be an excellent fellow to hire; but what exact good that is, it is for my employer to find out. What good I do, in the common sense of that word, must be aside from my main path, and for the most part wholly unintended. People say, practically, Begin where you are and such as you are, without aiming mainly to become of more worth, and with kindness aforethought go about doing good.

I say, rather than doing good, set about being good. The sun does not set about to do good, she does not seek to kindle her fires up to be a star of the sixth magnitude, steadily increasing her genial heat and beneficence 'til she is of such brightness that no mortal can look her in the face. Instead, she goes about in her own orbit, doing the system good—or rather, as a truer philosophy has discovered, the world going about her, getting good themselves—as she ignores them.

There is no odor so bad as that which arises from goodness tainted, as happens when one does good, rather than be good. It is human, it is divine, dead and putrefying flesh. If I knew for a certainty that a person was coming to my house with the conscious design of doing me good, I should run for my life, as from that dry and parching wind of the African deserts called the simoom, which fills the mouth and nose and ears and eyes with dust 'til you are suffocated, for fear that I should get some of their good done to me,—some of their virus mingled with my blood. No,—in this case I would rather suffer evil the natural way. A person is not a good person to me because they will feed me if I should be starving, or warm me if I should be freezing, or pull me out of a ditch if I should ever fall into one. I can find you a Newfoundland dog that will do as much. Philanthropy is not love for one's fellow person in the broadest sense. It does not simply just save people in need. For if philanthropy does not help us in our best estate, when we are most worthy to be helped? In a true philanthropic setting, it has never been sincerely proposed that any good be done to me.

The Jesuits were quite balked by those Natives, who, being burned at the stake after the Jesuits claimed their "divine right to inherit the land," still suggested new modes of torture to their tormentors. Being superior to physical suffering, they were also superior to any prize which the missionaries could offer; and the law to "do unto others as you would have done to you" fell with less persuasiveness on the ears of those Indigenous, who, for their part, did not think much about nor care how they were done unto; who loved their enemies after a new fashion, and came very near to freely forgiving them all that they did.

Be sure that you give the poor the aid they most need, though it be your example which leaves them far behind. If you give money, spend yourself with it, and do not merely abandon it to them. We make curious mistakes sometimes. Often the poor person is not so cold and hungry as they are dirty and ragged and gross. It is partly their taste, and not merely their misfortune. If you give them money, they will perhaps buy more rags with it. There are a thousand hacking at the branches of evil to one who is striking at the root, and it may be that one who bestows the largest amount of time and money on the needy is doing the most to produce that misery which they strive in vain to relieve. It is the pious slave-breeder devoting the proceeds of every tenth enslaved human to buy a Sunday's liberty for the rest. Some show their kindness to the poor by employing them in their kitchens. Would one not be kinder if they employed themselves in their own kitchen instead, and let the worker find a way to employ themselves as well? To what end do we labor for others? You boast of spending a tenth part of your income in charity; maybe you should spend the nine tenths so, and be done with it. But society still only recovers a tenth part of it, it is squandered as the roots persist. Is this phenomenon owing to the generosity of the givers, or the wastefulness of the receivers, or could we contribute it to the carelessness of the officers in charge of the system that keeps this oddity in place? What is truly broken?

Philanthropy is almost the only virtue which is sufficiently appreciated by all of humankind. Nay, it is greatly overrated; and it is our selfish vanity which overrates it. A poor man, one sunny day here in Concord, praised a fellow townsperson to me, because, as he said, they were kind to the poor; meaning to himself. The kind uncles and aunts of the race are more esteemed than its true spiritual fathers and mothers.

I would not subtract anything from the praise that is due to the subject of philanthropy, but merely request justice for all who, by their lives and everyday works, are a blessing to humankind. I do not value chiefly a person's uprightness and benevolence, which are, as it were, their stem and leaves. I want the flower and fruit of a person; that some fragrance be wafted over from them to me, and some ripeness flavor our intercourse. Their goodness must not be a partial and transitory act, but a constant superfluity, which costs them nothing and of which they are unconscious. This is a charity that hides a multitude of sins. The philanthropist too often surrounds humankind with the remembrance of their own cast-off griefs as an atmosphere, and calls it sympathy. We should impart our courage, and not our despair; our health and ease, and not our disease, and take care that this does not spread by contagion.

From what southern plains comes up the voice of wailing? Under what latitudes reside the heathen to whom we would send light? Who is that intemperate and brutal one whom we would redeem?

If anything ails a person, if they have a pain in their bowels even, they forthwith set about reforming the world. Being a microcosm themselves, they discover, and it is a true discovery, that the world has been eating green apples; and it pains them again to think of that children will nibble at them before they are truly ripe; and straightway they set out their drastic philanthropic plan to educate the Esquimaux and the Patagonian, and visits the Indian and Chinese villages; and thus, by a few years of philanthropic activity, they cure themselves of dyspepsia, the globe acquires a faint blush on one or both of its cheeks, as if it were beginning to be ripen, and life loses its crudity and is once more sweet and wholesome to live. I never dreamed of any enormity greater than I have committed. I never knew, and never shall know, a worse person than myself. I have destroyed culture for my want of saving others from eating green apples, which are perfectly delicious, though perhaps not my first choice. I did not seek to show them the joys of red apples, but rather, to save them from green ones.

Why must we chase the reforming of ailments rather than the growth of goodness? Rescue the drowning and tie your shoe- strings. Take your time, and set about some free labor.

I believe that what so saddens the reformer is not their sympathy for fellows in distress, but their private ail. Let this be righted, let the spring come to them, the morning rise over their couch, and let them forsake their never-ending charitable endeavors without apology. My excuse for not lecturing against the use of tobacco is, that I never chewed it; that is a penalty which reformed tobacco-chewers have to pay; though there are things enough I have chewed, which I could lecture against free labor.

Our manners have been corrupted by communication with the saints. Our hymn-books resound with a melodious cursing of God and enduring her forever. One would say that even the prophets and redeemers had merely consoled the fears of humans, rather than confirmed their hopes. There is nowhere recorded a simple and irrepressible satisfaction with the raw gift of life, any righteous praise of God. If, then, we would indeed restore humankind by truly botanic, magnetic, or natural means, let us first be as simple and well as Nature ourselves, dispel the clouds which hang over our own brows, and take up a little life into our pores. Do not endeavor to be an overseer of the poor, but endeavor to become one of the worthies of the world.

I read in the Gulistan, or Flower Garden, of Sheik Sadi of Shiraz:

> They asked a wise person, saying: "Of the many celebrated trees which the Most High God has created, they call none 'free,' except the cypress, which bears no fruit. What mystery is there in this?" He replied: "Each has its

appropriate produce, and appointed season, during which it is fresh and blooming, and in the absence of this season, it is dry and withered; to neither state is the cypress exposed, being always flourishing; and of this nature are the 'azads,' or religious independents... If thy hand has plenty, be liberal as the date tree; but if it affords nothing to give away, be an azad, or free person, like the cypress."

WHERE I LIVED, AND
WHAT I LIVED FOR

At a certain season of our life, we are accustomed to consider every spot as the possible site of a house. I have thus surveyed the country on every side within a dozen miles of where I live. In imagination I have bought all the farms in succession, for all were to be bought, and I knew their price. I walked over each farmer's premises, tasted their wild apples, discoursed on agricultural practices with them; took their farm at their price, at any price, mortgaging it from them in my mind;—even put a higher price on it,—took everything but a deed of it,—took their word for their deed, for I dearly love to talk,—cultivated it, and the owner too, to some extent, I trust, and withdrew when I had enjoyed it long enough, leaving them to carry it on. This experience entitled me to be regarded as a sort of real-estate actor by my friends. Wherever I sat, there I might live, and the landscape radiated from me accordingly. What is a house but a seat?—better if a country seat. I discovered many a site, which some might have thought too far from the village, but to my eyes the village was too far from it. Well, there I might live, I said; and there I did live, for an hour, a summer and a winter life; saw how I could let the years run off, buffet the winter through, and see the spring come in. The future inhabitants of this region, wherever they may place their houses, may be sure that they have been anticipated. An afternoon of daydreaming was sufficient to lay out the land into orchard, woodlot, and pasture, and to decide what fine oaks or pines should be left to stand before the door, and where each cut tree might be used to the best advantage; and then I let it lie, for a person is rich in proportion to the number of things which they can afford to let alone.

My imagination carried me so far that I was even refused the purchase of several farms,—but I never got my fingers burned by actual possession. The nearest that I came to actual possession was when I bought the Hollowell place, and had begun to sort my seeds, and collected materials with which to make a wheelbarrow to carry it on or off with; but before the owner gave me a deed of it, they changed their mind and wished to keep it, and they offered me ten dollars to release them from the contract. Now, to speak the truth, I had but ten cents in the world, and it surpassed my arithmetic to tell, if I was a man who had ten cents, or who had a farm, or ten dollars, or all of it together. However, I let them keep the ten dollars and the farm too, for I had carried it far enough; or rather, to be generous, I sold them the farm for just what I gave for it, and, as they were not rich themselves, made a present of ten dollars, and I still had my ten cents, and seeds, and materials for a wheelbarrow left. I found thus that I had been a rich man without any damage to my poverty. But I retained access to the landscape, and I have since annually carried off what it yielded without a wheelbarrow. With respect to landscapes,—

"I am monarch of all I survey,
My right there is none to dispute."

I have frequently seen a poet withdraw from a farm, having enjoyed the most valuable part, while the crusty farmer supposed that they had got a few wild apples only. Why, the owner does not know it for many years when a poet has put their farm in rhyme; the pot has fairly impounded it, milked it, skimmed it, and got all the cream, and left the farmer only the skimmed milk.

The real attractions of the Hollowell farm, to me, were; its complete retirement, being about two miles from the village, half a mile from the nearest neighbor, and separated from the highway by a broad field and bounded by the river, which the owner said protected it from spring frosts, by fog, though that was nothing to me; the gray color and ruinous state of the house and barn, and the dilapidated fences, which put such an interval between me and the last occupant; the hollow and lichen-covered apple trees, gnawed by rabbits, showing what kind of neighbors I should have; but above all, the recollection I had of it from my earliest voyages up the river, when the house was concealed behind a dense grove of red maples, through which I heard the house-dog bark. I was in haste to buy it, before the owner finished harvesting rocks, cutting down the hollow apple trees, and grubbing up some young birches which had sprung up in the pasture; in short, before they had made any more extractions of, or so-called improvements to, the land. I was ready to carry it on; like Atlas, to take the world on my shoulders, but I knew all the while that it would yield the most abundant crop of the kind I wanted if I could only afford to purchase it and let it alone, to let it be unmolested in my possession. For this curious world which we inhabit is more wonderful than it is convenient; more beautiful than it is useful; it is more to be admired and enjoyed than used. But it turned out as I have said.

All that I can say, then, with respect to farming on a large scale, (I have always cultivated a garden) was that I have my seeds ready. Many think that seeds improve with age. I have no doubt that time discriminates between the good and the bad; and when at last I shall plant, I shall be less likely to be disappointed. But I would say to my fellows, once for all, As long as possible live free and uncommitted. It makes but little difference whether you are committed to a farm or the county jail.

Old Cato says "When you think of getting a farm, turn it thus in your mind, not to buy greedily;...do not spare your pains to look at it, and do not think it enough to go round it once. The oftener you go there the more it will please you, if it is good." I think I shall not buy greedily, but go round and round it as long as I live, and be buried in it first, that it may please me the more at last.

The present was my next experiment of this kind, which I purpose to describe more at length; and for convenience, putting the experience of two years in the woods into one.

When first I took up my abode in the woods, that is, began to spend my nights as well as days there, which, by accident, was on Independence Day, or the Fourth of July, 1845, my house was not finished for winter, but was merely a defense against the rain, without plastering or chimney, the walls being of rough, weather-stained boards, with wide chinks, which made it cool at night. The upright white hewn studs and freshly planed door and window casings gave it a clean and airy look, especially in the morning, when its timbers were saturated with dew, so that I fancied that by noon some sweet gum would exude from them. To my imagination it retained throughout the day more or less of this auroral character, reminding me of a certain house on a mountain which I had visited the year before. This was an airy and unplastered cabin, fit to entertain a traveling god. The winds which passed over my dwelling were like those that sweep over the ridges of mountains, bearing the broken strains, or celestial parts only, of terrestrial music. The morning wind forever blows, the poem of creation is uninterrupted; but few are the ears that hear it.

The only house I had been the owner of before, if I except a boat, was a tent, which I used occasionally when making excursions in the summer, and this is still rolled up in my garret; but the boat, after passing from hand to hand, has gone down the stream of time. With this more substantial shelter about me, I had made some progress toward settling in the world. This frame, so slightly clad, was a sort of crystallization around me. I did not need to go outdoors to take the air, for the atmosphere within had lost none of its freshness. It was not so much within doors as behind a door where I sat, even in the rainiest weather. I have heard that "An abode without birds is like a tea made without water." Such was not my abode, for I found myself suddenly an intimate neighbor to the birds; not by having imprisoned one, but having caged myself near them. I was not only nearer to some of those which commonly frequent the garden and the orchard, but to those wilder and more thrilling songsters of the forest which never, or rarely, serenade a villager,—the wood-thrush, the veery, the scarlet tanager, the field-sparrow, the whippoorwill, and many others.

I was seated by the shore of a small pond, about a mile and a half south of the village of Concord and somewhat higher than it, in the midst of an extensive wood between that town and Lincoln, and about two miles south of our only field known to fame, Concord Battle Ground; but I was so low in the woods that the opposite shore, half a mile off, covered with wood, was my most distant horizon. Here and there, the pond's soft ripples or its smooth reflecting surface was revealed, while the mists, like ghosts, were stealthily withdrawing in every direction into the woods, as at the breaking up of some nocturnal convention. The very dew seemed to hang upon the trees later into the day than usual, as on the sides of mountains.

This small lake was a perfect neighbor inbetween the intervals of gentle rainstorms in August, when both air and water were perfectly still, and the sky overcast. Mid-afternoon had all the serenity of evening, and the wood-thrush sang around, and was heard from shore to shore. A lake like this is never smoother than at such a time; and the clear portion of the air above the water, full of light and reflections, becomes a lower heaven itself.

From a hilltop nearby, where the wood had been recently cut off, there was a pleasing vista southward across the pond, seen through a wide indentation in the hills. Here, the opposite sides sloping toward each other suggested a stream flowing out in that direction through a wooded valley, but stream there was none. Indeed, by standing on tiptoe I could catch a glimpse of some of the peaks of the still bluer and more distant mountain ranges in the north-west, through the valley, and also of some portion of the village. But in other directions, even from this point, I could not see over or beyond the woods which surrounded me.

It is well to have some water in your neighborhood, to give buoyancy to and float the ground. One value even of the smallest well is, that when you look into it you see that they layer of earth on which we stand is not a continent, but rather, a floating island on a watery planet.

Though the view from my door was still more contracted, I did not feel crowded or confined in the least. There was pasture enough for my imagination. "There are none happy in the world but beings who enjoy freely a vast horizon,"—said Damodara, when his herds required new and larger pastures.

Both place and time were changed in these woods, and I dwelt nearer to those parts of the universe and to those eras in history which had most attracted me. Where I lived was as far off as many a region viewed nightly by astronomers. We are wont to imagine rare and delectable places in some remote and more celestial corner of the system, behind the constellation of Cassiopeia's Chair, far from noise and disturbance. I discovered that my house actually resided in such a withdrawn, but forever new and unprofaned, part of the universe. If it were worth the while to settle in those parts near to the Pleiades or the Hyades, to Aldebaran or Altair, then I was really there already, or at an equal remoteness from the life which I had left behind.

"There was a shepherd that did live,
And held their thoughts as high
As the mountains whereon the flocks did feed,
As they pondered and looked by."

What should we think of the shepherd's life if their flocks always wandered to higher pastures than their thoughts?

Every morning was a cheerful invitation to make my life of equal simplicity, and I may say innocence, with Nature herself. I have been a worshipper as sincere as the Greeks as they worshiped Aurora, the Roman goddess of the dawn. I got up early and bathed in the pond; that was a religious exercise, and one of the best things which I did. They say that characters were engraven on the bathing tub of king Tching-thang to this effect: "Renew thyself completely each day; do it again, and again, and forever again." I can understand that. Morning brings back the heroic ages. I was as much affected by the faint hum of a mosquito making its invisible and unimaginable tour through my apartment at earliest dawn, when I was sitting with door and windows open, as I could be by any trumpet that ever sang of fame. It was Homer's requiem; itself an Iliad and Odyssey in the air, singing its own wrath and wanderings. There was something cosmical about it; a standing advertisement of the everlasting vigor and fertility of the world. The morning, which is the most memorable season of the day, is the awakening hour. Then there is least somnolence in us; and for an hour, at least, some part of us awakes which slumbers all the rest of the day and night. Little is to be expected of that day, if it can be called a day, to which we are not awakened by our Genius, but by the mechanical nudging of some servitor, by the ringing of factory bells. How sweet it is to be awakened to a higher life than we fell asleep from, and thus the darkness bears its fruit, and proves itself to be good and worthy, no less than the light. By our own newly-acquired force and rising aspirations from within, accompanied by the undulations of Nature's celestial music, we understand what it means to be alive. One who does not believe that each day contains an earlier, more sacred and auroral hour than they have yet seen, they have despaired of life, and are pursuing a descending and darkening way. After a partial cessation, the soul of a human, or its organs rather, are reinvigorated each dawning day, and their Genius tries again what noble life it can make. All memorable events, I should say, transpire in morning time and in a morning atmosphere. The Vedas say, "All intelligences awake with the morning." Poetry and art, and the fairest and most memorable of the actions of people, date from such an hour. All poets and heroes are the children of Aurora, and emit their music at sunrise. To they whose elastic and vigorous thoughts keep pace with the sun, the day is a perpetual morning. It matters not what the clocks say or the attitudes and labors of townspeople. Morning is when I am awake and there is a dawn in me. Moral reform is the effort to come out of a sleep. Why is it that one gives such a poor account of their day if they have not been slumbering properly? They are not such poor calculators. If they had not been overcome with drowsiness, they would have performed something. The millions are awake enough for physical labor; but only one in a million is awake enough for effective intellectual exertion, only one in a hundred millions to a poetic or divine life. To be awake is to be alive. I have never yet met anyone who was quite awake. How could I have looked them in the face?

We must learn to reawaken and keep ourselves awake, not by mechanical aids, but by an infinite expectation of the dawn, which does not forsake us in our soundest sleep. I am encouraged by the unquestionable ability of people to elevate their lives by conscious endeavors. It is something to be able to paint a particular picture, or to carve a statue, and so to make a few objects beautiful; but it is far more glorious to carve and paint the very atmosphere and medium through which we look, which morally we can do. To affect the quality of the day, that is the highest of arts. Everyone is tasked to make their life, even in its smallest details, worthy of the contemplation of their most elevated and critical hour.

I went to the woods because I wished to live deliberately, to front only the essential facts of life, and see if I could not learn what it had to teach, and not, when I came to die, discover that I had not lived. I did not wish to live what was not life, for living is so dear; nor did I wish to practice resignation, unless it was quite necessary. I wanted to live deep and suck out all the marrow of life, to live so sturdily and Spartan-like as to sift out all that was not true life, to cut a broad swath and shave close, to drive life into a corner, and reduce it to its lowest terms, and, if it proved to be meaningful, to then get the whole and genuine meaningfulness of it, and publish its meaningfulness to the world; or if it were sublime, to know it by experience, and be able to give a true account of it in my next excursion. For most people, it appears to me, are in a strange uncertainty about life, whether it was created by the devil or by gods, and have somewhat hastily concluded that it is the chief end of humans here to "glorify God and enjoy God forever."

Still we live in a basic manner, like ants; though the fable tells us that we were long ago changed into humans. Our life is frittered away by detail. An honest person has hardly need to count more than their ten fingers, or in extreme cases they may add their ten toes, and lump the rest. Simplicity, simplicity, simplicity! I say, let your affairs be as two or three, and not a hundred or a thousand; instead of a million, count half a dozen, and keep your accounts on your thumb nail. In the midst of this choppy sea of civilized life, such are the clouds and storms and quicksands and thousand-and-one items to be accounted for, that a person who manages to succeed must be a great calculator. Simplify, simplify. Instead of three meals a day, if it be necessary eat but one; instead of a hundred forks, five; and reduce other things in proportion. Our life is like a German Confederacy, made up of petty states, with its boundary forever fluctuating, so that even a German cannot tell you how it is bounded at any moment. The nation itself, with all its so called internal improvements, which, by the way are all external and superficial, is just such an unwieldy and overgrown establishment, cluttered with furniture and tripped up by its own traps, ruined by luxury and heedless expense; and the only cure for it is a more than Spartan simplicity of life and elevation of purpose. It lives too fast. People think that it is essential that the Nation have commerce, and export ice, and talk through a telegraph, and ride thirty miles an hour; but whether we should live like baboons or like humans is a little uncertain. If we do not lay out railroad sleepers, and forge rails, and devote days and nights to the work, but go to tinkering upon our lives to improve them, who will be left to build railroads? And if railroads are not built, how shall we get to heaven in season? But if we stay at home and mind our business, who will want railroads? We do not ride on the railroad; it rides upon us. Did you ever think what those sleepers are that underlie the railroad? Each one is a human laborer, and a tree; both human and tree are Nature, industrialized. The rails are laid on them, and they are covered with sand, and the cars run smoothly over them. They are sound sleepers, I assure you. And every few years a new lot is laid down and run over; and it continues that, if some have the pleasure of riding on a rail, others have the misfortune to be ridden upon. I am glad to know that it takes a gang of laborers to keep the sleepers down and level in their beds, for this is a sign that they will surely sometime find life and get up again.

Why should we live with such hurry and waste of life? We are determined to be starved before we are hungry. People say that a stitch in time saves nine, and so they take a thousand stitches to-day to save nine to-morrow. As for work, we haven't any of any consequence. If I should only give a few pulls at the parish bell- rope, as for a fire, there is hardly a person on their farm in the outskirts of Concord that would not forsake all and follow that sound, not mainly to save property from the flames, but, if we will confess the truth, much more to see it burn, or to see it put out, and have a hand in it, or feel like we have, at least. Hardly anyone takes a half hour's nap after dinner, but if they do, they wake and hold up their head and ask, "What's the news?" After a night's sleep the news is as indispensable as breakfast. "Pray tell me anything new that has happened to anyone, anywhere on this globe,"—and they read the news over their coffee and rolls; they read that a man has had his eyes gouged out this morning on the Wachito River; never recognizing that they themselves live in the dark unfathomed mammoth cave of this world, and have but the undeveloped rudiment of an eye.

For my part, I could easily do without the post-office. I think that there are very few important communications made through it. To speak critically, I never received more than one or two letters in my life that were worth the postage. The penny-post is, commonly, an institution through which you seriously offer a person that penny for their thoughts which is usually safely offered in jest. And I am sure that I never read any memorable news in a newspaper. If we read of someone being robbed, or murdered, or killed by accident, or one house burned, or one vessel wrecked, or one steamboat blown up, or one cow run over on the Western Railroad, or one mad dog killed,—we never need read of another. One is enough. If you are acquainted with the principle, what do you care for a myriad instances and applications? To a philosopher all news, as it is called, is gossip, and they who edit and read it are bored gossipers over their afternoon tea. Yet not just a few are greedy after this gossip. There was such a rush, as I hear, the other day at one of the offices to learn the foreign news by the last arrival, that several large squares of plate glass belonging to the establishment were broken by the pressure,—all to hear news which I seriously think a ready wit might write ahead of time by twelve months, or twelve years, with sufficient enough accuracy. As for Spain, for instance, if you know how to throw in names of current politicians and entertainers, from time to time in the right proportions, and serve up a bull-fight when other entertainments fail, it will be true to the letter, no matter the year. And as for England, almost the last significant scrap of news from that quarter was the revolution of 1649; and if you have learned the history of her crops for an average year, you never need attend to that thing again, unless your speculations are of a merely pecuniary character. If you ask someone who rarely looks into the newspapers, nothing new does ever happen in foreign parts, a French revolution not excepted.

What news! how much more important to know what that is which is never old!

Shams and delusions are esteemed for the most entertaining news, while reality is simply fabulous. If we would steadily observe realities only, and not allow ourselves to be deluded... life would be like a fairy tale and the Arabian Nights' Entertainments. If we respected only what is inevitable and has a right to be, music and poetry would resound along the streets. When we are unhurried and wise, we perceive that only great and worthy things have any permanent and absolute existence,—that petty fears and petty pleasures are but the shadow of reality. This is always exhilarating and sublime. By closing our eyes and slumbering in our minds throughout our days, and consenting to be deceived by shows, we establish and confirm our daily routines and habits, built on purely illusory foundations. Children, who play life, discern its true law and relations more clearly than adults, who fail to live it worthily, but who think that they are wiser by experience—that is, by failure.

I have read in a Hindoo book, that "there was a Queen's daughter, who, being expelled in infancy from her native city, was brought up by a forester, and, growing up to maturity in that state, imagined himself to belong to the barbarous race with which she lived. One of her mother's ministers having discovered him, revealed to her what he was, and the misconception of her character was removed, and he knew himself to be a queen, too. So the soul," continues the Hindoo philosopher, "from the circumstances in which it is placed, mistakes its own character, until the truth is revealed to it by some holy teacher, and then it knows themselves to be God, and only God, without needing other labels."

I perceive that we inhabitants of New England live the mundane lives that we do because our vision does not penetrate the surface of things. We think that that is which appears to be. If one should walk through their town and see only the reality, if they should give us an account of the realities they beheld there, we should not recognize the place in their description. Look at a meeting-house, or a court-house, or a jail, or a shop, or a dwelling-house, and say what that thing really is before a true gaze, and they would all go to pieces in your account of them. Only bricks, iron, glass, and wood. Humans hold truth remote, out of sight, in the outskirts of the system, behind the farthest star, before the universe and after it's perishing. We prefer euphemisms.

In eternity there is indeed something true and sublime. But all these times and places and occasions to be described are now and here. God culminates in the present moment, and will never be more divine in the lapse of all the ages. And we are enabled to apprehend what is sublime and noble only by the perpetual instilling and drenching of the reality that surrounds us. The universe constantly and obediently answers to our conceptions; whether we travel fast or slow, the track is laid for us. Let us spend our lives in conceiving, then. Let us spend one day as deliberately as Nature, and not be thrown off the track by every nutshell and mosquito's wing that falls on the rails. Let us rise early and fast, gently and without perturbation; let company come and let company go, let the bells ring and the children cry. Why should we knock under and go with the stream? Let us not be upset and overwhelmed in that terrible rapid and whirlpool called a dinner, uncomplicated until we make it so. Weather this danger and you are safe, for the rest of the way is down hill. With engaged nerves, with morning vigor, sail by it, looking another way, tied to the mast like Ulysses to press forward and avoid the siren calls of distraction. If the engine whistles, let it whistle 'til it is hoarse for its pains. If the bell rings, why should we run? We will consider what kind of music they are like. Let us settle ourselves, and work and wedge our feet downward through the mud and slush of opinion, and prejudice, and tradition, and delusion, and appearance, that sediment which covers the globe, through Paris and London, through New York and Boston and Concord, through church and state, through poetry and philosophy and religion, 'til we come to a hard bottom and rocks in place, which we can call reality, and say, "This is it, and there is no mistake;" and then begin, having a point of reference, below water and frost and fire, a place where you might pour foundation for a wall, or set a lamp-post safely, or perhaps a gauge, perhaps in the future, a "Realometer," that coming ages might know how deep a deposit of shams and appearances had gathered from time to time. If you stand face to face with a fact, you will see the sun glimmer on its surfaces, and feel its sweet edge dividing you through the heart and marrow, and so you will happily conclude your mortal career. Be it life or death, we crave only reality. If we are dying in reality, let us hear the rattle in our throats and feel cold in the extremities; if we are alive in reality, let us go about our business.

Time is but the stream I go a-fishing in. I drink at it; but while I drink I see the sandy bottom and detect how shallow it is. Its thin current slides away, but eternity remains. We are but a spoke in the wheel of time, rolling 'round and 'round. My life, a blip of heaven-on-earth; a gift with the fuse burning at both ends. I would drink deeper; like a fish in the sky, whose bottom is pebbly with stars. I have always been regretting that I was not as wise as the day I was born. The intellect is a cleaver; it discerns and rifts its way into the secret sacredness of things. I do not wish to be any more busy with my hands than is necessary. My head is my hands and feet. I feel all my best faculties concentrated in it. My instinct tells me that my head is an organ for burrowing, as some creatures use their snout and fore paws, and with it I would mine and burrow my way through these hills. I think that the richest vein is somewhere hereabouts; and here I will begin to mine.

READING

My residence was more favorable, not only to thought, but to serious reading, than a university; and though I was beyond the range of the ordinary circulating library, I had more than ever come within the influence of those books which circulate round the world, whose sentences were first written on bark, and are now merely copied from time to time on to linen paper. I kept Homer's Iliad on my table through the summer, though I looked at his pages only now and then. Incessant labor with my hands, at first, for I had my house to finish and my beans to hoe at the same time, made more study impossible. Yet I sustained myself by the prospect of such reading in future. I read one or two lighthearted books of travel in the intervals of my work, 'til that endeavor made me ask myself where it was that I lived.

The student may excessively read Homer or Æschylus in the Greek without danger of overindulgence or luxuriousness, for they will in some measure emulate their heroes, and consecrate morning hours to their pages. The modern cheap and fertile press has done little to bring us nearer to the heroic writers of antiquity. I believe that the adventurous student will always study classics, in whatever language they may be written and however ancient they may be. For what are the classics but the noblest recorded thoughts of humankind? They are the only oracles which are not decayed, and there are such answers to the most modern inquiry in them as current philosophers give. We might as well omit to study Nature because she is old. To read ancient books in a true spirit is a noble exercise, and one that will task the reader more than any exercise which the customs of the day esteem. It requires a training such as the athletes underwent, the steady intention almost of the whole life to this object. Books must be read as deliberately and reservedly as they were written. However much we may admire the orator's occasional bursts of eloquence during an enrapturing speech, the noblest written words commonly rest comfortably above the fleeting spoken language, as the solid sky with its stars is behind the clouds. There are the stars, and they who can, may read them. The astronomers forever comment on and observe them. They are not exhalations like our daily colloquies, social formalities, and vaporous breath. What is called orator's eloquence in the forum is commonly found to be rhetoric in the study. The orator yields to the inspiration of a transient occasion, and speaks to the mob before them, to those who can hear them; but the writer, whose more steady life is their occasion, and who would be much distracted by the same event and the same crowd which inspire the orator, speaks to the intellect and health of humankind, to all in any age who take the time to understand.

No wonder that Alexander carried the Iliad with him on his expeditions in a precious casket. A written word is the choicest of relics. Words may be breathed from all human lips;—not be represented on canvas or in marble only, but be carved out of the breath of life itself. Two thousand summers have imparted to the monuments of Grecian literature, but they do not show the wear of Grecian marble, or perhaps only a slightly maturer golden and autumnal tint, for these written words have carried their own serene and celestial atmosphere into all lands to protect them against the corrosion of time. Books are the treasured wealth of the world and the fit inheritance of generations and nations. Books, the oldest and the best, stand naturally and rightfully on the shelves of every cottage. They have no cause of their own to plead, but while they enlighten and sustain the reader their common sense will not refuse them. Their authors are a natural and irresistible aristocracy in every society, and, more than royals or emperors, exert an influence on humankind. When the business trader has earned, by enterprise and industry, their coveted leisure and independence, and is admitted to the circles of wealth and fashion, they turn inevitably at last to those still higher but yet inaccessible circles of intellect and genius. They become sensible to the imperfection of culture and the vanity and insufficiency of all their riches, and further prove their good sense by the pains which they take to secure for their children that intellectual culture whose want they so keenly feel; and thus it is that they become the founder of a family, whether biological or selected from the masses.

That age will be rich indeed when those relics which we call Classics, and the still older and more than classic but even less known Scriptures of the nations, shall have still further accumulated, when the Vaticans shall be filled with Vedas and Zendavestas and Bibles, with Homers and Dantes and Shakespeares, and all the centuries to come shall have successively deposited their trophies in the forum of the world. By such a pile we may hope to scale heaven at last.

The works of the great poets have never yet been read by mankind, for only great poets can read them. They have only been read as the multitude read the stars, at most astrologically, not astronomically. Most have learned to read to serve a paltry convenience, as they have learned to cipher in order to keep accounts and not be cheated in trade; but of reading as a noble exercise they know little or nothing; yet this only is reading, in a high sense, not that which lulls us as a luxury and suffers the nobler faculties to sleep the while, but what we have to stand on tip-toe to read and devote our most alert and wakeful hours to.

I think that having learned our letters we should read the best that is in literature, and not be forever repeating our abc's, sitting on the lowest and foremost form all our lives. Most are satisfied if they read or hear read to them, the wisdom of one good book, perhaps the Bible, and for the rest of their lives vegetate their faculties in what is called easy reading, or perhaps even "easy watching." There are those who, like goats, can digest all sorts of this procured and mush-brained entertainment, even after the fullest dinner, for they cannot let anything pass them without consuming. If others are the machines to provide this provender, they are the machines to consume it. They read the nine thousandth tale about Zebulon and Sephronia, and how they loved as none had ever loved before, and neither did the course of their true love run smooth,—at any rate, how it did run and stumble, and get up again and go on! "The Skip of the Tip-Toe- Hop," a Romance of the Middle Ages, by the celebrated author 'M.G. Millhouse' was released as a nation-sweeping book series; and then a great rush to the box office, now that it has been turned into a play. All this they read and watch with saucer eyes, erect and with primitive curiosity, but without extracting the moral. The result is dullness of sight, a stagnation of the vital circulations, and a general deliquium and sloughing off of all the intellectual faculties. This sort of gingerbread is baked daily and with more short-cuts than pure wheat or rye in almost every oven, and it always finds a surer market, eager to consume.

I know a woodchopper, of middle age, who takes a French paper, not for news as he says, but to "keep himself in practice," he being a Canadian by birth; and when I ask him what he considers the best thing he can do in this world, he says, beside this, to keep up and add to his English. This is about as much as the college bred generally do or aspire to do, and they take an English newspaper for the purpose. One who has just come from reading perhaps one of the best English books will find how many with whom they can converse about it? Or suppose they come from reading a Greek or Latin classic in the original, they will find nobody at all to speak to, but must keep silence about it. Indeed, there is hardly the professor in our colleges, who, if they have mastered the difficulties of the language, has proportionally mastered the difficulties of the wit and poetry of a Greek poet. Most do not know that any nation but the Hebrews have had a scripture. A person, anyone, will go considerably out of their way to pick up a silver dollar; but here are golden words, which the wisest ancestors of antiquity have uttered, and whose worths have been assured by the wise of every succeeding age;— and yet we choose the daily news, social gossip, the jester shows, and easy- reading books, which are for children and beginners; and our reading, our conversation and thinking, are all on a very low level, worthy only of manikins. Mind you, enjoy yourself. But don't forget to give your head something of substance, for it withers on a diet of romance novels. Plato's Dialogues, which contain what was immortal in him, lie on the next shelf, and yet we mostly never read them. We are like the titmouse, who flies always close to the ground, rather than soaring up into the open sky.

How many a person has begun a new era in their life from the reading of a single book! The book exists for us perchance which will explain our miracles and reveal new ones. The at-present unutterable things we may find somewhere uttered. These same questions that disturb and puzzle and confound us have in their turn occurred to all the wise ones before us; not one has been omitted; and each has answered them, according to their ability, by their words and their life. Moreover, with wisdom we shall learn liberality. The solitary hired worker on a farm in the outskirts of Concord, who has had their second birth and peculiar religious experience, and is driven as they believe into the silent gravity and exclusiveness by their faith, may think it is not true for all; but Zoroaster, thousands of years ago, travelled the same road and had the same experience; but he, being wise, knew it to be universal. Let one humbly commune with Zoroaster then, and even with Jesus Christ, and let "our church" go by the board—we have nothing to gain from these dilutions of what our ancestors offered us as divine and universal spiritual truth. We have our own access line to the divine.

It appears to me that humans are altogether too much insisted upon. The egotism of our race prohibits us from taking wider views of the universe. I do not value any view of the universe into which humans and the institutions of people enter very largely and absorb much of the attention.

We boast that we belong to the nineteenth century and are making the most rapid strides of any nation. But consider how little this village does for its own culture. I do not wish to flatter my townspeople, nor to be flattered by them, for that will not advance either of us. We need to be provoked,—goaded like oxen, as we are, into a trot. We have a somewhat decent system of common schools for children and infants; but excepting the half-starved college, and the puny beginning of a library suggested by the state, no school for ourselves. We spend more on almost any single article of bodily aliment than on our total mental aliment. It is time that we had uncommon schools, that we did not leave off our education when we begin to be adults. It is time that villages were universities, and their elder inhabitants be the fellows of universities, paid with leisure—to let them pursue liberal studies the rest of their lives, to repay to them for the service of their wisdom granted. Shall the world be confined to one Paris or one Oxford forever? Cannot students be boarded here and get a liberal education under the skies of Concord? Can we not hire a philosopher to lecture to us? Alas! what with foddering the cattle and tending the store, we are kept from school too long, and our education is sadly neglected. The village should be the patron of the fine arts. It is rich enough, but it spends frivolously. It wants only the magnanimity and refinement. It can spend money enough on such things as farmers and traders value, but it is thought Utopian to propose spending money for things which the wise know to be of far more worth. This town has spent seventeen thousand dollars on a town-house, thank fortune or politics, but probably it will not spend so much on living wit, the true substance to put into that shell, in a hundred years. The one hundred and twenty-five dollars annually subscribed for a Lyceum in the winter is better spent than any other equal sum raised in the town. If we live in the nineteenth century, why should we not enjoy the advantages which the nineteenth century offers? Why should our life be in any respect provincial? If we will read newspapers, why not skip the gossip of Boston and take the best newspaper in the world at once?— not be sucking the pap of "neutral family" papers. Let the reports of all the learned societies come to us, and we will see if they know any thing, if they shall stand the test of time. Why should we leave it to the media to select our daily reading? As the nobleperson of cultivated taste surrounds themself with whatever conduces to their culture,—genius—learning—wit— books—paintings—statuary—music—philosophical instruments, and the like; so let the village do,—not stop short at a few tools and a puny library because our pilgrim forefounders got through a cold winter once on a bleak rock with these. To act collectively is according to the spirit of our institutions; and I am confident that, as our circumstances are more flourishing, our means are greater than the royal's. We can hire all the wise in the world to come and teach, and board them round the while, and not be provincial at all. That is the uncommon school we want. Instead of nobles directing our education towards building us into industry machines, encouraging us to "relax" our minds in the evenings with schmuck, utterly fatigued from a long day of doing everything but learning nothing; let us instead create noble villages; let us learn to think for ourselves. If it is necessary, omit one bridge over the river, go round a little there, and throw one arch at least over the darker gulf of ignorance which surrounds us.

SOUNDS

But while we are confined to books, though the most select and classic, and read only particular written languages, which are themselves but dialects which are narrow and limited in perspective, we are in danger of forgetting the language which all things and events speak without metaphor, which alone is copious and standard. Much is published, but little printed. The rays which stream through the shutter will be no longer remembered when the shutter is wholly removed. No method nor discipline can supersede the necessity of being forever on the alert. What is a course of history, or philosophy, or poetry, no matter how well selected, or the best society, or the most admirable routine of life, compared with the discipline of looking always at what is to be seen? Will you be a reader, a student merely, or a seer? Read your fate, see what is before you, and walk on into futurity.

I did not read books the first summer; I hoed beans. But there were times when I could not afford to sacrifice the bloom of the present moment to any work, whether of the head or hands. I love a broad margin to my life. Sometimes, in a summer morning, having taken my accustomed bath, I sat in my sunny doorway from sunrise 'til noon, rapt in a revery, amidst the pines and hickories and sumacs, in undisturbed solitude and stillness, while the birds sang around or flitted noiseless through the house, until by the sun falling in at my west window, or the noise of some traveler's wagon on the distant highway, I was reminded of the lapse of time. I grew in those seasons like corn in the night, and they were far better than any work of the hands would have been. They were not time subtracted from my life, but so much over and above my usual allowance. I realized what the Eastern cultures mean by contemplation and the forsaking of works. For the most part, I minded not how the hours went. The day advanced as if to light some work of mine; it was morning, and lo, now it is evening, and nothing memorable is accomplished. Instead of singing like the birds, I silently smiled at my incessant good fortune. As the sparrow had its trill, sitting on the hickory before my door, so had I my chuckle or suppressed warble which they might hear out of my nest. My days were not days of the week, bearing the stamp of any heathen deity, nor were they minced into hours and fretted by the ticking of a clock; for I lived like the Indigenous Peoples, of whom it is said that "for yesterday, to-day, and to-morrow they have only one word, and they express the variety of meaning by pointing backward for yesterday, forward for to-morrow, and overhead for the passing day." This was sheer idleness to my fellow-townspeople, no doubt; but if the birds and flowers had tried me by their standard, I should not have been found wanting. One must find their occasions in themself, it is true. The natural day is very calm, and will not disapprove of their curious loafing about.

I had this advantage, at least, in my mode of life, over those who were obliged to look abroad for amusement, to society and the theatre, that my life itself had become my amusement and never ceased to be novel. It was a drama of many scenes and without an end. If we were always indeed getting our living, and regulating our lives according to the last and best mode we had learned, we should never be troubled with dissatisfaction and boredom. Follow your genius closely enough, and it will not fail to show you a fresh prospect every hour. Housework was a pleasant pastime. When my floor was dirty, I rose early, and, setting all my furniture out of doors on the grass, bed and bedstead making but one budget, dashed water on the floor, and sprinkled white sand from the pond on it, and then with a broom scrubbed it clean and white; and by the time the villagers had broken their fast the morning, the sun had dried my house sufficiently to allow me to move in again, and my meditations were almost uninterrupted. It was pleasant to see my whole household effects out on the grass, making a little pile like a nomad's pack, and my three- legged table, from which I did not remove the books and pen and ink, standing amid the pines and hickories. They seemed glad to get out themselves, and as if unwilling to be brought in. I was sometimes tempted to stretch an awning over them and take my seat there. It was worth the while to see the sun shine on these things, and hear the free wind blow on them; so much more interesting most familiar objects look out of doors than in the house. A bird sits on the next bough, life-everlasting grows under the table, and blackberry vines run round its legs; pine cones, chestnut burs, and strawberry leaves are strewn about. It looked as if this was the way these forms came to be transferred to our furniture, to tables, chairs, and bedsteads,— because they once stood in their midst.

My house was on the side of a hill, immediately on the edge of the larger wood, in a young forest of pitch pines and hickories, and half a dozen rods from the pond, to which a narrow footpath led down the hill. In my front yard grew the strawberry, blackberry, and life-everlasting, johnswort and goldenrod, shrub-oaks and sand-cherry, blueberry and groundnut. Near the end of May, the sand-cherry (Cerasus pumila,) adorned the sides of the path with its delicate flowers arranged in umbels cylindrically about its short stems, which last, in the fall, weighed down with good sized and handsome cherries, fell over in wreaths like rays on every side. I tasted them out of compliment to Nature, though they were scarcely palatable. The sumac (Rhus glabra,) grew luxuriantly about the house, pushing up through the embankment which I had made, and growing five or six feet the first season. Its broad pinnate tropical leaf was pleasant though strange to look on. The large buds, suddenly pushing out late in the spring from dry sticks which had seemed to be dead, developed themselves as by magic into graceful green and tender boughs, an inch in diameter; and sometimes, as I sat at my window, so heedlessly did they grow and tax their weak joints, I heard a fresh and tender bough suddenly fall like a fan to the ground, when there was not a breath of air stirring, broken off by its own weight. In August, the large masses of berries, which, when in flower, had attracted many wild bees, gradually assumed their bright velvety crimson hue, and by their weight again bent down and broke the tender limbs.

As I sit at my window this summer afternoon, hawks are circling about my clearing; the tantivy of wild pigeons, flying by twos and threes athwart my view, or perching restless on the white- pine boughs behind my house, gives a voice to the air; a fishhawk dimples the glassy surface of the pond and brings up a fish; a mink steals out of the marsh before my door and seizes a frog by the shore; the sedge is bending under the weight of the reed- birds flitting hither and thither; and for the last half hour I have heard the rattle of railroad cars, now dying away and then reviving like the beat of a partridge, conveying travelers from Boston to the country. For I did not live so out of the world as that boy who, as I hear, was put out to a farmer in the east part of the town, but ere long ran away and came home again, quite down at the heel and homesick. He had never seen such a dull and out-of-the-way place; the folks were all gone off; why, you couldn't even hear the whistle! I doubt if there is such a place in Massachusetts now:—

> "In truth, our village has become a butt
> For one of those fleet railroad shafts, and o'er
> Our peaceful plain its soothing sound is—
> Concord," as my friend Ellery Channing writes.

The Fitchburg Railroad touches the pond about a hundred rods south of where I dwell. I usually go to the village along its causeway, and am, as it were, re-lated to society by this link. The workers on the freight trains, who go over the whole length of the road, bow to me as to an old acquaintance, they pass me so often, and apparently they take me for an employee; and so I am. I too would happily be a track-repairer of sorts, somewhere in the orbit of the earth, though not work-ing with wood or steel.

The whistle of the locomotive penetrates my woods, summer and winter, sounding like the scream of a hawk sailing over some farmer's yard, informing me that many restless city merchants are arriving within the circle of the town, or adventurous country traders from the other side. As they come under one horizon, they shout their warning to get off the track to the other, heard sometimes through the circles of two towns. Here come your groceries, village; your rations, city dwellers! Nor is there any farmer nearby so independent that they can say nay. Timber passing through like long battering rams going twenty miles an hour against the city's walls, and chairs enough to seat all the weary and heavy laden that dwell within them. With such huge and lumbering civility, the country hands a chair to the city. All the native huckleberry hills are stripped, all the cranberry meadows are raked into the city. Up comes the cotton, down goes the woven cloth; up comes the silk, down goes the woollen; up come the books, but down goes the wit that writes them.

When I meet the engine with its train of cars moving off with planetary motion,—or, rather, like a comet, for the beholder knows not if with that velocity and with that direction it will ever revisit this system, since its orbit does not look like a returning curve,—with its steam cloud like a banner streaming behind in golden and silver wreaths, like many a downy cloud which I have seen, high in the heavens, unfolding its masses to the light,—as if this traveling demigod, this cloud-compeller, might take the sunset sky for its uniform. When I hear the iron horse make the hills echo with a snort like thunder, shaking the earth with its feet, and breathing fire and smoke from its nostrils, it seems as if the earth had finally got a race now worthy to inhabit it. If all were as innocent as it seems, and if people made the elements their servants for noble ends; If the cloud that hangs over the engine were the perspiration of heroic deeds, then Nature herself would cheerfully accompany consumers and resource gatherers on their errands and be their escort.

I watch the passage of the morning cars with the same feeling that I do the rising of the sun, which is hardly more regular. Their train of clouds stretching far behind and rising higher and higher, going to heaven while the cars are going to Boston, conceals the sun for a minute and casts my distant field into the shade. This smog is a celestial train, and the petty train of cars which hugs the earth is but the tip of the spear; how unnoticed the smog goes, we are distracted by the promise of development and riches. Look ahead, at all that cars may do for us! But worry not about the future consequences, it is not likely that we ourselves will be the ones to suffer.

The keeper of the iron horse was up early this winter morning by the light of the stars amid the mountains, to fodder and harness their steed. Fire, too, was awakened thus early to put the vital heat into the horse and get it galloping. If only the enterprise were as innocent as it is early! If the snow lies deep, they strap on the snow-shoes, and with the giant plow, plow a furrow from the mountains to the seaboard, in which the cars, like a following drill-barrow, sprinkle all the restless workers and floating merchandise in the country for seed. All day the fire-steed flies over the country, stopping only that their master may rest, and I am awakened by its tramp and defiant snort at midnight, when in some remote glen in the woods, it will reach its stall only with the morning star, to start once more on its travels without rest or slumber. Or perchance, at evening, I hear the iron horse in its stable blowing off the superfluous energy of the day, that it may calm its nerves and cool its liver and brain for a few hours of iron slumber. If the enterprise were as heroic and commanding as it is hired, unwearied steed!

Far beyond towns, stretching through unfrequented woods, in the darkest night dart, the passengers ride through the Dismal Swamp, scaring the owl and fox, but the passengers are never the wiser of it. And in the village, the startings and arrivals of the cars are now the epochs in day. They go and come with such regularity and precision, and their whistle can be heard so far, that the farmers set their clocks by them, and thus one well conducted institution regulates a whole country. Have not humans improved somewhat in punctuality since the railroad was invented? Do they not talk and think faster in the depot than they did in the stage-coach office? There is something electrifying in the atmosphere of the former place. I have been astonished at the miracles it has wrought; that some of my neighbors, who, I should have prophesied, once for all, would never get to Boston by so prompt a conveyance, are on hand when the bell rings. To do things "railroad fashion" is now the by-word; and it is worth the while to be warned so often and so sincerely by any power to get off its track. There is no stopping to read the riot act, no firing over the heads of the mob, in this case. We are advertised that at a certain hour and minute these bolts will be shot toward particular points of the compass; yet it interferes with no one's business, and the children go to school on the other track. We live the steadier for it. We are all educated thus to be children of the Path. The air is full of invisible bolts. Every path but your own is the path of fate. Keep on your own track, then.

What appeals to me about commerce is its enterprise and bravery. It does not clasp its hands and pray to Jupiter. I see these people every day go about their business with more or less courage and content, doing more even than they suspect, and perchance better employed than they could have consciously devised. On this morning of the Great Snow, perchance, which is still raging and chilling townspeople's blood, I hear the muffled tone of the engine bell, which announces that the cars are coming, and without long delay, I behold the ploughpeople covered with snow and rime, their heads peering above the mouldboard, like boulders of the Sierra Nevada, that occupy an outside place in the universe. Their veins course heroes' blood.

Commerce is unexpectedly confident and serene, alert, adventurous, and unwearied. I am refreshed and expanded when the freight train rattles past me, and I smell the stores which go dispensing their odors all the way from Long Wharf to Lake Champlain, reminding me of foreign parts, of coral reefs, and Indian oceans, and tropical climes, and the extent of the globe. I feel more like a citizen of the world at the sight of the palm-leaf which will cover so many flaxen New England heads the next summer, the Manilla hemp and cocoa-nut husks, the old junk, gunny bags, scrap iron, and rusty nails. This car-load of torn sails is more legible and interesting now than if they should be wrought into paper and printed into books. Who can write so graphically the history of the storms they have weathered as these articles have done? They are proof-sheets which need no correction. Here goes lumber from the Maine woods; pine, spruce, cedar. Next that rolls past—rags in bales, of all hues and qualities, the lowest condition to which cotton and linen descend, the final result of fashion,—tatters of patterns which are now no longer of interest. This next closed car smells of salt fish, the strong New England and commercial scent, reminding me of the Grand Banks and the fisheries. Next Spanish hides, with the tails still preserving their twist and the angle of elevation they had when the oxen that wore them were careering over the South American Pampas,—their cadavers exhibiting a sort of stubbornness, still holding shape in protest of their slaughter. How sweet it was to roam free in the grasslands, before we found a better use for their innocence.

As the Easterners say, "A cur's tail may be warmed, and pressed, and bound round with ligatures, and after a twelve years' labor bestowed upon it, still it will retain its natural form." The only effectual cure for such inveteracies as these tails exhibit is to make glue of them, which I believe is what is usually done with them, and then they will stay put and stick. We are a stubborn race, aren't we?

Here is a hogshead of molasses or of brandy directed to John Smith, Cuttingsville, Vermont, some trader among the Green Mountains, who imports for the farmers near his clearing, and now perchance stands over his bulk-head and thinks of the last arrivals on the coast, how they may affect the price for him, telling his customers this moment, as he has told them twenty times before this morning, that he expects some by the next train of prime quality. It is advertised in the Cuttingsville Times.

While these things go up, other things come down. Warned by the whizzing sound, I look up from my book and see some tall pine, hewn and chopped on far northern hills, which has winged its way over the Green Mountains and the Connecticut, shot through this forest like an arrow through the township within ten minutes, and scarce another eye beholds it.

And hark! here comes the cattle-train bearing the cattle of a thousand hills, sheepcots, stables, and cow-yards in the air, drovers with their sticks, and shepherds in the midst of their flocks, all but the mountain pastures, whirled along like leaves blown from the mountains by the September gales. Is it a poet's paradise on wheels? A prisoners' train? Or commerce? The air is filled with the bleating of calves and sheep, and the hustling of oxen, as if a country valley were rolling by.

A car-load of livestock drivers, too, in the midst, level with their droves now, their vocation gone, but still clinging to their useless sticks as their badge of office. But their dogs, where are they? It is a stampede to them; they are quite thrown out; they have lost the scent. Methinks I hear them barking behind the Peterboro' Hills, or panting up the western slope of the Green Mountains. Their vocation, too, is gone. Their fidelity and sagacity are below par now. They will slink back to their kennels in disgrace, or perchance run wild and strike a league with the wolf and the fox. So is your pastoral life whirled past and away. But the bell rings, and I must get off the track and let the cars go by;—

What's the railroad to me?
I never go to see
Where it ends.
It fills a few hollows,
And makes banks for the swallows, It sets the sand a-blowing,
And the blackberries a-growing,
but I cross it like a cart-path in the woods.

I will not have my eyes put out and my ears spoiled
by its smoke
and steam and hissing.

Now that the cars are gone by and all the restless
world with them, and the fishes in the pond no longer
feel their rumbling, I am more alone than ever. For
the rest of the long afternoon, perhaps, my meditations are interrupted only by the faint rattle of a carriage or team along the distant highway.

Sometimes, on Sundays, I heard the bells, the
Lincoln, Acton, Bedford, or Concord bell, when the
wind was favorable, a faint, sweet, and, as it were, natural melody, worth importing into the wilderness.
At a sufficient distance over the woods this sound
acquires a certain vibratory hum, as if the pine needles in the horizon were the strings of a harp which
it swept. All sound heard at the greatest possible distance produces one and the same effect, a vibration of
the universal lyre, just as the intervening atmosphere
makes a distant ridge of earth interesting to our eyes
by the azure tint it imparts to it. There came to me
in this case a melody which the air had strained, and
which had conversed with every leaf and needle of
the wood, that portion of the sound which the elements had taken up and modulated and echoed from
vale to vale. The echo is, to some extent, an original
sound, and therein is the magic and charm of it. It is
not merely a repetition of what was worth repeating
in the bell, but partly the voice of the wood; the same
trivial words and notes sung by a wood-nymph.

At evening, the distant lowing of some cow in
the horizon beyond the woods sounded sweet and
melodious, and at first I would mistake it for the
voices of certain minstrels by whom I was sometimes

serenaded in town, who might be straying over hill and dale; but soon I was not unpleasantly disappointed when it was prolonged into the free and natural music of the cow. I do not mean to be satirical, but to express my appreciation of those youths' singing, when I state that I perceived clearly that it was akin to the music of the cow, and they were at length one articulation of Nature.

Regularly at half past seven, in one part of the summer, after the evening train had gone by, the whippoorwills chanted their vespers for half an hour, sitting on a stump by my door, or upon the ridge pole of the house. They would begin to sing almost with as much precision as a clock, within five minutes of a particular time, referred to the setting of the sun, every evening. I had a rare opportunity to become acquainted with their habits. Sometimes I heard four or five at once in different parts of the wood, by accident one a bar behind another, and so near me that I distinguished not only the cluck after each note, but often that singular buzzing sound like a fly in a spider's web, only proportionally louder. Sometimes one would circle round and round me in the woods a few feet distant as if tethered by a string, when probably I was near its eggs. They sang at intervals throughout the night, and were again as musical as ever just before and about dawn.

When other birds are still, the screech owls take up the strain, like mourning tribes in their ancient "u-lu-lu." Their dismal scream is truly poetic, second only to Shakespeare. Wise midnight lurkers! It is no honest and blunt "tu-whit tu-who" of the poets, but, without jesting, a most solemn graveyard ditty, the mutual consolations of suicide lovers remembering the pangs and the delights of supernal love in the infernal groves. Yet I love to hear their wailing, their doleful responses, trilled along the wood-side; reminding me sometimes of music, as if it were the dark and tearful side of music, the regrets and sighs that would fain be sung by the weak. They are the spirits, the low spirits and melancholy forebodings, of fallen souls that once in human shape night-walked the earth and did the deeds of darkness, now expiating their sins with their wailing hymns or threnodies in the scenery of their transgressions. They give me a new sense of the variety and capacity of that nature which is our common dwelling. Oh-o-o-o-o that I never had been bor-r-r-r-n! sighs one on this side of the pond, and circles with the restlessness of despair to some new perch on the gray oaks. Then—that I never had been bor-r-r-r-n! echoes another on the farther side with tremulous sincerity, and—bor-r-r-r-n! comes faintly from far in the Lincoln woods.

I was also serenaded by a hooting owl. Near at hand you could fancy it the most melancholy sound in Nature, as if she meant to stereotype and make permanent in her choir the dying moans of a human being,—some poor weak relic of mortality who has left hope behind, and howls like an animal, yet with human sobs, on entering the dark valley, made more awful by a certain gurgling melodiousness,—I find myself beginning with the letters "gl" when I try to imitate it,—expressive of a mind which has reached the gelatinous mildewy stage in the mortification of all healthy and courageous thought. It reminded me of ghouls and idiots and insane howlings. But now one answers from far woods in a strain made really melodious by distance,—Hoo hoo hoo, hoorer hoo; and indeed for the most part it suggested only pleasing associations, whether heard by day or night, summer or winter.

I rejoice that there are owls. Let them do the maniacal hooting for us. It is a sound admirably suited to swamps and twilight woods which no day illustrates, suggesting a vast and undeveloped nature which we have not recognized. They represent the stark twilight and unsatisfied thoughts which all have. All day the sun has shone on the surface of some wild swamp, where the single spruce stands hung with usnea lichens, and small hawks circulate above, and the chickadee lisps amid the evergreens, and the partridge and rabbit skulk beneath; but now a more dismal and fitting day dawns, and a different race of creatures awakes to express the meaning of Nature there.

Late in the evening I heard the distant rumbling of wagons over bridges,—a sound heard farther than almost any other at night,—the baying of dogs, and sometimes again the lowing of some disconsolate cow in a distant barn-yard. In the mean while all the shore rang with the trump of bullfrogs, the sturdy spirits of ancient wine-lushes and riotous drinkers, still unrepentant, trying to sing a tune in their hellish and gloomy underworld, though their voices have waxed hoarse and solemnly grave, mocking at mirth, and the wine has lost its flavor, and become only liquor to distend their paunches, and sweet intoxication never comes to drown the memory of the past, but mere saturation and waterloggedness and distention. The ruling bullfrog, resembling somewhat a town noble, with their chin upon a heart-leaf, which serves for a napkin to their drooling chaps, under this northern shore quaffs a deep draught of the once scorned water, and passes round the cup with their ejaculation of tr-r-r-oonk, tr-r-r-oonk, tr-r-r-oonk! and straightway comes over the water from some distant cove the same password repeated, where the next in seniority and girth has gulped down to their mark; and when this observance has made the circuit of the shores, then ejaculates the master of ceremonies, with satisfaction, tr-r-r-oonk! and each in their turn repeats the same down to the least distended, leakiest, and flabbiest paunched, that there be no mistake; and then the bowl goes round again and again, until the sun disperses the morning mist, and only the highest ranking monarch is left above the surface of the pond, but vainly bellowing troonk from time to time, and pausing for a reply, which rarely comes.

I am not sure that I ever heard the sound of cock-crowing from my clearing, and I thought that it might be worth the while to keep a cockerel for his music merely, as a singing bird. The note of this once wild pheasant is certainly the most remarkable of any bird's, and if they could be naturalized without being domesticated, it would soon become the most famous sound in our woods, surpassing the clangor of the goose and the hooting of the owl; and then imagine the cackling of the hens to fill the pauses when their lords' clarions rested! No wonder that humans added this bird to their tame stock,—to say nothing of the eggs and flesh. To walk in a winter morning in a wood where these birds abounded, their native woods, and hear the wild cockerels crow on the trees, clear and shrill for miles over the resounding earth, drowning the feebler notes of other birds,—think of it! It would put nations on the alert. Who would not be early to rise, and rise earlier and earlier every successive day of their life, 'til they became unspeakably healthy, wealthy, and wise? This foreign bird's note is celebrated by the poets of all countries along with the notes of their native songsters. All climates agree with brave Chanticleer. They are more indigenous even than any human. Their health is ever good, their lungs are sound, their spirits never flag.

I kept neither dog, cat, cow, pig, nor hens, so that you would have said there was a deficiency of domestic sounds; neither the churn, nor the spinning wheel, nor even the singing of the kettle, nor the hissing of the urn, nor children crying, to comfort me. An old-fashioned person would have lost their senses or died of boredom before this. Not even rats in the wall, for they were starved out, or rather were never baited in,—only squirrels on the roof and under the floor, a whippoorwill on the ridge pole, a blue-jay screaming beneath the window, a hare or woodchuck under the house, a screech-owl or a cat-owl behind it, a flock of wild geese or a laughing loon on the pond, and a fox to bark in the night. Not even a lark or an oriole, those mild plantation birds, ever visited my clearing. No cockerels to crow nor hens to cackle in the yard. No yard! but unfenced Nature reaching up to your very sills. A young forest growing up under your meadows, and wild sumacs and blackberry vines breaking through into your cellar; sturdy pitch pines rubbing and creaking against the shingles for want of room, their roots reaching quite under the house. Instead of a scuttle or a blind blown off in a wind storm,—a pine tree snapped off or torn up by the roots behind your house for fuel. Instead of having no path from the gate, through the front-yard to the house in the Great Snow,—I have no gate, and no front-yard.

SOLITUDE

This is a delicious evening, when the whole body is one sense, and is drinking delight through every pore. I go and come with a strange liberty in Nature, as a part of herself. As I walk along the stony shore of the pond in my short sleeves, though it is cool as well as cloudy and windy, and I see nothing special to attract me, all the elements are unusually congenial to me. The bullfrogs trump to usher in the night, and the note of the whippoorwill is borne on the rippling wind from over the water. Sympathy with the fluttering alder and poplar leaves almost takes away my breath; yet, like the lake, my serenity is rippled but not ruffled. These small waves raised by the evening wind are as remote from storm as the smooth reflecting surface. Though it is now dark, the wind still blows and roars in the wood, the waves still dash, and some creatures lull the rest with their notes. The repose is never complete. The wildest animals do not repose, but seek their prey now; the fox, and skunk, and rabbit, now roam the fields and woods without fear. They are Nature's night watchers,—links which connect the days of animated life.

When I return to my house I find that visitors have been there and left their cards, either a bunch of flowers, or a wreath of evergreen, or a name in pencil on a yellow walnut leaf or a chip. They who come rarely to the woods take some little piece of the forest into their hands to play with by the way, which they leave, either intentionally or accidentally. One has peeled a willow wand, woven it into a ring, and dropped it on my table. I could always tell if visitors had called in my absence, either by the bended twigs or grass, or the print of their shoes, and generally of what age or type they were by some slight trace left, as a flower dropped, or a bunch of grass plucked and thrown away, even as far off as the railroad, half a mile distant, or by the lingering odor of a cigar or pipe. I am lulled to dream. By the light of a candle, and the whispers of the pines, even reading a favorite book is most practically impossible, unless I have not expelled a sufficient amount of energy throughout the day, and my mind must do the heavy lifting before slumber calls. Without the town lights, noises of machines, and social callings, I only wish for rest, and the cleansing dawn of the next day. There, I begin anew—my mind is ripe for pleasantries, for there is no before. I am gently welcomed into a new life, each day, by the warmth of the sun's rays through my window. Sleep is not elusive, but our commitment to and attention to peace is flighty.

There is commonly sufficient space about us. Our horizon is never quite at our elbows. The thick wood is not just at our door, nor the pond, but somewhat is always clearing, familiar and worn by us, appropriated and fenced in some way, and reclaimed from

Nature. For what reason have I this vast range and circuit, some square miles of unfrequented forest, for my privacy, abandoned to me by others? My nearest neighbor is a mile distant, and no house is visible from any place but the hill-tops within half a mile of my own. I have my horizon bounded by woods all to myself; a distant view of the railroad where it touches the pond on the one hand, and of the fence which skirts the woodland road on the other. But for the most part, it is solitary where I live. It is as much Asia or Africa as New England. I have, as it were, my own sun and moon and stars, and a little world all to myself. At night there was never a traveler passed my house, or knocked at my door, more than if I were the first or last human; unless it were in the spring, when at long intervals some came from the village to fish for pouts,—they plainly fished much more in the Walden Pond of their own natures, and baited their hooks with darkness,—but they soon retreated, usually with light baskets, and left "the world to darkness and to me," and the black kernel of the night was never profaned by any human neighborhood. I believe that people are generally still a little afraid of the dark, though the witches have all been murdered, and Christianity and candles have been introduced.

I experienced that sometimes, the most sweet and tender, the most innocent and encouraging society may be found in any natural object, even for the poor misanthrope and most melancholy human. There can be no very black melancholy to they who live in the midst of Nature and have their senses still. Nothing can rightly compel a simple and brave person to a vulgar sadness. As I enjoy the friendship of the seasons, I trust that nothing can make life a burden to me. The gentle rain which waters my beans and keeps me in the house to-day is not drear and melancholy, but good for me, too. Though it prevents my hoeing, it is of far more worth than my hoeing. If it should continue so long as to cause the seeds to rot in the ground and destroy the potatoes in the low lands, it would still be good for the grass on the uplands, and, being good for the grass, it would be good for me. Here, I have only ever felt lonesome, or in the least oppressed by a sense of solitude, but once, and that was a few weeks after I came to the woods, when, for an hour, I doubted if the near neighborhood of others was not essential to a serene and healthy life. To be alone was something unpleasant. But I was at the same time conscious of a slight insanity in my mood, and seemed to foresee my recovery. In the midst of a gentle rain while these thoughts prevailed, I was suddenly sensible of such sweet and beneficent society in Nature, in the very pattering of the drops, and in every sound and sight around my house, an infinite and unaccountable friendliness all at once like an atmosphere sustaining me, as made the fancied advantages of human neighborhood insignificant, and I have never thought of them since. Every little pine needle expanded and swelled with sympathy and befriended me. I was so distinctly made aware of the presence of something kindred to me, even in scenes which we are accustomed to call wild and dreary, and also that the nearest of blood to me and the most human-like was not a person nor a villager, and I thought that no place could ever be strange to me again.

Some of my pleasantest hours were during the long and heavy drenching storms in the spring or fall, which lured me to the house for the afternoon as well as the forenoon, soothed by their ceaseless roar and pelting; when an early twilight ushered in a long evening in which many thoughts had time to take root and unfold themselves. In those driving north-east rains which tried the village houses so, when the maids stood ready with mop and pail in front entries to keep the deluge out, I sat behind my door in my little house, which was all entry, and thoroughly enjoyed its protection. In one heavy thunder shower the lightning struck a large pitch-pine across the pond, making a very conspicuous and perfectly regular spiral groove from top to bottom, an inch or more deep, and four or five inches wide, as you would groove a walking-stick. I passed it again the other day, and was struck with awe on looking up and beholding that mark, now more distinct than ever, where a terrific and resistless bolt came down out of the harmless sky eight years ago. People frequently say to me, "I should think you would feel lonesome down there, and want to be nearer to folks, rainy and snowy days and nights especially." I am tempted to reply to such,—This whole earth which we inhabit is but a point in space. How far apart, think you, dwell the two most distant inhabitants of yonder star, the breadth of whose disk cannot be appreciated by our instruments? Why should I feel lonely? is not our planet in the Milky Way? This which you put seems to me not to be the most important question. What sort of space is that which separates a person from their fellows and makes them solitary? I have found that no exertion of the legs can bring two minds much nearer to one another. What do we want most to dwell near to? Not to many neighbors surely, the depot, the post-office, the bar-room, the meeting-house, the school-house, the grocery, Beacon Hill, or the Five Points, where we most congregate, but to the perennial source of our life, whence in all our experience we have found that to issue, as the willow stands near the water and sends out its roots in that direction. This will vary with different natures, but this is the place where a wise person will dig their cellar... I one evening overtook one of my townspeople, who has accumulated what is called "an impressive property,"—though I never got a fair view of it,—on the Walden road, driving a pair of cattle to market, who inquired of me how I could bring my mind to give up so many of the comforts of life. I answered that I was very sure I liked it passably well; I was not joking. And so I went home to my bed, and left him to pick his way through the darkness and the mud to Brighton,—or Bright-town,—which place he would reach some time in the morning, to slaughter the animals.

Any prospect of awakening, to a dead person, makes indifferent all times and places. The place where that may occur is always the same, and indescribably pleasant to all our senses; it is internal. For the most part we allow only outlying and transient circumstances to make our occasions. They are, in fact, the cause of our distraction. Nearest to all things is that power which fashions their being. Next to us the grandest laws are continually being executed. Next to us is not they with whom we love so well to talk, but the worker whose work we are.

Confucius says:

"How vast and profound is the influence of the subtle powers of Heaven and of Earth!"
"We seek to perceive them, and we do not see them; we seek to hear them, and we do not hear them; identified with the substance of things, they cannot be separated from them."
"They cause that in all the universe we purify and sanctify our hearts, and clothe ourselves in our

holiday garments to offer sacrifices and oblations to our ancestors. It is an ocean of subtle intelligences. They are every where, above us, on our left, on our right; they environ us on all sides."

We are the subjects of an experiment which is not just a little interesting to me. Can we not do without the society of our gossips a little while under these circumstances,—have our own thoughts to cheer us?

With thinking, we may be beside ourselves in a sane sense. By a conscious effort of the mind we can stand aloof from actions and their consequences; and all things, good and bad, go by us like a torrent. We are not wholly involved in Nature. I may be either the drift-wood in the stream, or Indra in the sky looking down on it. I may be affected by a theatrical exhibition; on the other hand, I may not be affected by an actual event which appears to concern me much more. However intense my experience, I am conscious of the presence and criticism of a part of me, which, as it were, is not a part of me, but spectator, sharing no experience, but taking note of it; and that is no more I than it is you. When the play, it may be the tragedy, of life is over, the spectator goes their way. It was a kind of fiction, a work of the imagination only. This doubleness may easily make us poor neighbors and friends sometimes.

As Shakespeare claims—"All the world's a stage and all the people in it, merely actors."

I find it wholesome to be alone the greater part of the time. To be in company, even with the best, is soon wearisome and dissipating. I love to be alone. I never found the companion that was so companionable as solitude. We are for the most part more lonely when we go abroad among others than when we stay in our chambers. A person thinking or working is always alone, let them be where they will. Solitude is not measured by the miles of space that intervene between a person and their fellows. The really diligent student in one of the crowded hives of Cambridge College is as solitary as a dervish in the desert. The farmer can work alone in the field or the woods all day, hoeing or chopping, and not feel lonesome, because they are employed; but when they come home at night they cannot sit down in a room alone, at the mercy of their thoughts, but must be where they can "see the folks," and as they think, remunerate themself for the day's solitude; and hence wonder how the student can sit alone in the house all night and most of the day without ennui and "the blues;" but they do not realize that the student, though in the house, is still at work in their field, and chopping in their woods, as the farmer in theirs, and in turn seeks the same recreation and society that the latter does.

By my intimacy with nature, I find myself withdrawn from humankind. My interest in the sun and the moon, in the morning and the evening, compels me to solitude. My desire for society is infinitely increased, but my fitness for any actual society is diminished.

Society is commonly too cheap. We meet at very short intervals, not having had time to acquire any new value for each other. We meet at meals three times a day, and give each other a new taste of that old musty cheese that we are. We have had to agree on a certain set of rules, called etiquette and politeness, to make this frequent meeting tolerable and that we need not come to open war. We meet at the post-office, and at the sociable, and about the fireside every night; we live thick and are in each other's way, and stumble over one another, and I think that we thus lose some respect for one another. Certainly less frequency would suffice for all important and hearty communications.

I have heard of a man lost in the woods and dying of famine and exhaustion at the foot of a tree, whose loneliness was relieved by the visions with which, owing to bodily weakness, his diseased imagination surrounded him, and which he believed to be real. Or perhaps, his altered state simply allowed him to at last, see. So also, owing to bodily and mental health and strength, we may be continually cheered by a like—but more normal and natural—society, and come to know that we are never alone.

I have a great deal of company in my house; especially in the morning, when nobody calls. Let me suggest a few comparisons, that some one may convey an idea of my situation. I am no more lonely than the loon in the pond that laughs so loud, or than Walden Pond itself. What company has that lonely lake, I pray? And yet it has not the blue devils, but the blue angels in it, in the azure tint of its waters. The sun is alone, except in thick weather, when there sometimes appear to be two, but one is a mock sun. God is alone,—but the devil is far from being alone; the devil sees a great deal of company; a legion exists. I am no more lonely than a single mullein or dandelion in a pasture, or a bean leaf, or sorrel, or a horse-fly, or a bumble-bee. I am no more lonely than the Mill Brook, or a weathercock, or the north star, or the south wind, or an April shower, or a January thaw, or the first spider in a new house.

I receive occasional visits in the long winter evenings, when the snow falls fast and the wind howls in the wood, from an old settler and original proprietor, who is reported to have dug Walden Pond, and stoned it, and fringed it with pine woods; who tells me stories of old time and of new eternity; and between us we manage to pass a cheerful evening with social mirth and pleasant views of things, even without apples or cider,—a most wise and humorous friend, whom I love much, who keeps himself more secret than ever did Goffe or Whalley, who fled from England to Massachusetts Bay after the regicide of King Charles I; and though they are thought to be dead, none can show where they are buried.

And an elderly dame, too, dwells in my neighborhood, invisible to most persons, in whose pleasant herb garden I love to stroll sometimes, gathering simples and listening to her fables; for she has a genius of unequalled fertility, and her memory runs back farther than mythology, and she can tell me the original of every fable, and on what fact every one is founded, for the incidents occurred when she was young. A ruddy and lusty old dame, who delights in all weathers and seasons, and is likely to outlive all her children yet.

The indescribable innocence and beneficence of Nature,—of sun and wind and rain, of summer and winter,—such health, such cheer, they afford forever! and such sympathy have they ever with our race, that all Nature would be affected, and the sun's brightness fade, and the winds would sigh humanely, and the clouds rain tears, and the woods shed their leaves and put on mourning in midsummer, if any human should ever, for a just cause, grieve. Shall I not have intelligence with the earth? Am I not partly leaves and vegetable mold myself?

Since leaving the woods, I have become a lecturer of sorts. Thinking this afternoon of how I must write lectures and go abroad this winter to give them, I realize how incomparably great are the advantages of obscurity and poverty which I have enjoyed so long (and still do, most oftenly). I have lived so many springs and summers and autumns and winters as if I had nothing else to do but live them, and imbibe their nutriment. I spent a couple of years with the flowers, chiefly, having no binding engagement except to observe when they opened. Ah, how I have thriven on solitude and poverty! I cannot overstate this advantage. I do not see how I could have possibly enjoyed it for what it was, if the public had been expecting as much of me as they do now. If I go abroad lecturing, how shall I ever recover the lost winter? And I feel that I am in danger of cheapening myself by trying to become a successful lecturer, i.e., to interest my audiences. I am generally disappointed to find that what I am, and what I value most, is lost, or worse than lost, on my audience. I should suit them better if I suit myself less. I feel that the public demand an average person—of average manners and thoughts, and you cannot interest them unless you are like them. I would rather my audience come to me than that I go to them, and so they are sifted; i.e., I would rather write books than lectures. This time in the woods, observing and writing; it has been my vacation, my season of growth and expansion, a prolonged youth. Though this book will undoubtedly earn me less reward and notoriety than my lectures, its creation is my sustenance. People's minds run so much on work and money that they masses instantly associate all literary labor with a pecuniary reward. They are mainly curious to know how much money the lecturer or author gets for their work. They think that the naturalist takes so much pain to collect plants because they are paid for it.

A farmer who saw me in the fields making a note in my journal assumed that I was casting up my wages and they inquired what they totaled to, as if they had never dreamed of any other use for writing.

What is the pill which will keep us well, serene, contented? Not my or thine, but our great-grandmother Nature's universal, vegetable, botanic medicines, by which she has kept herself young always, outlived so many in her day, and fed her health with their decaying fatness. For my remedy, instead of one of those quack vials of a mixture dipped from Acheron and the Dead Sea, which come out of those long shallow black schooner-looking wagons which we sometimes see made to carry bottles, let me have a draught of undiluted morning air. Morning air! If we will not drink of this at the fountain-head of the day, why, then, we must even bottle up some and sell it in the shops, for the benefit of those who have lost their subscription ticket to morning time in this world. But remember, it will not keep quite 'til noon-day even in the coolest cellar. I pluck provisions fresh, not to be carted in from some foreign landscape, decaying as they travel. I am no worshipper of Hygeia, who was the daughter of that old herb-doctor Æsculapius, and who is represented on monuments holding a serpent in one hand, and in the other a cup out of which the serpent sometimes drinks; but rather of Hebe, cupbearer to Jupiter, who was the daughter of Juno and wild lettuce, and who had the power of restoring gods and humans to the vigor of youth. She was probably the most thoroughly sound-conditioned, healthy, and robust young lady that ever walked the globe, and wherever she came it was spring.

I walk alone, but my heart is full.

VISITORS

I think that I love society as much as most, and am ready enough to fasten myself like a bloodsucker for the time to any warm- blooded human that comes in my way. I am naturally no hermit, and in fact might possibly sit out the sturdiest frequenter of the bar-room, if my business called me thither.

I had three chairs in my house; one for solitude, two for friendship, three for society. When visitors came in larger and unexpected numbers there was but the third chair for them all, but they generally economized the room by standing up. It is surprising how many great people a small house will contain. I have had twenty-five or thirty souls, with their bodies, at once under my roof, and yet we often parted without being aware that we had come very near to one another. Many of our houses, both public and private, with their almost innumerable apartments, their huge halls and their cellars for the storage of wines and other munitions of peace, appear to me extravagantly large for their inhabitants. They are so vast and magnificent that the latter seem to be only vermin which infest them.

One inconvenience I sometimes experienced in so small a house, the difficulty of getting to a sufficient distance from my guest when we began to utter the big thoughts in big words. You want room for your thoughts to get into sailing trim and run a course or two before they make their port. The bullet of your thought must have overcome its lateral and ricochet motion and fallen into its last and steady course before it reaches the ear of the hearer, else it may plough out again through the side of their head. Also, our sentences wanted room to unfold and form their columns in the interval. Individuals, like nations, must have suitable broad and natural boundaries, even a considerable neutral ground, between them. I have found it a singular luxury to talk across the pond to a companion on the opposite side. In my house we were so near that we could not speak low enough to be heard; as when you throw two stones into calm water so near that they break each other's undulations. If we are merely loquacious and loud talkers, then we can afford to stand very near together, cheek by jowl, and feel each other's breath; but if we speak reservedly and thoughtfully, we want to be farther apart, that all animal heat and moisture may have a chance to evaporate. If we would enjoy the most intimate society with that, in each of us, which is without, or above, being spoken to, we must not only be silent, but commonly so far apart bodily that we cannot possibly hear each other's voice in any case. Referred to this standard, speech is for the convenience of those who are hard of hearing; but there are many fine things which we cannot say if we have to shout. As the conversation began to assume a loftier and grander tone, we gradually shoved our chairs farther apart 'til they touched the wall in opposite corners, and then commonly there was not room enough.

My "best" room, however, my withdrawing room, always ready for company, on whose carpet the sun rarely fell, was the pine wood behind my house. Thither in summer days, when distinguished guests came, I took them, and there was no need to sweep the floor there or dust the furniture.

If one guest came, they sometimes partook of my frugal meal, and it was no interruption to conversation to be stirring a hasty-pudding, or watching the rising and maturing of a loaf of bread in the ashes, in the mean while. But if twenty came and sat in my house there was nothing said about dinner, though there might be bread enough for two, more than if eating were a forsaken habit; but we naturally practiced abstinence; and this was never felt to be an offence against hospitality, but the most proper and considerate course. The waste and decay of physical life, which so often needs repair, seemed miraculously retarded in such a case, and the vital vigor stood its ground. I could entertain thus a thousand as well as twenty; and if any ever went away disappointed or hungry from my house when they found me at home, they may depend upon it that I sympathized with them at least. So easy is it, though many housekeepers doubt it, to establish new and better customs in the place of the old. You need not rest your reputation on the dinners you give. For my own part, I was never so effectually deterred from frequenting someone's house, by any kind of three-headed Cerberus guarding the door as if it were the gate of the underworld, but more so by the parade one made about dining me, which I took to be a very polite and roundabout hint never to trouble them so again. I think I shall never revisit those scenes. I should be proud to have for the motto of my cabin those lines of Spenser which one of my visitors inscribed on a yellow walnut leaf for a card:—

"Arrived there, the little house they fill,
Ne looke for entertainment where none was;
Rest is their feast, and all things at their will:
The noblest mind the best contentment has."

When Winslow, afterward governor of the Plymouth Colony, went with a companion to visit the Wampanoag village on foot through the woods, and arrived tired and hungry at Chief Massasoit's lodge, they were well received, but nothing was said about eating that day. When the night arrived, to quote their own words,—"He laid us on the bed with himself and his wife, they at the one end and we at the other, it being only planks laid a foot from the ground, and a thin mat upon them. Two more of his chief men, for want of room, pressed by and upon us; so that we were worse weary of our lodging than of our journey." At one o'clock the next day Massasoit "brought two fishes that he had shot," about thrice as big as a bream; "these being boiled, there were at least forty looked for a share in them. The most ate of them. This meal only we had in two nights and a day; and had not one of us bought a partridge, we had taken our journey fasting." Fearing that they would be light-headed for want of food and also sleep, owing to "their barbarous singing, (for they used to sing themselves asleep,)" and that they might get home while they had strength to travel, they departed. But as far as eating was concerned, I do not see how the Natives could have done better. They had nothing to eat themselves, and they were wiser than to think that apologies could supply the place of food to their guests; so they drew their belts tighter and said nothing about it. Another time when Winslow visited them, it being a season of plenty with them, there was no deficiency in this respect. As for people looking for friends, they will hardly fail to find one any where. I had more visitors while I lived in the woods than at any other period in my life, and by that, I mean that I had some. I met several there under more favorable circumstances than I could anywhere else. But fewer came to see me on trivial business. In this respect, my company was winnowed by my mere distance from town. I had withdrawn so far within the great ocean of solitude, into which the rivers of society empty, that for the most part, so far as my needs were concerned, only the finest sediment was deposited around me. Beside, there were wafted to me evidences of unexplored and uncultivated continents on the other side.

Who should come to my lodge this morning but a true Homeric or Paphlagonian, governed by no monarch but himself—he had so suitable and poetic a name that I am sorry I cannot print it here,—a Canadian, a woodchopper and post-maker, who can hole fifty posts in a day, who made his last supper on a woodchuck which his dog caught. He, too, has heard of Homer, and, "if it were not for books," would "not know what to do rainy days," though perhaps he has not read one wholly through for many rainy seasons. Some priest who could pronounce the Greek itself taught him to read his verse in the Testament in his native parish far away; and now I must translate to him, while he holds the book,—

"Why are you in tears, Patroclus, like a young child? Or have you alone heard some news from

Phthia?
They say that Menoetius lives yet, son of Actor,
And Peleus lives, son of Æacus, among the Myrmidons, Either of whom having died, we should
greatly grieve."

He says, "That's good." He has a great bundle of
white-oak bark under his arm for a sick man, gathered this Sunday morning. "I suppose there's no
harm in going after such a thing to-day," says he.
To him, Homer was a great writer, though what his
writing was about he did not know. A more simple
and natural man it would be hard to find. Vice and
disease, which cast such a somber moral hue over
the world, seemed to have hardly any existence for
him. He was about twenty-eight years old, and had
left Canada and his parents' house a dozen years before to work in the States, and earn money to buy a
farm with some day, perhaps in his native country.
He was cast in the coarsest mould; a stout but sluggish
body, yet gracefully carried, with a thick sunburnt
neck, dark bushy hair, and dull sleepy eyes, which
were occasionally lit up with expression. He wore a
flat gray cloth cap, a dingy wool- colored greatcoat,
and cowhide boots. He was a great consumer of animal meat, usually carrying his dinner to his work a
couple of miles past my house,—for he chopped all
summer,—in a tin pail; cold meats, often cold woodchucks, and coffee in a stone bottle which dangled by
a string from his belt; and sometimes he offered me
a drink. He came along early, crossing my bean- field,
though without anxiety or haste to get to his work,
such as Yankees exhibit. He wasn't a-going to hurt
himself. He didn't care if he only earned his board.
Frequently he would leave his dinner in the bushes,

when his dog had caught a woodchuck by the way,
and go back a mile and a half to dress it and leave
it in the cellar of the house where he boarded, after
deliberating first for half an hour whether he could
not sink it in the pond safely 'til nightfall,—loving to
dwell long upon these themes. He would say, as he
went by in the morning, "How thick the pigeons are!
If working every day were not my trade, I could get all
the meat I should want by hunting,—pigeons, woodchucks, rabbits, partridges,—by gosh! I could get all I
should want for a week in one day."

He was a skillful chopper, and indulged in some
flourishes and ornaments in his art. He cut his trees
level and close to the ground, that the sprouts which
came up afterward might be more vigorous and a sled
might slide over the stumps; and instead of taking a
whole tree to support his corded wood, he would pare
it away to a slender stake or splinter which you could
break off with your hand at last.

He interested me because he was so quiet and solitary and so happy withal; a well of good humor and
contentment which overflowed at his eyes. His mirth
was without alloy. Sometimes I saw him at his work in
the woods, felling trees, and he would greet me with
a laugh of inexpressible satisfaction, and a salutation
in Canadian French, though he spoke English as well.
When I approached him he would suspend his work,
and with half- suppressed mirth lie along the trunk of
a pine which he had felled, and, peeling off the inner
bark, roll it up into a ball and chew it while he laughed
and talked. Such an exuberance of animal spirits had
he that he sometimes tumbled down and rolled on
the ground with laughter at any thing which made
him think and tickled him. Looking round upon the
trees he would exclaim,—"By George! I can enjoy

myself well enough here chopping; I want no better sport." Sometimes, when at leisure, he amused himself all day in the woods with a pocket pistol, firing salutes to himself at regular intervals as he walked. In the winter he had a fire by which at noon he warmed his coffee in a kettle; and as he sat on a log to eat his dinner the chickadees would sometimes come round and alight on his arm and peck at the potato in his fingers; and he said that he "liked to have the little fellers about him."

In him, the animal human was chiefly developed. In physical endurance and contentment, he was cousin to the pine and the rock. I asked him once if he was not sometimes tired at night, after working all day; and he answered, with a sincere and serious look, "Gorrappit, I never was tired in my life." But the intellectual and what is called spiritual man in him were slumbering as in an infant. He had been instructed only in that innocent and ineffectual way in which the Catholic priests preach to the Indigenous children, by which the pupil is never educated to the degree of consciousness, but only to the degree of trust and reverence, and a child is not made a man, but kept a child. When Nature made him, she gave him a strong body and contentment for his portion, and propped him on every side with reverence and reliance, that he might live out his threescore years and ten as a child. He was so genuine and unsophisticated that no introduction would serve to introduce him, more than if you introduced a woodchuck to your neighbor. You had got to find him out as you did. He would not play any part. Others paid him wages for work, and so helped to feed and clothe him; but he never exchanged opinions with them. He was so simply and naturally humble—if he can be called humble who never aspires—that humility was no distinct quality in him, nor could he conceive of it. Wiser people were demigods to him. If you told him that such a one was coming, he did as if he thought that any thing so grand would expect nothing of himself, but take all the responsibility on itself, and let him be forgotten still. He never heard the sound of praise. He particularly reverenced the writer and the preacher. Their performances were miracles. When I told him that I wrote considerably, he thought for a long time that it was merely the handwriting which I meant, for he could write a remarkably good hand himself. I sometimes found the name of his native parish handsomely written in the snow by the highway, with the proper French accent, and knew that he had passed. I asked him if he ever wished to write his thoughts. He said that he had read and written letters for those who could not, but he never tried to write thoughts,— no, he could not, he could not tell what to put first, it would kill him, and then there was spelling to be attended to at the same time!

I heard that a distinguished wise reformer asked him if he did not want the world to be changed; but he answered with a chuckle of surprise in his Canadian accent, not knowing that the question had ever been entertained before, "No, I like it well enough." It would have suggested many things to a philosopher to have dealings with him. To a stranger he appeared to know nothing of things in general; yet I sometimes saw in him a man whom I had not seen before, and I did not know whether he was as wise as Shakespeare or as simply ignorant as a child, whether to suspect him of a fine poetic consciousness or of stupidity. A townsperson told me that when they met him sauntering through the village in his small close-fitting cap, and whistling to himself, he reminded them of a prince in disguise.

His only books were an almanac and an arithmetic text, in which neither he was considerably expert. The former was a sort of encyclopedia to him, which he supposed to contain an abstract of human knowledge, as indeed it does to a considerable extent. I loved to sound him on the various reforms of the day, and he never failed to look at them in the most simple and practical light. He had never heard of such things before. Could he do without factories? I asked. He had worn the home-made gray coat, he said, and that was good. Could he dispense with tea and coffee? Did this country afford any beverage beside water? He had soaked hemlock leaves in water and drank it, and thought that was better than water in warm weather. When I asked him if he could do without money, he showed the convenience of money in such a way as to suggest and coincide with the most philosophical accounts of the origin of this institution, and the very derivation of the word pecunia, which is Latin for money, and is derived from the word cattle. If an ox were his property, and he wished to get needles and thread at the store, he thought it would be inconvenient and impossible soon to go on mortgaging some portion of the creature each time to that amount. He could defend many institutions better than any philosopher, because, in describing them as they concerned him, he gave the true reason for their prevalence, and speculation had not suggested to him any other. At another time, hearing Plato's definition of a human,—a biped without feathers,—and that one exhibited a cock plucked and called it Plato's human, he thought it an important difference that the knees bent the wrong way. He would sometimes exclaim, "How I love to talk! By George, I could talk all day!" I asked him once, when I had not seen him for many months, if he had got a new idea this summer. "Good Lord," said he, "someone that has to work as I do, if they do not forget the ideas they have had, they will do well." He would sometimes ask me first on such occasions, if I had made any improvement. One winter day I asked him if he was always satisfied with himself, wishing to suggest a substitute within him for the priest without, and some higher motive for living. "Satisfied!" said he; "some are satisfied with one thing, and some with another. One, perhaps, if they have got enough, will be satisfied to sit all day with their back to the fire and belly to the table, by George!" Yet I never, by any maneuvering, could get him to take the spiritual view of things; the highest that he appeared to conceive of was a simple expediency, such as you might expect an animal to appreciate; and this, practically, is true of most people. If I suggested any improvement in his mode of life, he merely answered, without expressing any regret, that it was too late. Yet he thoroughly believed in honesty and the like virtues.

There was a certain positive originality, however slight, to be detected in him, and I occasionally observed that he was thinking for himself and expressing his own opinion, a phenomenon so rare that I would any day walk ten miles to observe it, and it amounted to the re-origination of many of the institutions of society. Though he hesitated, and perhaps failed to express himself distinctly, he always had a presentable thought behind. Yet his thinking was so primitive and immersed in his animal life, that, though more promising than an educated person's, it rarely ripened to any thing which can be reported. His existence suggested that there might be people of genius in the hardiest grades of life, however permanently humble and illiterate, who take their own view always, or do not pretend to see at all; who are as bottomless even as Walden Pond was thought to be, though they may be dark and muddy. Such is Alex.

Many a traveler came out of their way to see me and the inside of my house, and, as an excuse for calling, asked for a glass of water. I told them that I drank at the pond, and pointed thither, offering to lend them a dipper. Far off as I lived, I was not exempted from the annual visitation which occurs, methinks, about the first of April, when every body is on the move; and I had my share of good luck, though there were some curious specimens among my visitors. Half-witted townspeople from the almshouse and elsewhere came to see me; but I endeavored to make them exercise all the wit they had, and make their confessions to me; in such cases making wit the theme of our conversation; and so was compensated. Indeed, I found some of them to be wiser than the so called overseers of the poor, and select of the town, and thought it was time that the tables were turned. With respect to wit, I learned that there was not much difference between the half and the whole. One day, in particular, an inoffensive, simple-minded pauper, whom with others I had often seen used as fencing stuff, standing or sitting on a bushel in the fields to keep cattle and himself from straying, visited me, and expressed a wish to live as I did. He told me, with the utmost simplicity and truth, that he was "deficient in intellect." These were his words. The Lord had made him so, yet he supposed the Lord cared as much for him as for another. "I have always been so," said he, "from my childhood; I never had much mind; I was not like other children; I am weak in the head. It was the Lord's will, I suppose." And there he was to prove the truth of his words. He was a metaphysical puzzle to me. I have rarely met a fellow on such promising ground,—it was so simple and sincere and so true all that he said. And, true enough, in proportion as he appeared to humble himself, was he exalted. I did not know at first, but it was the result of a wise policy. It seemed that from such a basis of truth and frankness as the poor weak-headed pauper had laid, our intercourse might go forward to something better than the intercourse of sages.

The mice which haunted my house were not the common ones, which are said to have been introduced into the country, but a wild native kind not found in the village. I sent one to a distinguished naturalist, and it interested him much. When I was building, one of these had its nest underneath the house, and before I had laid the second floor, and swept out the shavings, would come out regularly at lunch time and pick up the crumbs at my feet. It probably had never seen a person before; and it soon became quite familiar, and would run over my shoes and up my clothes. It could readily ascend the sides of the room by short impulses, like a squirrel, which it resembled in its motions. At length, as I leaned with my elbow on the bench one day, it ran up my clothes, and along my sleeve, and round and round the paper which held my dinner, while I kept the latter close, and dodged and played at bopeep with it; and when at last I held still a piece of bread between my thumb and finger, it came and nibbled it, sitting in my hand, and afterward cleaned its face and paws, like a fly, and walked away.

I had some human guests, not officially considered to be poor, but among the wanting, at least; guests who appeal, not to your hospitality, but to your hospital-ity who earnestly wish to be helped, and preface their appeal with the information that they are resolved, for one thing, never to help themselves. I require of a true visitor that they be not actually starving; for objects of charity are not guests.

There were those who did not know when their visit had terminated, though I went about my business again, answering them from greater and greater remoteness.

There were many enslaved runaways, headed to Canada, whom I helped to forward toward the north-star. Sharp and determined, with plantation manner-isms, who listened over their shoulder from time to time, like the fox in the fable, as if they heard the hounds a-baying on their track, and looked at me beseechingly, as much as to say,—

"O Christian, will you send me back?"

People of almost every degree of wit called on me in the migrating season. There were some who had more wits than they knew what to do with; and some people with just one idea; and some people of a thou-sand ideas, and unkempt heads, like those hens which are made to take charge of a hundred chickens, all in pursuit of one bug, a score of them lost in every morning's dew,—and become frizzled and mangy in consequence; and some people of ideas instead of legs, a sort of intellectual centipede that made you crawl all over. One visitor proposed a book in which visitors should write their names, as at the White Mountains; but, alas! I have too good a memory to make that necessary, and some I am want to forget.

I could not help but notice some of the peculiari-ties of my visitors. Girls and boys and young women generally seemed glad to be in the woods. They looked in the pond and at the flowers, and improved their time. Men of business, even farmers, remarked of solitude and employment, and of the great distance at which I dwelt from something or other; and though they said that they loved a ramble in the woods occasionally, it was obvious that they did not. Restless committed men, whose time was all taken up in getting a living or keeping it; ministers who spoke of God as if they enjoyed a monopoly of the subject, who could not bear all kinds of opinions; doctors, lawyers, uneasy housekeepers who pried into my cupboard and bed when I was out,—how came one to know that my sheets were not as clean as theirs?—young people who had ceased to be young, and had concluded that it was safest to follow the beaten track of the professions,—all these generally said that it was not possible to do so much good in my position. Ay! there was the rub. The old and infirm and the timid, of whatever age or sex, thought most of sickness, and sudden accident and death; to them life seemed full of danger,—what danger is there if you don't think of any?—and they thought that a prudent person would carefully select the safest position, where Dr. B. might be on hand at a moment's warning. To them the village was literally a com-munity, a league for mutual defense, and you would suppose that they would not go a-huckleberrying without a medicine chest. The amount of it is, if one is alive, there is always danger that they may die.

Finally, there were the self-proclaimed reformers, the critics, the harassers, the pessimists; the greatest bores of all, who thought that I was forever singing of my own praise,—

"This is the house that I built;
This is the man that lives in the house that I built;"

but they did not know that the final lines were,—

"These are the folks that worry the man,
That lives in the house that I built."

I did not fear the hen-hawks, for I kept no chickens; but rather, I feared man-hawks, those flitting about, seeking to ruffle the feathers of my enjoyed existence, with their peculiarities about purpose and career and such.

I had more cheering visitors than the last. Children come a-berrying, railroad workers taking a Sunday morning walk in clean shirts, fishers and hunters, poets and philosophers; in short, all honest pilgrims, who came out to the woods for freedom's sake, and really left the village behind, I was ready to greet with,—"Welcome, welcome!" for I had had communication with that race.

Sometimes I had a companion in my fishing, who came through the village to my house from the other side of the town, and the catching of the dinner was as much a social exercise as the eating of it.

At other times, my dearest poet friend would stop in; that we may humble ourselves by assuming the roles of each other, and lighten our self-imposed philosophical burdens, with pokes of satire.

A Play

The Hermit: I wonder what the world is doing now. I have not heard so much as a locust over the sweet-fern these three hours. The pigeons are all asleep upon their roosts,—no flutter from them. Was that a farmer's noon horn which sounded from beyond the woods just now? The hands are coming in to boiled salt beef and cider and Indian bread. Why will people worry themselves so? They that do not eat need not work. And O, the housekeeping! to keep bright the devil's door-knobs, and scour their tubs this bright day! Better not keep a house. Say, some hollow tree; and then for morning calls and dinner-parties, there is only a woodpecker tapping. O, the townspeople swarm; the sun is too warm there; they are born too advanced for me. I have water from the spring, and a loaf of brown bread on the shelf.—Hark! I hear a rustling of the leaves. Is it some ill-fed village hound yielding to the instinct of the chase? or the lost pig which is said to be in these woods, whose tracks I saw after the rain?

The Poet: See those clouds; how they hang! That's the greatest thing I have seen to-day. There's nothing like it in old paintings, nothing like it in foreign lands,— unless when we were off the coast of Spain. That's a true Mediterranean sky. I thought, as I have my living to get, and have not eaten to-day, that I might go a-fishing. That's the true industry for poets. It is the only trade I have learned. Come, let's get along.

The Hermit: I cannot resist. My brown bread will soon be gone. I will go with you gladly soon, but I am just concluding a serious meditation. I think that I am near the end of it. Leave me alone, then, for a while. But that we may not be delayed, you shall be digging the bait meanwhile. Angle-worms are rarely to be met with in these parts, where the soil was never fattened with manure; the race is nearly extinct. The sport of digging the bait is nearly equal to that of catching the fish, when one's appetite is not too keen; and this you may have all to yourself to-day. I would advise you to set in the spade down yonder among the ground-nuts, where you see the johnswort waving. I think that I may warrant you one worm to every three sods you turn up, if you look well in among the roots of the grass, as if you were weeding. Or, if you choose to go farther, it will not be unwise, for I have found the increase of fair bait to be very nearly as the squares of the distances.

The Hermit (Now Alone): Let me see; where was I? Methinks I was nearly in this frame of mind; the world lay about at this angle. Shall I go to heaven or a-fishing? If I should soon bring this meditation to an end, would another so sweet occasion be likely to offer? I was as near being resolved into the essence of things as ever I was in my life. I fear my thoughts will not come back to me. My thoughts have left no track, and I cannot find the path again. What was it that I was thinking of? It was a very hazy day. I will just try these three sentences of Con-fut-see; they may fetch that state about again. I know not whether it was the dumps or a budding ecstasy. Mem. There never is but one opportunity of a kind.

The Poet: How now, Hermit, is it too soon? I have got just thirteen whole ones, beside several which are imperfect or undersized; but they will do for the smaller fry; they do not cover up the hook so much. Those village worms are quite too large; a shiner may make a meal off one without finding the skewer.

The Hermit: Well then, if you've got the worms, then my meditation is finished. Shall we go to the River Concord? There's good sport there if the water be not too high.

[Applause]

THE BEAN-FIELD

Meanwhile my beans, the length of whose rows, added together, was seven miles already planted, were impatient to be hoed, for the earliest had grown considerably before the latest were in the ground. What was the meaning of this so steady and self-respecting, this small Herculean labor, I knew not. I came to love my rows, my beans, though so many more than I wanted. They attached me to the earth, and so I got strength like Antæus, who, in wrestling Hercules, gained strength each time he touched the ground. But why should I raise them? Only Heaven knows. This was my curious labor all summer,—to make this portion of the earth's surface, which had before yielded only cinquefoil, blackberries, johnswort, sweet wild fruits, pleasant flowers, and the like, produce instead this pulse. What shall I learn of beans or beans of me? I cherish them, I hoe them, early and late I have an eye to them; and this is my day's work. It is a fine broad leaf to look on. My supportive companions are the dews and rains which water this dry soil, and what fertility is in the soil itself, which for the most part is lean and depleted. My enemies are leaf-eating worms, cool days, and most of all, wood-chucks. The last have nibbled for me a quarter of an acre clean. But what right had I to oust johnswort and the rest, and break up their ancient herb garden? Soon, however, the remaining beans will be too tough for them, and will go forward to meet new foes.

When I was four years old, as I well remember, I was brought from Boston to Concord, through these very woods and this field, to the pond. It is one of the oldest scenes stamped on my memory. And now today, my flute has waked the echoes over that very same water. The pines still stand here older than I; or, if some have fallen, I have cooked my supper with their stumps, and a new growth is rising all around, preparing another aspect for new infant eyes. Almost the same johnswort springs from the same peren-nial root in this pasture, and even I have at length helped to clothe that fabulous landscape of my infant dreams, and one of the results of my presence and influence is seen in these bean leaves, corn blades, and potato vines.

I planted about two acres and a half, and in the course of the summer it appeared by the arrow-heads which I turned up in hoeing, that an extinct nation had anciently dwelt here and planted corn and beans long before colonizers came to clear the land and exhaust the soil, for New Englanders gen-erally rather to start afresh than maintain a land with permaculture practices. The last use of this land was likely fifteen years or so ago, and yet it has still not recovered from the pillage.

Before yet any woodchuck or squirrel had run across the road, or the sun had got above the shrub oaks, while all the dew was on, though the farmers warned me against it,—and yet I would advise you to do all your work if possible while the dew is on,—I began to level the ranks of haughty weeds in my bean field and throw dust upon their heads. Early in the morning I worked barefooted, dabbling like a malleable artist in the dewy and crumbling sand, but later in the day the sun blistered my feet. The sun lighted me to hoe beans, pacing slowly backward and forward over that yellow gravelly upland, between the long green rows, fifteen rods long, with one end terminating in a patch of oak shrubs where I could rest in the shade, the other in a blackberry field where the green berries deepened their tints by the time I had made another bout. Removing the weeds, putting fresh soil about the bean stems, and encouraging this weed which I had sown, making the yellow soil express its summer thoughts in bean leaves and blossoms rather than in wormwood and piper and millet grass, making the earth say beans instead of grass,—this was my daily work. As I had little aid from horses or cattle, or hired help, or improved implements of agriculture, and used no manure. I was much slower, and became much more intimate with my beans than usual.

But labor of the hands, even when pursued to the verge of drudgery, is perhaps never the worst form of idleness. It has a constant and imperishable moral, and to the scholar it yields a classic result. A very *gricola laboriosus* was I to travelers bound westward through Lincoln and Wayland to nobody knows where; they sitting at their ease in gigs, with elbows on knees, and reins loosely hanging in festoons; I the home-staying, laborious native of the soil. But soon my homestead was out of their sight and thought. It was the only open and cultivated field for a great distance on either side of the road; so they made the most of it; and sometimes the human specimen in the field heard more of travelers' gossip and comment than was meant for his ear:

"Beans so late! peas so late!"—for I continued to plant when others had begun to hoe,—the ministerial farmer had not suspected it.
"Corn, my child, for fodder; corn for fodder."

"Does he live there?" asks the black bonnet of the gray coat; and the hard-featured farmer reins up their grateful dobbin to inquire what you are doing where they see no manure in the furrow, and recommends a little chip dirt, or any little waste stuff, or it may be ashes or plaster. But here were two acres and a half of trenches, and only a hoe for cart and two hands to draw it,—there being an aversion to other carts and horses,—and chip dirt far away. Fellow-travelers as they rattled by compared it aloud with the fields which they had passed, so that I came to know how I stood in the agricultural world. This was one field not bothered to be included in the official agriculture census report. But, by the way, who estimates the value of the crop which nature yields in the still wilder fields unimproved by humans? The crop of English hay is carefully weighed, the moisture calculated, the silicates and the potash; but in all dells and pond holes in the woods and pastures and swamps grows a rich and various crop only unreaped by human. Mine was, as it were, the connecting link between wild and cultivated fields; as some states are colonized, and others half-colonized, and others completely rudimentary, so my field was, though not in a bad sense, a half-cultivated field. They were beans cheerfully returning to their wild and primitive state that I cultivated, and my hoe played the Ranz des Vaches for them.

Near at hand, upon the topmost spray of a birch, sings the brown-thrasher—or red mavis, as some love to call them—all the morning, glad of your society, that would find out another farmer's field if yours were not here. While you are planting the seed, they cry,—"Drop it, drop it,—cover it up, cover it up,—pull it up, pull it up, pull it up." But this was not corn, and so it was safe from such enemies as they. You may wonder what their rigmarole, their amateur Paganini performances on one string or on twenty, have to do with your planting, but yet I prefer it to leached ashes or plaster. It was a cheap sort of top dressing in which I had entire faith.

As I drew a still fresher soil about the rows with my hoe, I disturbed the ashes of unchronicled nations who in primeval years lived under these heavens, and their small implements of war and hunting were brought to the light of this modern day. They lay mingled with other natural stones, some of which bore the marks of having been burned by Indigenous fires, and some by the sun, and also bits of pottery and glass brought hither by the recent cultivators of the soil. When my hoe tinkled against the stones, that music echoed to the woods and the sky, and was an accompaniment to my labor which yielded an instant and immeasurable crop. It was no longer beans that I hoed, nor I that hoed beans.

The night-hawk circled overhead in the sunny afternoons like a mote in the eye, or in heaven's eye, falling from time to time with a swoop and a sound as if the heavens had opened up, torn at last to very rags and tatters, and yet a perfect sky remained; Small imps that fill the air and lay their eggs on the ground on bare sand or rocks on the tops of hills, where few have found them, gracefully carried up by ripples from the pond, as leaves are raised by the wind to float in the heavens; such kindredship is in Nature. The hawk is an aerial sister of the wave which she sails over and surveys, her perfect air-inflated wings answering to the elemental unfledged wing tips of the sea's waves. Or sometimes I watched a pair of hen-hawks circling high in the sky, alternately soaring and descending, approaching, and leaving one another, as if they were the embodiment of my own thoughts. Or I was attracted by the passage of wild pigeons from this wood to that, with a slight quivering winnowing sound and carrier haste; or from under a rotten stump my hoe turned up a sluggish portentous and outlandish spotted salamander, a trace of Egypt and the Nile, yet our contemporary. When I paused to lean on my hoe, these sounds and sights I heard and saw anywhere in the row, a part of the inexhaustible entertainment which the country offers.

On gala days, the town fires its great guns, which echo like popguns to these woods, and some waifs of martial music occasionally penetrate thus far. To me, away there in my bean- field at the other end of the town, the big guns sounded as if a puffball had burst; and when there was a military turnout of which I was ignorant, I have sometimes had a vague sense all the day of some sort of itching and disease in the horizon, as if some eruption would break out there soon, either scarlatina or canker-rash. It seemed by the distant hum as if somebody's bees had gone away from the hive, and that all the neighbors, according to false advice, were endeavoring to call them down into the hive again by rattling their domestic utensils on the front porch, as if some clamoring would scare these wild and free creatures back. And when the sound died quite away, and the hum had ceased, and the most favorable breezes told no tale, I knew that they had got the last of them safely into the town hive, and that now their minds were bent on the honey with which it was smeared.

I felt proud to know that the liberties of Massachusetts and of our motherland were in such safe keeping; and as I turned to my hoeing again I was filled with an inexpressible confidence, and pursued my labor cheerfully with a calm trust in the future. Spending such a fortune on defense; we must be safe from all of the worst evils, yes?

When there were several bands of musicians, it sounded as if all the village was a vast bellows, and all the buildings expanded and collapsed alternately with a loud, bellowing racket. But sometimes it was a really noble and inspiring strain that reached these woods, and the trumpet that sings of fame, and I felt inspired to stab and skewer a fellow human—an enemy imagined, or perhaps prescribed—and looked round for a woodchuck or a skunk to exercise my chivalry upon. These martial strains seemed as far away as Palestine, and reminded me of a march of crusaders in the horizon. This was one of the great days in town; though the sky had, from my clearing, only the same everlastingly magnificent look that it wears daily, and I saw no difference in it.

It was a singular experience—that long acquaintance which I cultivated with beans, what with planting, and hoeing, and harvesting, and threshing, and picking over and selling them,—the last was the hardest of all,—I might add eating, for I did taste. I was determined to know beans. When they were growing, I used to hoe from five o'clock in the morning 'til noon, and commonly spent the rest of the day about other affairs. Consider the intimate and curious acquaintance one makes with various kinds of weeds,—it will bear some detail in the account, for there was no little detail in the labor,—disturbing their delicate organizations so ruthlessly, and making such invidious distinctions with my hoe, leveling whole ranks of one species, and sedulously cultivating another. That's Roman wormwood,—that's pigweed, —that's sorrel,—that's piper-grass,—have at him, chop him up, turn his roots upward to the sun, don't let him have a fibre in the shade, if you do he'll turn himself t'other side up and be as green as a leek in two days. A long war, not with cranes, but with weeds, those Trojans who had sun and rain and dews on their side. Daily the beans saw me come to their rescue armed with a hoe, and thin the ranks of the enemies; filling up trenches with the conquered corpses. Many a victim fell before my weapon and rolled in the dust, though only time shall tell who is the true and hardiest victor. Human attempts to control the landscape thus far have been cute, at best. And is it I who holds the gavel to determine which are called "weeds?" Are my beans not weeds to the buttercups?

Those summer days which some of my contemporaries devoted to the fine arts in Boston or Rome, and others to contemplation in India, and others to trade in London or New York, I thus, with the other farmers of New England, devoted to agriculture. Not that I wanted beans to eat, whether they mean sustenance or as counters for voting, for I am by nature a Pythagorean and they are not permitted to eat beans; but still, this has nothing to do with anything and I care not what I am supposed to be doing. I exchanged them for rice, for some must work in fields if only for the sake of tropes, literary inspiration, and expression. It was on the whole, a rare amusement, which, continued too long, might have become a sensual indulgence.

Though I gave them no manure, and did not hoe them all once, I hoed them unusually well as far as I went, and was paid for it in the end, as Evelyn says, "there is no compost or additive whatsoever comparable to this continual motion, redigging, and turning of the mould with the spade." "The earth," he adds elsewhere, "especially if fresh, has a certain magnetism in it, by which it attracts the salt, power, or virtue (call it either) which gives it life; all dungings and other sordid temperings being but the afterthoughts to this improvement." Moreover, this being one of those "worn-out and exhausted lay fields which enjoy their sabbath," had perchance, as Sir Kenelm Digby thinks likely, attracted "vital spirits" from the air, which I believe may be less of the air, and more in the ground, and of the fungal nature. I harvested twelve bushels of beans.

But to be more particular, for it is complained that Mr. Coleman has reported chiefly the expensive experiments of proper farmers in his census, my outgoes were,—

For a hoe:	$0.54
Ploughing, harrowing, and furrowing:	7.50
	Too much
Beans for seed:	3.12½
Potatoes for seed:	1.33
Peas for seed:	0.40
Turnip seed:	0.06
White line for crow fence:	0.02
Horse cultivator and boy, three hours:	1.00
Horse and cart to get crop:	0.75

————

In all:	$14.72½[e]

e. According to the Consumer Price Index, this amount would equate to roughly $475 in 2022.

My income was from:

Nine bushels and twelve quarts of beans sold:	$16.94
Five large potatoes:	2.50
Nine small:	2.25
Grass:	1.00
Stalks:	0.75

———

In all: $23.44[f]

Leaving a pecuniary profit, as I have elsewhere said, of:
$8.71½.[g]

This is the result of my experience in raising beans. Plant the common small white bush bean about the first of June, in rows three feet by eighteen inches apart, being careful to select fresh round and unmixed seed. First look out for worms, and replace vacancies by planting anew. Then look out for woodchucks, if it is an exposed place, for they will nibble off the earliest tender leaves almost clean as they go; and again, when the young tendrils make their appearance, they have notice of it, and will shear them off with both buds and young pods, sitting erect like a squirrel. But above all, harvest as early as possible, if you would escape frosts and have a fair and salable crop; you may save much loss by this means. A smaller, early profit is never a loss when compared to the possible profits of later, for the latter is not guaranteed.

This further experience also I gained. I said to myself, I will not plant beans and corn with so much industry another summer, but other seeds; sincerity, truth, simplicity, faith, innocence, and the like, and see if they will not grow in this soil, even with less

f. According to the Consumer Price Index, this amount would equate to roughly $756 in 2022.
g. According to the Consumer Price Index, this amount would equate to roughly $281 in 2022.

toil and cultivation, and sustain me. Alas! I said this to myself; but now another summer is gone, and another, and another, and I am obliged to say to you, Reader, that the seeds which I planted, if indeed they were the seeds of those virtues, were wormeaten or had lost their vitality, and so did not come up. Commonly, one will only be brave as their parents were brave, or timid. This generation is very sure to plant corn and beans each new year precisely as the Indigenous did centuries ago and taught the first settlers to do, as if there were a fate in it. I saw an old man the other day, to my astonishment, making the holes with a hoe for the seventieth time at least, and not for himself to lie down in! But why should not the New Englander try new adventures, and not lay so much stress on their grain, their potato and grass crop, and their orchards,—raise other crops than these? Why concern ourselves so much about our beans for seed, and not be concerned at all about a new generation of people? We should really be fed and cheered if when we met a person we were to see that some of the qualities which I have named, which are for the most part aimlessly floating in the air, had taken root and grown in them, to be prized more than beans. Our ambassadors should be instructed to send home such virtuous seeds as these, and Congress help to distribute them over all the land. We should never cheat and insult and banish one another by our meanness, if there were present the tiniest kernel of worth and friendliness. But most people I do not meet at all, for they seem not to have time; they are busy about their beans. If we could see and hear, we would not see a fellow leaning on a hoe or a spade as a staff between work intervals, like a mushroom, but rather as partially risen out of the earth, something more than erect, like swallows walking on the ground:

"And as they spoke, their wings would now and then
Spread, as they meant to fly, then close again,"

And so we should suspect that we might be conversing with an angel, if we had the time to spare for such trivial matters between our important business of selling beans.

Ancient poetry and mythology suggest, at least, that agriculture was once a sacred art; but it is pursued with irreverent haste and heedlessness by us, our object being to have large farms and large crops merely. We have no festival, nor procession, nor ceremony, not excepting our dusty Cattle-shows and so-called Thanksgivings, by which the farmer might express a sense of the sacredness of their calling, or be reminded of its sacred origin. It is the profit and the feast which tempt them. By avarice and selfishness, and a groveling habit, from which none of us is free, by regarding the soil as property, or the means of acquiring property chiefly, the landscape is deformed, agriculture is degraded with us, and the farmer leads the scrappiest of lives. They know Nature, but as a robber of her beauty and innocence. The train cars of timber wail as they pass through the forest, like a mother cow's cries as she is separated from her calf, and she watches her nipper dragged away, both of them bellowing, so that we may employ her to meet our odd obsession with drinking the mammary fluids of other species. But her cries are quickly forgotten, for we prefer to feast upon the tender veal of her youngling while dipping bakery goods in her stolen milk, than to face the realities of the industries that provide the products we deem necessary. We spear God to appease our comforts.

Some neighbors farm timber, which seems necessary, but their methods perplex me, as a lover of woodlands. One may think that no care needs to be taken to preserve forests—for can't we just plant more trees? But this overlooks the nobler trees, the slow- growing, scarce trees that can't beat out other fresh seedlings. The proprietor of wood lots often treats their stock like a horse driver—by standing before it and beating them in the face all the way across the field.

The sun looks upon our cultivated fields and on the prairies and forests without distinction. They all reflect and absorb the rays alike, and the former make but a small part of the glorious picture which the sun beholds in a daily course. To the sun, the earth is all equally cultivated like a garden. Therefore we should receive the benefit of its light and heat with a corresponding trust and magnanimity. This broad field which I have looked at so long, it looks not to me as the principal cultivator, but away from me to influences more genial to it, which water and make it green. These beans have results which are not harvested by me. Do they not grow for woodchucks partly? Shall I not rejoice also at the abundance of the weeds whose seeds are the granary of the birds? It matters little comparatively whether the fields fill the farmer's barns. The true agriculturalist will cease from anxiety, as the squirrels manifest no concern whether the woods will bear chestnuts this year or not, and finish their labor with every day, relinquishing all claim to the produce of their fields, and sacrificing in their mind not only their first, but their last fruits also.

THE VILLAGE

After hoeing, or perhaps after reading and writing, in the forenoon, I usually bathed again in the pond, swimming across one of its coves for a stint, and washed the dust of labor from my person, or smoothed out the last wrinkle which study had made, and for the afternoon, was absolutely free. Every day or two I strolled to the village to hear some of the gossip which is incessantly going on there, circulating either from mouth to mouth, or from newspaper to newspaper, and which, taken in homœopathic doses, was really as refreshing in its way as the rustle of leaves and the peeping of frogs. As I walked in the woods to see the birds and squirrels, so I walked in the village to see the people and children; instead of the wind among the pines I heard the carts rattle. In one direction from my house there was a colony of muskrats in the river meadows; under the grove of elms and buttonwoods in the other horizon was a village of busy townspeople, as curious to me as if they had been prairie dogs, each sitting at the mouth of its burrow, or running over to a neighbor's to gossip. I went there frequently to observe their habits. The village appeared to me a great news room; and on one side, to support it, as once at Redding & Company's on State Street, they kept nuts and raisins, or salt and meal and other groceries. Some have such a vast appetite for the former commodity, that is, the news, and such sound digestive organs, that they can sit forever in public avenues without stirring, and let it simmer and whisper through them like the Etesian winds, or as if inhaling ether, it only producing numbness and insensibility to pain,—otherwise it would often be painful to hear,—without affecting the consciousness. I hardly ever failed, when I rambled through the village, to see a row of such worthies, either sitting on a ladder sunning themselves, with their bodies inclined forward and their eyes glancing along the line this way and that, from time to time, with a voluptuous expression, or else leaning against a barn with their hands in their pockets, like caryatides, as if to prop up the structure. They, being commonly out of doors, heard whatever was in the wind. These are the coarsest mills, in which all gossip is first rudely digested or cracked up before it is emptied into finer and more delicate hoppers within doors.

I observed that the vitals of the village were the grocery, the bar-room, the post-office, and the bank; and, as a necessary part of the machinery, they kept a bell, a big gun, and a fire-engine, at convenient places; and the houses were so arranged as to make the most of humankind, in lanes and fronting one another, so that every traveler had to run the gantlet, and every woman, man, and child might get a lick at them. Of course, those who were stationed nearest to the head of the line, where they could most see and be seen, and have the first blow at them, paid the highest prices for their places; and the few straggling inhabitants in the outskirts, where long gaps in the line began to occur, and the traveler could get over walls or turn aside into cow paths, and so escape.

Signs were hung out on all sides to allure the traveler; some to catch them by the appetite, as the tavern and victualling cellar; some by the fancy, as the dry goods store and the jeweler's; and others by the hair or the feet or the skirts, as the barber, the shoemaker, or the tailor. Besides, there was a still more terrible standing invitation to call at every one of these houses, and company expected about these times. For the most part I escaped wonderfully from these dangers, either by proceeding at once boldly and without deliberation to the goal, as is recommended to those who run the gantlet, or by keeping my thoughts on high things, like Orpheus, who, "loudly singing the praises of the gods to his lyre, drowned the voices of the Sirens, and kept out of danger." Sometimes I bolted suddenly, and nobody could tell my whereabouts, for I did not stand much about gracefulness, and never hesitated at a gap in a fence. I was even accustomed to make an irruption into some houses, where I was well entertained, and after learning the kernels and very last sieve-ful of news, what had subsided, the prospects of war and peace, and whether the world was likely to hold together much longer, I was let out through the rear avenues, and so escaped to the woods again.

It was very pleasant, when I stayed late in town, to launch myself into the night, especially if it was dark and tempestuous, and set sail from some bright village parlor or lecture room towards my snug harbor in the woods, with a bag of rye or cornmeal upon my shoulder, leaving only my outer self at the helm to do the navigating, or even tying up the helm when it was plain sailing, so that I might lend my mind to a merry crew of thoughts. I also had many a genial thought by the cabin fire "as I sailed." I was never cast away nor distressed in any weather, though I encountered some severe storms. It is darker in the woods, even in common nights, than most suppose. I frequently had to look up at the opening between the trees above the path in order to learn my route, and, where there was no cart-path, to feel with my feet the faint track which I had worn, or steer by the known relation of particular trees which I felt with my hands, passing between two pines for instance, not more than eighteen inches apart, in the midst of the woods, invariably, in the darkest night. Sometimes, after coming home thus late in a dark and muggy night, when my feet felt the path which my eyes could not see, dreaming and absent-minded all the way, until I was aroused by having to raise my hand to lift the latch, I have not been able to recall a single step of my walk, and I have thought that perhaps my body would find its way home if its master should forsake it, as the hand finds its way to the mouth without assistance. Several times, when a visitor chanced to stay into evening, and it proved a dark night, I was obliged to conduct them to the cart-path in the rear of the house, and then point out to them the direction they were to pursue, and instructing that they were to be guided rather by their feet than their eyes.

One very dark night, I directed two young friends who had been fishing in the pond. They lived about a mile off through the woods, and were quite used to the route. A day or two after one of them told me that they wandered about the greater part of the night, close by their own premises, and did not get home 'til toward morning, by which time, as there had been several heavy showers in the mean while, and the leaves were very wet, they were drenched to their skins. I have heard of many going astray even in the village streets, when the darkness was so thick that you could cut it with a knife, as the saying is. Some who live in the outskirts, having come to town a-shopping in their wagons, have been obliged to put up for the night; and many have gone half a mile out of their way, feeling the sidewalk only with their feet, and not knowing when they turned.

It is a surprising and memorable, as well as valuable experience, to be lost in the woods any time. Often in a snow storm, even by day, one will come out upon a well-known road and yet find it impossible to tell which way leads to the village. Though they know that they have traveled it a thousand times, they cannot recognize a feature in it, but it is as strange to them as if it were a road in Siberia. By night, of course, the perplexity is infinitely greater. In our most trivial walks, we are constantly, though unconsciously, steering like pilots by certain well-known beacons and headlands, and if we go beyond our usual course we still carry in our minds the bearing of some neighboring cape; and not 'til we are completely lost, or turned round,—for one needs only to be turned round once with their eyes shut in this world to be lost,—do we appreciate the vastness and strangeness of Nature. Every individual has to learn the points of compass again as often as they awake, whether from sleep or any abstraction. Not 'til we are lost,—or in better terms, not 'til we have lost the world,—do we begin to find ourselves, and realize where we are and the infinite extent of our relations.

Every larger tree in town which I knew and admired is being gradually culled out and carried to the mill. I miss them as surely and with the same feeling that I do the old friendly inhabitants of the village, sitting out on their porches, awaiting any visitor that should stop for a tea and chat. To me, those trees were something more than timber; to their owners, not so. I attended the felling, or rather, the funeral, of one old citizen of the town—a giant great elm. I was the chief mourner there, or perhaps the only mourner. How have the mighty fallen! Its history extends back over more than half the whole history of the town. Since its kindred could not conveniently attend, I attended. Methinks its fall marks an epoch in the history of the town. How much of old Concord falls with it! The town clerk will not chronicle its fall, but I will. Instead of erecting a monument to it, we take all possible pains to obliterate its stump—the only monument of a tree which is commonly allowed to stand. No longer will our eyes rest on its massive gray trunk, like a Corinthian support column; no longer shall we sit or walk in the shade of its lofty, spreading canopy. Is it not sacrilege to cut down the last elderly tree which has so long looked over Concord beneficently?

The things which make a town beautiful—rivers, trees, meadows, rocks, etc.—they have a high value which dollars and cents do not currently represent. If the inhabitants of a town are wise, they seek to preserve these things, though it may seem costly compared to dividing and selling them to the next town over. I do not think one fit to be the founder of a town who does not foresee the value of these things, but only legislates them as products. Thank God that people cannot yet fly, and lay waste to the sky as well as the earth! We are safe on that side for the present.

Townspeople have been talking now for a week at the post office about the age of the great elm, hacked down, as if it were some great mystery. I stooped down and read its years to them (127 years, in rings), but they heard me only as much as the wind that once sighed through its branches. In front of me, they continued to guess, and surmised that it might be two hundred years old—yet they never stooped for themselves to read the inscription left behind, nor consider my readings. Truly, they love darkness rather than light.

A sermon should be given to the town on economy of fuel. What right has my neighbor to burn ten cords of fresh wood, when I burn only one, gathered from downed trees in the forest? Thus, robbing our half-naked town of our precious coverings. Are they so much colder than I? It is expensive to maintain them in our midst.

One afternoon, near the end of the first summer, when I went to the village to get a shoe from the cobbler's, I was seized and put into jail, because, as I have elsewhere related, I did not pay a tax to, or recognize the authority of, the state which buys and sells men, women, and children like crops at the door of its senate-house. I do not find it my task to right all wrongs, but I do not either see it fit to contribute to wrongdoing.

I had gone down to the woods for my own purposes. But, wherever one goes, others will pursue and paw at them with their dirty institutions, and, if they can, constrain one to belong to their desperate odd-fellow society. It is true, I might have resisted forcibly with more or less effect, might have run "amok" against society; but I preferred that society should run "amok" against me, it being the desperate party.

However, I was released the next day, for my acquaintances found it terribly shameful to have a relative in jail, and paid my bail. I obtained my mended shoe, and returned to the woods in season to get my dinner of huckleberries on Fair-Haven Hill. I was never molested by any person but those who represented the state. I had no lock nor bolt except for on the desk which held my papers, not even a nail to put over my latch or windows. I never fastened my door night or day, though I was to be absent several days; not even when the next fall I spent a fortnight in the woods of Maine. And yet my house was more respected than if it had been surrounded by a file of soldiers. The tired rambler could rest and warm themselves by my fire, the literary amuse themselves with the few books on my table, or the curious, by opening my closet door, see what was left of my dinner, and what prospect I had of a supper. Yet, though many people of every class came this way to the pond, I suffered no serious inconvenience from these sources, and I never missed anything but one small book, a volume of Homer, which perhaps was improperly gilded, and this I trust a soldier of our camp has found invaluable use of by this time. I am convinced, that if all were to live as simply as I then did, thieving and robbery would be unknown. These take place only in communities where some have got more than is sufficient while others have not enough. The Homers would soon get properly distributed. As to how we may end crime, perhaps we turn to our leaders, as Confucius says—

"Nec bella fuerunt, Faginus astabat dum scyphus ante dapes."

"Nor wars did any molest, When only beechen bowls were in request."

"You who govern public affairs, what need have you to employ punishments? Love virtue, and the people will be virtuous. The virtues of a superior one are like the wind, and the virtues of a common one are like the grass. The grass, when the wind passes over it, bends."

THE PONDS

Sometimes, having had a surfeit of human society and gossip, and worn out all my village friends, I rambled still farther westward than I habitually dwell, into yet more unfrequented parts of the town, "to fresh woods and pastures new," or, while the sun was setting, made my supper of huckleberries and blueberries on Fair Haven Hill, and laid up a store for several days. The fruits do not yield their true flavor to the purchaser of them, nor to one who raises them for the market. There is but one way to obtain it, yet few take that way. If you would know the flavor of huckleberries, ask the shepherd or the partridge. It is a vulgar error to suppose that you have tasted huckleberries if you never plucked them. A huckleberry never reaches Boston; they have not been known there since they grew on her three hills. The ambrosial and essential part of the fruit is lost with the bloom which is rubbed off in the market cart, and they become mere provender. As long as Eternal Justice reigns, not one innocent huckleberry can be transported thither from the country's hills.

Occasionally, after my hoeing was done for the day, I joined some impatient companion who had been fishing on the pond since morning, as silent and motionless as a duck or a floating leaf, and, after practicing various kinds of philosophy, had concluded commonly, by the time I arrived, that he belonged to the ancient sect of Seenobites.

There was one older fisher who came around, excellent and skilled in all kinds of woodcraft, who was pleased to look upon my house as a building erected for the convenience of fishers; and I was equally pleased when he sat in my doorway to arrange his lines. Once in a while, we sat together on the pond, he at one end of the boat, and I at the other; but not many words passed between us, for he had grown deaf in his later years, but he occasionally hummed a psalm, which harmonized well enough with my philosophy. Our intercourse was thus altogether one of unbroken harmony, far more pleasing to remember than if it had been carried on by speech.

When, as was commonly the case, I had none to commune with, I used to raise the echoes by striking with a paddle on the side of my boat, filling the surrounding woods with circling and dilating sound, stirring them up as the keeper of a menagerie of wild beasts, until I elicited a growl from every wooded vale and hill-side.

In warm evenings I frequently sat in the boat playing the flute, and saw the perch, which I seemed to have charmed, hovering around me, and the moon traveling over the ribbed bottom, which was strewed with the wrecks of the forest.

Formerly I had come to this pond adventurously, from time to time in my younger years, in dark summer nights, with a companion, and making a fire close to the water's edge, which we thought attracted the fishes, we caught pouts with a bunch of worms strung on a thread; and when we had done, far in the night, threw the burning branches high into the air like skyrockets, which, coming down into the pond, were quenched with a loud hissing, and we were suddenly groping in total darkness. Through this, whistling a tune, we took our way to the haunts of humankind again, back into civilization. But now, this shore is my home.

Sometimes, after staying in a village parlor 'til the family had all retired, I have returned to the woods, and, thinking of the next day's dinner, spent the hours of midnight fishing from a boat by moonlight, sere-naded by owls and foxes, and hearing, from time to time, the creaking note of some unknown bird close at hand. These experiences were very memorable and valuable to me,—anchored in forty feet of water, and twenty or thirty rods from the shore, surrounded sometimes by thousands of small perch and shiners, dimpling the surface with their tails in the moon-light, and communicating by a long flaxen line with mysterious nocturnal fishes which had their dwelling forty feet below, or sometimes dragging sixty feet of line about the pond as I drifted in the gentle night breeze, now and then feeling a slight vibration along it, indicative of some life prowling about its extrem-ity, of dull uncertain blundering purpose there, and slow to make up its mind. At length you slowly raise, pulling hand over hand, some horned pout squeak-ing and squirming to the upper air. It was very queer, especially in dark nights, when your thoughts had wandered to vast and cosmogonic themes in other spheres, to feel this faint jerk, which came to inter-rupt your dreams and link you to Nature again. It seemed as if I might next cast my line upward into the air, as well as downward into this element, which was scarcely more dense. Thus I caught two fishes as it were with one hook.

The scenery of Walden is on a humble scale, and, though very beautiful, does not approach to grandeur, nor can it much concern one who has not long frequented it or lived by its shore; yet this pond is so remarkable for its depth and purity as to merit a particular description. It is a clear and deep green well, half a mile long and a mile and three quarters in circumference, and contains about sixty-one and a half acres; a perennial spring in the midst of pine and oak woods, without any visible inlet or outlet except by the clouds and evaporation. The surrounding hills rise abruptly from the water to the height of forty to eighty feet, though on the south-east and east they attain to about one hundred and one hundred and fifty feet respectively, within a quarter and a third of a mile. They are exclusively woodland. All our Concord waters have two colors at least; one when viewed at a distance, and another, more proper, close at hand. The first depends more on the light, and follows the sky. In clear weather, in summer, they appear blue at a little distance, especially if agitated, and at a great distance all appear alike. In stormy weather they are sometimes of a dark slate color. The sea, however, is said to be blue one day and green another without any perceptible change in the atmosphere. I have seen our river, when, the landscape being covered with snow, both water and ice were almost as green as grass.

Some consider blue "to be the color of pure water, whether liquid or solid." But, looking directly down into our waters from a boat, they are seen to be of very different colors. Lying between the earth and the heavens, it partakes of the color of both. Viewed from a hill-top it reflects the color of the sky; but near at hand it is of a yellowish tint next the shore where you can see the sand, then a light green, which gradually deepens to a uniform dark green in the body of the pond. In some lights, viewed even from a hill-top, it is of a vivid green next the shore. Some have referred this to the reflection of the verdure; but it is equally green there against the railroad sand-bank, and in the spring, before the leaves are expanded, and it may be simply the result of the prevailing blue mixed with the yellow of the sand. Such is the color of its iris. This shallow, shore hugging portion is also, where in the spring, the ice being warmed by the heat of the sun reflected from the bottom, and also transmitted through the earth, melts first and forms a narrow canal about the still frozen middle.

At times, I have discerned a matchless and indescribable light blue, such as watered or changeable silks and sword blades suggest, more cerulean than the sky itself, alternating with the original dark green on the opposite sides of the waves, which last appeared but muddy in comparison. It is a vitreous greenish blue, as I remember it, like those patches of the winter sky seen through cloud vistas in the west before sundown. Yet a single glass of its water held up to the light is as colorless as an equal quantity of air. It is well known that a large plate of glass will have a green tint, owing, as the makers say, to its "body," but a small piece of the same will be colorless. How large a body of Walden water would be required to reflect a green tint I have never proved. The water of our river is black or a very dark brown to one looking directly down on it, and, like that of most ponds, imparts to the body of one bathing in it a yellowish tinge; but this water is of such crystalline purity that the body of the bather appears of an alabaster whiteness, still more unnatural, which, as the limbs are magnified and distorted withal, produces a monstrous effect, making fit studies for a Michael Angelo.

The water is so transparent that the bottom can easily be discerned at the depth of twenty-five or thirty feet. Paddling over it, you may see, many feet beneath the surface the schools of perch and shiners, perhaps only an inch long, yet the former easily distinguished by their transverse bars, and you think that they must be ascetic fish that find a subsistence there. Once, in the winter, many years ago, when I had been cutting holes through the ice in order to catch pickerel, as I stepped ashore I tossed my axe back on to the ice, but, as if some evil genius had directed it, it slid four or five rods directly into one of the holes, where the water was twenty-five feet deep. Out of curiosity, I lay down on the ice and looked through the hole, until I saw the axe a little on one side, standing on its head, with its helve erect and gently swaying to and fro with the pulse of the pond; and there it might have stood erect and swaying 'til in the course of time the handle rotted off, if I had not disturbed it. Making another hole directly over it with an ice chisel which I had, and cutting down the longest birch which I could find in the neighborhood with my knife, I made a slip-noose, which I attached to its end, and, letting it down carefully, passed it over the knob of the handle, and drew it by a line along the birch, and so pulled the axe out again.

The shore is composed of a belt of smooth rounded white stones like paving stones, excepting one or two short sand beaches, and is so steep that in many places a single leap will carry you into water over your head; and were it not for its remarkable transparency, that would be the last to be seen of its bottom 'til it rose on the opposite side. Some think it is bottomless. It is nowhere muddy, and a casual observer would say that there were no weeds at all in it; and of noticeable plants, except in the little meadows recently overflowed, which do not properly belong to it, a closer scrutiny does not detect a flag nor a bulrush, nor even a lily, yellow or white, but only a few small heart-leaves and potamogetons, and perhaps a water-target or two; all which however a bather might not perceive; and these plants are clean and bright like the element they grow in. The stones extend a rod or two into the water, and then the bottom is pure sand, except in the deepest parts, where there is usually a little sediment, probably from the decay of the leaves which have been wafted on to it so many successive falls, and a bright green weed is brought up on anchors even in midwinter.

We have one other pond just like this, White Pond, in Nine Acre Corner, about two and a half miles westerly; but, though I am acquainted with most of the ponds within a dozen miles of this centre I do not know any with a third of this pure and well-like character. Perhaps on that spring morning when Adam and Eve were driven out of Eden, Walden Pond was already in existence, and it was covered by a gentle spring rain, a tingly mist, and a warm southerly wind, and it was visited by myriads of ducks and geese, which had not heard of the fall. Even then, it had clarified its waters and colored them of the hue they now wear, and obtained a patent from heaven to be the only Walden Pond in the world and distiller of celestial dews. Who knows in how many unremembered nations' literatures this has been the Castalian Fountain? or what nymphs presided over it in the Golden Age? It is a gem of the holiest waters.

Yet perchance the first who came to this well have left some trace of their footsteps. I have been surprised to detect encircling the pond, even where a thick wood has just been cut down on the shore, a narrow shelf-like path in the steep hill- side, alternately rising and falling, approaching and receding from the water's edge, as old probably as the race of humankind here, worn by the feet of aboriginal hunters, and still from time to time unwittingly trodden by the present occupants of the land. This is particularly distinct to one standing on the middle of the pond in winter, just after a light snow has fallen, appearing as a clear undulating white line, unobscured by weeds and twigs, and very obvious a quarter of a mile off in many places where in summer, it is hardly distinguishable close at hand. The snow reprints it, as it were, in clear white type alto- relievo. The ornamented grounds of prestigious villas which will one day be built here may still preserve some trace of this.

The pond rises and falls, but whether regularly or not, and within what period, nobody knows, though, as usual, many pretend to know. It is commonly higher in the winter and lower in the summer, though not corresponding to the general wet and dryness. I can remember when it was a foot or two lower, and also when it was at least five feet higher, than when I lived by it. But the pond has risen steadily for two years, and now, in the summer of '52, is just five feet higher than when I lived there, or as high as it was thirty years ago, and fishing goes on again in the meadow. This makes a difference of level, at the outside, of six or seven feet; and yet the water shed by the surrounding hills is insignificant in amount, and this overflow must be referred to causes which affect the deep springs. This same summer the pond has begun to fall again. It is remarkable that this fluctuation, whether periodical or not, appears thus to require many years for its accomplishment. I have observed one rise and a part of two falls, and I expect that a dozen or fifteen years hence the water will again be as low as I have ever known it. Flint's Pond, a mile eastward, allowing for the disturbance occasioned by its inlets and outlets, and the smaller intermediate ponds also, sympathize with Walden, and recently attained their greatest height at the same time with the latter. The same is true, as far as my observation goes, of White Pond.

This rise and fall of Walden at long intervals serves this use at least; the water standing at this great height for a year or more, though it makes it difficult to walk round it, kills the shrubs and trees which have sprung up about its edge since the last rise, pitch-pines, birches, alders, aspens, and others, and, falling again, leaves an unobstructed shore; for, unlike many ponds and all waters which are subject to a daily tide, its shore is cleanest when the water is lowest. On the side of the pond next my house, a row of pitch pines fifteen feet high has been killed and tipped over as if by a lever, and thus a stop put to their encroachments; and their size indicates how many years have elapsed since the last rise to this height. By this fluctuation the pond asserts its title to a shore, and thus the shore is shorn, and the trees cannot hold it by right of possession. These are the lips of the lake on which no beard grows. It licks its chaps from time to time. When the water is at its highest, the alders, willows, and maples send forth a mass of fibrous red roots several feet long from all sides of their stems in the water, and to the height of three or four feet from the ground, in the effort to maintain themselves; and I have known

the high-blueberry bushes about the shore, which
commonly produce no fruit, bear an abundant crop
under these circumstances.

Some have been puzzled to tell how the shore became so regularly maintained. My townspeople have
all heard the tradition; the oldest people tell me that
they heard it in their youth—that anciently, the Indigenous Peoples were holding a pow-wow upon a hill
here, which rose as high into the heavens as the pond
now sinks deep into the earth, and while they were
thus engaged, the hill shook and suddenly sank, and
only one old squaw, named Walden, escaped. From
her, the pond was named. It has been conjectured that
when the hill shook these stones rolled down its side
and became the present shore. It is very certain, at
any rate, that once there was no pond here, and now
there is one. As for the stones, I observe that the surrounding hills are remarkably full of the same kind of
stones, so that they have been obliged to pile them up
in walls on both sides of the railroad cut nearest the
pond; and, moreover, there are most stones where
the shore is most abrupt;—one might even suppose
that it was called originally called Walled-in Pond.

The pond was my well, already dug. For four
months in the year its water is as cold as it is pure at
all times; and I think that it is then as good as any,
if not the best, in the town. In the winter, all water
which is exposed to the air is colder than springs and
wells which are protected from it. Moreover, in summer, Walden never becomes so warm as most water
which is exposed to the sun, on account of its depth.
In the warmest weather I usually placed a pailful in
my cellar, where it became cool in the night, and remained so during the day; though I also resorted to
a spring in the neighborhood. It was as good when a

week old as the day it was dipped, and had no taste of the pump. Whoever camps for a week in summer by the shore of a pond, needs only bury a pail of water a few feet deep in the shade of his camp to have the luxury of ice.

There have been caught in Walden pickerel, one weighing as much as seven pounds, to say nothing of another which carried off a reel with great velocity, which the fisher safely measured in at eight pounds, at a distance. Perch and pouts, some of each weighing over two pounds, shiners, chivins or roach (Leuciscus pulchellus), a very few breams, and a couple of eels, one weighing four pounds,—I am thus particular because the weight of a fish is commonly its only title to fame, and these are the only eels I have heard of here;—also, I have a faint recollection of a little fish some five inches long, with silvery sides and a greenish back, somewhat dace-like in its character, which I mention here chiefly to link my facts to fable. Nevertheless, this pond is not very fertile in fish. Its pickerel, though not abundant, are its chief boast. I have seen at one time, lying on the ice, pickerel of at least three different kinds; a long and shallow one, steel- colored, most like those caught in the river; a bright golden kind, with greenish reflections and remarkably deep, which is the most common here; and another, golden-colored, and shaped like the last, but peppered on the sides with small dark brown or black spots, intermixed with a few faint blood-red ones, very much like a trout. These are all very firm fish, and weigh more than their size promises. The shiners, pouts, and perch also, and indeed all the fishes which inhabit this pond, are much cleaner, handsomer, and firmer-fleshed than those in the river and most other ponds, as the water is purer, and they can easily be distinguished. Probably many ichthyologists would make new varieties of some of them. There are also a clean race of frogs and tortoises, and a few muscles in it; muskrats and minks leave their traces about it, and occasionally a traveling mud-turtle visits it. Sometimes, when I pushed off my boat in the morning, I disturbed a great mud-turtle which had burrowed herself under the boat in the night. Ducks and geese frequent it in the spring and fall, the white-bellied swallows (Hirundo bicolor) skim over it, and the peetweets (Totanus macularius) "teter" along its stony shores all summer. I have sometimes disturbed a fishhawk sitting on a white-pine over the water; but I doubt if this pond is ever profaned by the wing of a gull. At most, it tolerates one annual loon. These are all the animals of consequence which frequent it now.

You may see from a boat, in calm weather, near the sandy eastern shore, where the water is eight or ten feet deep, and also in some other parts of the pond, some circular heaps half a dozen feet in diameter by a foot in height, consisting of small stones less than a hen's egg in size, where all around is bare sand. At first you wonder if the Indigenous Peoples could have formed them on the ice for any purpose, and so, when the ice melted, they sank to the bottom; but they are too regular and some of them plainly too fresh for that. They are similar to those found in rivers; but as there are no suckers nor lampreys here, I know not by what fish they could be made. Perhaps they are the nests of the chivin. These lend a pleasing mystery to the bottom.

The shore is irregular enough not to be monotonous. I have in my mind's eye the western indented with deep bays, the bolder northern, and the beautifully scalloped southern shore, where successive capes overlap each other and suggest unexplored coves between. The forest has never so good a setting, nor is so distinctly beautiful, as when seen from the middle of a small lake amid hills which rise from the water's edge; for the water in which it is reflected not only makes the best foreground in such a case, but, with its winding shore, the most natural and agreeable boundary to it. There is no rawness nor imperfection in its edges, as where the axe has cleared a part, or a cultivated field abuts on it. The trees have ample room to expand on the water side, and each sends forth its most vigorous branch in that direction. There, Nature has woven a natural hem, and the eye rises by soft gradations from the low shrubs of the shore to the highest trees. There are few traces of a human's hand to be seen. The water laves the shore as it did a thousand years ago.

A lake is the landscape's most beautiful and expressive feature. It is earth's eye; and when looking into it, the beholder measures the depth of their own nature. The fluviatile trees next the shore are the slender eyelashes which fringe it, and the wooded hills and cliffs around are its overhanging brows.

Standing on the smooth sandy beach at the east end of the pond, in a calm September afternoon, when a slight haze makes the opposite shore line indistinct, I have seen whence came the expression, "the glassy surface of a lake." When you invert your head, it looks like a thread of finest gossamer stretched across the valley, and gleaming against the distant pine woods, separating one stratum of the atmosphere from another. You would think that you could walk dry under it to the opposite hills, and that the swallows which skim over might perch on it. Indeed, they sometimes dive below this line, as it were by mistake, and are undeceived. As you look over the pond westward you are obliged to employ both your hands to defend your eyes against the reflected as well as the true sun, for they are equally bright; and if, between the two, you survey its surface critically, it is literally as smooth as glass, except where the skater insects, at equal intervals scattered over its whole extent, by their motions in the sun produce the finest imaginable sparkle on it, or, perchance, a duck plumes itself, or, as I have said, a swallow skims so low as to touch it. It may be that in the distance a fish describes an arc of three or four feet in the air, and there is one bright flash where it emerges, and another where it strikes the water; sometimes the whole silvery arc is revealed; or here and there, perhaps, is a thistle-down floating on its surface, which the fishes dart at and so dimple it again. It is like molten glass cooled but not congealed, and the few motes in it are pure and beautiful like the imperfections in glass.

You may often detect a yet smoother and darker water, separated from the rest as if by an invisible cobweb, with a boom of the water nymphs, resting on it. From a hill-top you can see a fish leap in almost any part; for not a pickerel or shiner picks an insect from this smooth surface but it manifestly disturbs the equilibrium of the whole lake. It is wonderful with what elaborateness this simple fact is observed,—piscine murder reveals clear truth,—and from my distant perch I distinguish the circling undulations when they are half a dozen rods in diameter. You can even detect a water-bug (Gyrinus) ceaselessly progressing over the smooth surface a quarter of a mile off; for they furrow the water slightly, making a conspicuous ripple bounded by two diverging lines, but the skaters glide over it without rippling it perceptibly. When the surface is considerably agitated there are no skaters nor water-bugs on it, but apparently, in calm days, they leave their havens and adventurously glide forth from the shore by short impulses 'til they completely cover it. It is a soothing employment, on one of those fine days in the fall when all the warmth of the sun is fully appreciated, to sit on a stump on such a height as this, overlooking the pond, and study the dimpling circles which are incessantly inscribed on its otherwise invisible surface amid the reflected skies and trees. Over this great expanse there is no true disturbance, but rather it is thus at once gently smoothed away, as the trembling circles seek the shore and all is smooth again. Not a fish can leap or an insect fall on the pond without being reported in circling dimples, in lines of beauty, as it were the constant welling up of its fountain, the gentle pulsing of its life, the heaving of its chest. The thrills of joy and thrills of pain are undistinguishable. How peaceful the phenomena of the lake! Ay, every leaf and twig and stone and cobweb sparkles now at mid-afternoon as when covered with dew in a spring morning. Every motion of an oar or an insect produces a flash of light; and if an oar falls, how sweet the echo!

In such a day, in September or October, Walden is a perfect forest mirror, set round with stones as precious to my eye as if fewer or rarer. Nothing so fair, so pure, and at the same time so large, as a lake, perchance, lies on the surface of the earth. Sky water. It needs no fence. Nations come and go without defiling it. It is a mirror which no stone can crack, whose quicksilver will never wear off, whose gilding Nature continually repairs; no storms, no dust, can dim its surface ever fresh;—a mirror in which all impurity presented to it sinks, swept and dusted by the sun's hazy brush.

The pond retains no breath that is breathed on it, but sends its own to float as clouds high above its surface, and be reflected in its bosom still.

A field of water reveals the spirit that is in the air. It is continually receiving new life and motion from above. It is intermediate in its nature between land and sky. On land, only the grass and trees wave, but the water itself is rippled by the wind. I see where the breeze dashes across it by the streaks or flakes of light. It is remarkable that we can look down on its surface. We shall, perhaps, look down thus on the surface of air at length, and mark where a still subtler spirit sweeps over it.

The skaters and water-bugs finally disappear in the latter part of October, when the severe frosts have come; and then on a calm day in November, usually, there is absolutely nothing to ripple the surface. One November afternoon, in the calm at the end of a rain storm of several days' duration, when the sky was still completely overcast and the air was full of mist, I observed that the pond was remarkably smooth, so that it was difficult to distinguish its surface; though it no longer reflected the bright tints of October, but the somber November colors of the surrounding hills. Though I passed over it as gently as possible, the slight undulations produced by my boat extended almost as far as I could see, and gave a ribbed appearance to the reflections. But, as I was looking over the surface, I saw here and there at a distance a faint glimmer, as if some skater insects which had escaped the frosts might be collected there, or, perchance, the surface, being so smooth, betrayed where a spring welled up from the bottom. Paddling gently to one of these places, I was surprised to find myself surrounded by myriads of small perch, about five inches long, of a rich bronze color in the green water, sporting there, and constantly rising to the surface and dimpling it, sometimes leaving bubbles on it. In such transparent and seemingly bottomless water, reflecting the clouds, I seemed to be floating through the air as in a balloon, and their swimming impressed me as a kind of flight or hovering, as if they were a compact flock of birds passing just beneath my level on the right or left, their fins, like sails, set all around them. There were many such schools in the pond, apparently improving the short season before winter would draw an icy shutter over their broad skylight, sometimes giving to the surface an appearance as if a slight breeze struck it, or a few rain-drops fell there. When I approached carelessly and alarmed them, they made a sudden splash and rippling with their tails, as if one had struck the water with a brushy bough, and instantly took refuge in the depths. As winter approached, the wind rose, the mist increased, and the waves began to run, and the perch leaped much higher than before, half out of water, a hundred black points, three inches long, at once above the surface. Even as late as the fifth of December, one year, I saw some dimples on the surface, and thinking it was going to rain hard immediately, the air being full of mist, I made haste to take my place at the oars and row homeward; already the rain seemed rapidly increasing, though I felt none on my cheek, and I anticipated a thorough soaking. But suddenly the dimples ceased, for they were produced by the perch, which the noise of my oars had seared into the depths, and I saw their schools dimly disappearing; so I spent a dry afternoon after all.

An old man who used to frequent this pond nearly sixty years ago, when it was dark with surrounding forests, tells me that in those days he sometimes saw it all alive with ducks and other water fowl, and that there were many eagles about it. He came here a-fishing, and used an old log canoe which he found on the shore. It was made of two white-pine logs dug out and pinned together, and was cut off square at the ends. It was very clumsy, but lasted a great many years before it became water-logged and perhaps sank to the bottom. He did not know whose it was; it belonged to the pond. He used to make a cable for his anchor of strips of hickory bark tied together. An old potter, who lived by the pond before the Revolution, told him once that there was an iron chest at the bottom, and that they had seen it. Sometimes it would come floating up to the shore; but when you went toward it, it would go back into deep water and disappear. I remember that when I first looked into these depths there were many large tree trunks to be seen indistinctly lying on the bottom, which had either been blown over formerly, or left on the ice at the last cutting, when wood was cheaper; but now they have mostly disappeared.

When I first paddled a boat on Walden, it was completely surrounded by thick and lofty pine and oak woods, and in some of its coves, grape vines had run over the trees next the water and formed bowers under which a boat could pass. The hills which form its shores are so steep, and the woods on them were then so high, that, as you looked down from the west end, it had the appearance of an amphitheatre for some kind of sylvan spectacle. I have spent many an hour, when I was younger, floating over its surface as the west wind willed, having paddled my boat to the middle, and lying on my back across the seats, in a summer forenoon, dreaming awake, until I was aroused by the boat touching the sand, and I arose to see what shore my fates had impelled me to; days when idleness was the most attractive and productive industry. Many a forenoon have I stolen away, preferring to spend thus the most valued part of the day; for I was rich, if not in money, in sunny hours and summer days, and spent them lavishly; nor do I regret that I did not waste more of them in the workshop or the teacher's desk. But since I left, those shores have been much laid to waste by the woodchoppers, and now for many a year there will be no more rambling through the aisles of the wood, with occasional vistas through which you see the water. My Muse may be excused if she is silent henceforth. How can you expect the birds to sing when their groves are cut down?

Now the trunks of trees on the bottom, and the old log canoe, and the dark surrounding woods, are gone, and the villagers, who scarcely know where it lies, instead of going to the pond to bathe or drink, are thinking to bring its water, which should be as sacred as the Ganges at least, to the village in a pipe, to wash their dishes with!—to earn their Walden by the turning of a valve or drawing of a plug! That devilish Iron Horse, whose ear-rending neigh is heard throughout the country and town, has already muddied the nearby Boiling Spring with its foot, and now it presents itself here to chop off all the woods on Walden shore, that Trojan horse, with a thousand workers in its belly, introduced by mercenary Greeks! Where is the country's champion, the Moore of Moore Hill, to meet the Trojan Iron Horse and thrust an avenging lance between the ribs of the bloated pest?

Nevertheless, of all the characters I have known, perhaps Walden wears best, and best preserves its purity. Though the woodchoppers have laid bare first this shore and then that, and others have built their pig sties by it, and the railroad has infringed on its border, and the ice-harvesters have skimmed it once, it is itself unchanged, the same water which my youthful eyes fell on; all the change is in me. It has not acquired one permanent wrinkle after all its ripples. It is perennially young, and I may stand and see a swallow dip apparently to pick an insect from its surface as of yore. It struck me again tonight, as if I had not seen it almost daily for more than twenty years,—Why, here is Walden, the same woodland lake that I discovered so many years ago; where a forest was cut down last winter another is springing up by its shore as lustily as ever; the same thought is welling up to its surface that was then; it is the same liquid joy and happiness to itself and its Maker, ay, and it may be to me. It is the work of a brave God surely, in whom there was no deception! She rounded this water with her hand, deepened and clarified it in her thought, and in her will, bequeathed it to Concord. I see by its face that it is visited by her reflection; and I can almost say, Walden, is it you?

> It is no dream of mine,
> To ornament a line;
> I cannot come nearer to God and Heaven
> Than I live to Walden even.
> I am its stony shore,
> And the breeze that passes o'er;
> In the hollow of my hand
> Are its water and its sand,
> And its deepest resort
> Lies high in my thought.

The cars never pause to look at it; yet I fancy that the engineers and firefighters, and those passengers who have a season ticket and see it often, are better off for the sight. The engineer does not forget at

night, or their nature does not, that they have be-
holden this vision of serenity and purity once at
least during the day. Though seen but once, it helps
to wash out the engine's soot. One proposes that it
be called "God's Drop."

Flint's, or Sandy Pond, in Lincoln, our greatest
lake and inland sea, lies about a mile east of Walden.
It is much larger, being said to contain one hundred
and ninety-seven acres, and is more fertile in fish; but
it is comparatively shallow, and not remarkably pure.
A walk through the woods thither was often my recreation. It was worth the while, if only to feel the wind
blow on your cheek freely, and see the waves run, and
remember the life of mariners. I went a-chestnutting
there in the fall, on windy days, when the nuts were
dropping into the water and were washed to my feet;
and one day, as I crept along its sedgy shore, the fresh
spray blowing in my face, I came upon the forgotten wreck of a boat, the sides gone, and hardly more
than the impression of its flat bottom left amid the
rushes; yet its model was sharply defined, as if it were
a large decayed pad, with its veins. It was as impressive a wreck as one could imagine on the sea-shore,
and had as good a moral. It is by this time, mere
vegetable mould and indistinguishable pond shore,
through which rushes and seedlings have pushed up.
I used to admire the ripple marks on the sandy bottom, at the north end of this pond, made firm and
hard to the feet of the wader by the pressure of the
water, and the rushes which grew in native file, in
waving lines, corresponding to these marks, rank behind rank, as if the waves had planted them. There
also I have found, in considerable quantities, curious
balls, composed apparently of fine grass or roots, of
pipewort perhaps, from half an inch to four inches in

diameter, and perfectly spherical. These wash back and forth in shallow water on a sandy bottom, and are sometimes cast on the shore. They are either solid grass, or have a little sand in the middle. At first you would say that they were formed by the action of the waves, like a pebble; yet the smallest are made of equally coarse materials, half an inch long, and they are produced only at one season of the year. Moreover, the waves, I suspect, do not so much construct as wear down a material which has already acquired consistency. They preserve their form when dry for an indefinite period.

Flint's Pond! Such is the poverty of our nomenclature. What right had the unclean and stupid farmer, whose farm abutted on this sky water, whose shores he has ruthlessly laid bare, to give his name to it? Some skin-flint, who loved better the reflecting surface of a dollar, or a bright cent, in which he could see his own brazen face; who regarded even the wild ducks which settled in it as trespassers; his fingers grown into crooked and horny talons from the long habit of grasping harpy-like. I go there not to see him nor to hear of him; who never saw it, who never bathed in it, who never loved it, who never protected it, who never spoke a good word for it, nor thanked God that she had made it. Rather let it be named from the fishes that swim in it, the wild fowl or quadrupeds which frequent it, the wild flowers which grow by its shores, or some wild woman or child the thread of whose history is interwoven with its own; not from him who could show no title to it other than the deed which a like-minded neighbor or legislature gave him,—him who thought only of its money value; whose presence perchance cursed all the shore; who exhausted the land around it, and would fain have exhausted the waters within it; who regretted only that it was not English hay or cranberry meadow,—there was nothing to redeem it, forsooth, in his eyes,—and would have drained and sold it for the mud at its bottom. It did not turn his mill, and it was no privilege to him to behold it. I respect not his labors, his farm where every thing has its price; who would carry the landscape, who would carry his God to market, if he could get any thing for her; on whose farm nothing grows free, whose fields bear no crops, whose meadows no flowers, whose trees no fruits, but dollars; who loves not the beauty of his fruits, whose fruits are not ripe for him 'til they are turned to dollars. Give me the poverty that enjoys true wealth. Farmers are respectable and interesting to me in proportion as they are poor,—poor farmers. A model farm! where the house stands like a fungus in a muck-heap, chambers for humans, horses, oxen, and swine, cleansed and uncleansed, all contiguous to one another! Such is a model farm.

No, no; if the fairest features of the landscape are to be named after people, let them be the noblest and worthiest people alone. Let our lakes receive as true names at least as the Icarian Sea, where Icarus fashioned wings of feathers and wax to escape King Minos, but flew too close to the sun, melted his wings, and fell into the sea. "Still the shore" a "brave attempt resounds."

Goose Pond, of small extent, is on my way to Flint's; and Fair- Haven, an expansion of Concord River, said to contain some seventy acres, is a mile south-west; and White Pond, of about forty acres, is a mile and a half beyond Fair-Haven. This is my lake country.

These, with Concord River, are my water privileges; and night and day, year in year out, they grind whatever grist I carry to them, returning my thoughts to me, refined.

Since the woodcutters, and the railroad, and I myself have profaned Walden, perhaps the most attractive, if not the most beautiful, of all our lakes, the gem of the woods, is White Pond;—a poor name from its commonness, whether derived from the remarkable purity of its waters or the color of its sands. In these as in other respects, however, it is a lesser twin of Walden. They are so much alike that you would say they must be connected under ground. It has the same stony shore, and its waters are of the same hue. As at Walden, in sultry dog-day weather, looking down through the woods on some of its bays which are not so deep but that the reflection from the bottom tinges them, its waters are of a misty bluish-green or glaucous color. About fifteen years ago, you could see the top of a pitch-pine projecting above the surface in deep water, many rods from the shore. It was even supposed by some that the pond had sunk, and this was one of the primitive forests that formerly stood there.

I find that even so long ago as 1792, in a "Topographical Description of the Town of Concord," by one of its citizens, in the Collections of the Massachusetts Historical Society, the author, after speaking of Walden and White Ponds, adds: "In the middle of the latter may be seen, when the water is very low, a tree which appears as if it grew in the place where it now stands...the top of this tree is broken off, and at that place measures fourteen inches in diameter."

In the spring of '49, I talked with the resident who lives nearest the pond in Sudbury, who told me that it was they who got out this tree ten or fifteen years before. As near as they could remember, it stood twelve or fifteen rods from the shore, where the water was thirty or forty feet deep. It was in the winter, and she had been cutting out ice in the forenoon, and had resolved that in the afternoon, with the aid of her neighbors, they would finally take out the old pitch-pine. They sawed a channel in the ice toward the shore, and began hauling it over and along and out on to the ice with oxen; but, before they had gone far, they were surprised to find that it was wrong end upward, with the stumps of the branches pointing down, and the small end firmly fastened in the sandy bottom. It was about a foot in diameter at the big end, and she had expected to get a good saw-log, but it was so rotten as to be fit only for fuel, if for that. She had some of it in her shed then. There were marks of an axe and of woodpeckers on the butt. She thought that it might have been a dead tree on the shore, but was finally blown over into the pond, and after the top had become waterlogged, while the butt-end was still dry and light, had drifted out and sunk wrong end up. Her father, eighty years old, could not remember when it was not there. Several pretty large logs may still be seen lying on the bottom, where, owing to the undulation of the surface, they look like huge water snakes in motion.

This pond has rarely been profaned by a boat, for there is little in it to tempt a fisher. Instead of the white lily, which requires mud, or the common sweet flag, the blue flag (Iris versicolor), grows thinly in the pure water, rising from the stony bottom all around the shore, where it is visited by humming birds in June; and the color both of its bluish blades and its flowers, and especially their reflections, are in singular harmony with the glaucous water.

White Pond and Walden are great crystals on the surface of the earth, Lakes of Light. If they were permanently congealed, and small enough to be clutched, they would, perchance, be carried off by business people, like precious stones, to adorn the heads of emperors; but being liquid, and ample, and through deed "secured to us and our successors forever," we disregard them, and run after the diamond of Kohinoor instead. They are too pure to have a market value; they contain no muck. How much more beautiful than our lives, how much more transparent than our characters, are they! We never learned meanness of them. How much fairer than the pool before the farmer's door, in which their ducks swim! Hither the clean wild ducks come. Nature has no human inhabitant who appreciates her. The birds with their plumage and their notes are in harmony with the flowers, but what modern human conspires with the wild luxuriant beauty of Nature? She flourishes most alone, far from the towns where we reside. Talk of heaven! Yet we disgrace Earth.

HIGHER LAWS

As I came home through the woods with my string of fish, trailing my pole, it being now quite dark, I caught a glimpse of a woodchuck stealing across my path, and felt a strange thrill of primal delight, and was strongly tempted to seize and devour them raw; not that I was hungry then, except for that wildness which they represented. The wildest scenes had become unaccountably familiar. I found in myself, and still find, an instinct toward a higher, or, as it is named, spiritual life, as do most, and another toward a primitive one, and I reverence them both.

I love the wild not less than the refined spiritual life. I like sometimes to take rank hold on life and spend my day more as the animals do. They early introduce us to and detain us in scenery with which otherwise, we should have little acquaintance. We are most interested when science reports what we know instinctively, for that alone is a true humanity, or account of human experience.

They mistake who assert that the country dweller has few amusements, because they have not so many public festivals, or that children do not play so many games as they do in the towns,—for here the more primitive but solitary amusements of hunting and foraging have not yet been replaced with engineered toys. But already a world change is taking place, an overlooking and irreverence of the natural, replaced with textiles and businesses, and we sprawl our tiles outward into the woods. Besides the Humane Society, perhaps the hunter is the greatest friend of the animals hunted, for they care to preserve the habitat of their prey; but perhaps that is owing, not to an increased humanity, but to an increased scarcity of game.

When at the pond, I wished sometimes to add fish to my fare for variety. I have actually fished from the same kind of necessity that the first fishers did. Whatever arguments against fishing I could conjure, concerned my philosophy more than my feelings; I feel little emotion for the pescatarian variety. I did not pity the fishes nor the worms—this was simply habit. But I had long felt concerned about fowling, and sold my gun before I went to the woods. During the last years that I carried a gun, my excuse was that I was studying ornithology, and sought only new or rare birds. But I confess that I am now inclined to think that there is a finer way of studying ornithology than this. It requires so much closer attention to the habits of the birds, that, if for that reason only, I have been willing to omit the gun. Yet I am compelled to doubt if equally valuable sports are ever substituted for hunting and fishing; and when some of my friends have asked me anxiously about their children, whether they should let them hunt, I have answered, yes,—remembering it being a requirement of my natural education, the first tickle of interest, which lay the first block of the foundation for the sacred chapel which housed my adult reverence for Her.

We cannot but pity the child who has never fired a gun; they are no more humane, as they usually still feast upon the enslaved flesh of farmed animals, rather than wild animals, while their natural education has been sadly neglected. This was my answer with respect to those youths who were bent on this pursuit, trusting that they would soon outgrow it. No humane being, past the thoughtless age of childhood, will wantonly murder any creature which holds its life by the same tenure that they do. The hare in its extremity cries in terror like a child.

Such is oftenest the young adult's introduction to the forest, and the most original part of themselves. They go thither at first as a hunter and fisher, until at last, if they have the seeds of a better life in them, they distinguish their proper objects, as a poet or naturalist it may be, and leaves the gun and fish-pole behind. But the mass of people remain always children, in this respect.

In my boating as of late, I have several times scared up a couple of ducks, and they allowed me to come quite near. But, I have not seen them for some days. Would you know the end of our friendship? Goodwin shot them, and his family, who never sailed the river, ate them. Of course, they know not what they did. But what if I should eat their canary? The spectator who admiringly watches the matador shares their deed in slaughter. The ducks belonged to me, just as much as to anyone, but it was considered of more importance that Goodwin and his family should taste the flavor of them dead, than that I should enjoy the beauty of them alive.

I have been surprised to consider that the only obvious employment, except wood-chopping, ice-cutting, or the like business, which detained my fellow citizens at Walden Pond for more than half day, was fishing. Commonly they did not think that they were lucky, or well paid for their time, unless they got a long string of fish, though they had the opportunity of seeing the pond all the while. They might go there a thousand times before the sediment of fishing would sink to the bottom and leave their purpose pure; but no doubt such a clarifying process would be going on all the while. The governor and their council faintly remember the pond, for they went a-fishing there when they were children; but now they are too old and dignified to go a-fishing, and so they know it no more forever. Yet even they expect to go to heaven at last. If the legislature regards it, they go to the pond chiefly to regulate the number of hooks to be used there. Thus, even in civilized communities, the embryo adult passes straight through the hunter stage of development.

I have found repeatedly, of late years, that I cannot fish without falling a little in self-respect. I have tried it again and again. I have skill at it, and, like many of my fellows, a certain instinct for it, which revives from time to time, but always when I have finished, I feel that it would have been better if I had not fished. I think that I do not mistake. It is a faint announcement, yet so are the first streaks of morning. There is unquestionably this instinct in me which belongs to the lower orders of creation; yet with every year I am less a fisher, though without more humanity or even wisdom; at present I am no fisher at all. It is the poetry of observing the fishes which is their chief use; their flesh is their lowest use. But I see that if I were to live in a wilderness I should again be tempted to become a fisher and hunter in earnest. Beside, there is something essentially unclean about this diet and the eating of all flesh, and I began to see where associated housework commences, to keep the house sweet and free from all ill odors and sights. Having been my own butcher and scullion and cook, as well as the guest for whom the dishes were served up, I can speak from an unusually complete experience. The practical objection to animal food in my case was its uncleanness; and, besides, when I had caught and cleaned and cooked and eaten my fish, they seemed not to have fed me essentially. It was insignificant and unnecessary, and cost more than it came to. A little bread or a few potatoes would have done as well, with less trouble, blood, and filth. Like many of my contemporaries, I had rarely for many years used animal food, or tea, or coffee, etc.; not so much because of any ill effects which I had traced to them, but as because they were not agreeable to my imagination. The repugnance to animal food is not the effect of experience, but is an instinct. It appeared more beautiful to live low and fare hard in many respects; and though I never did so, I went far enough to please my imagination. I believe that every person who has ever been earnest to preserve their higher or poetic faculties in the best condition has been particularly inclined to abstain from animal food, and from much decadent food of any kind. It is a significant fact, stated by entomologists, I find it in Kirby and Spence, that "some insects in their perfect state, though furnished with organs of feeding, make no use of them;" and they lay it down as "a general rule, that almost all insects in this state eat much less than in that of larvæ. The voracious caterpillar when transformed into a butterfly," ... "and the gluttonous maggot when become a fly," content themselves with a drop or two of honey or some other sweet liquid. The abdomen under the wings of the butterfly still represents the larva. This is the tid-bit which tempts his insectivorous fate. The gross feeder is a person in the larva state; and there are whole nations in that condition, nations without fancy or imagination, whose vast abdomens betray them. Suckling at the teats of other species, and breeding animals, forcing them to live unnaturally in work camps, and then slaughtering them well before their time, for a taste.

It is hard to provide and cook so simple and clean a diet as will not offend the imagination; but this, I think, is to be fed when we feed the body; they should both sit down at the same table. Yet perhaps this may be done. The fruits eaten temperately need not make us ashamed of our appetites, nor interrupt the worthiest pursuits. But put an extra condiment into your dish, and it will poison you. It is not worth the while to live by rich cookery. Most would feel shame if caught preparing with their own hands precisely such a dinner, whether of animal or vegetable food, as is every day prepared for them by others. Yet 'til this is otherwise, we are not civilized, and, if gentlemen and ladies, still are not true men and women. This certainly suggests what change is to be made. It may be vain to ask why the imagination will not be reconciled towards flesh and fat. I am satisfied that it is not. Is it not a disappointment that human is labeled as an omnivorous animal? True, humans can and do live, in a great measure, by preying on other animals; but this is a miserable way,—as any one who will go to snaring rabbits, or slaughtering lambs, may learn,—and one will be regarded as a benefactor of their race who

shall teach people to confine themselves to a more innocent and wholesome diet. Whatever my own practice may be, I have no doubt that it is a part of the
destiny of the human race, in its gradual improvement, to leave off breeding and eating animals, just as
we have come around to mostly stop murdering and
eating each other.

If one listens to the faintest but constant suggestions of their genius, which are certainly true, as they
grow more resolute and faithful, their most joyful
road lies ahead. The faintest assured objection which
one healthy person feels at their dietary and life
choices will at length prevail over the arguments and
shallow customs of humankind. No one ever followed
their genius 'til it misled them. If the day and the night
are such that you greet them with gratefulness, and
life emits a fragrance like flowers and sweet-scented
herbs, is more elastic, more starry, more immortal,—
that is your success. All nature is your congratulation,
and you have cause momentarily to bless yourself.
The greatest personal gains and values are farthest
from being appreciated by society. We easily come to
doubt if they exist. We soon forget them. They are
the highest reality. Perhaps the facts most astounding
and most real are never communicated by human to
human. The true harvest of my daily life is somewhat
as intangible and indescribable as the tints of morning or evening. It is a little star-dust caught, a segment
of the rainbow which I have clutched.

Yet, for my part, I was never unusually squeamish;
I could sometimes eat a fried rat with a good relish,
if it were necessary. I am glad to have drunk water so
long, for the same reason that I prefer the natural sky
to an opium-eater's heaven. I would fain keep sober
always; and there are infinite degrees of drunkenness.

I believe that water is the only drink for a wise person; wine is not so noble a liquor; and think of dashing the hopes of a morning with a cup of warm coffee, or of an evening with a dish of tea! Ah, how low I fall when I am tempted by them! Even music may be intoxicating. It is better to enjoy things by sensitivity, rather than excess. Such apparently slight causes destroyed Greece and Rome, and will destroy England and America. Of all drunkenness, who does not prefer to be intoxicated perpetually by the air they breathe? I have found that coarse labors compel me to eat and drink coarsely also, which is my most serious objection to these types of labors. But to tell the truth, I find myself at present somewhat less particular in these respects. I carry less religion to the table, ask no blessing; not because I am wiser than I was, but, I am obliged to confess, because, however much it is to be regretted, with years I have grown more coarse and indifferent. Perhaps these questions are entertained only in youth, as most believe of poetry. My practice is "nowhere," my opinion is here. Nevertheless, I am far from regarding myself as one of those privileged ones to whom the Ved refers when it says, that "they who have true faith in the Omnipresent Supreme Being may eat all that exists," that is, they are not bound to inquire what is their food, or who prepares it.

Who has not sometimes derived an inexpressible satisfaction from their food in which appetite had no share? I have been thrilled to think that I owed a mental perception to the commonly gross sense of taste, that I have been inspired through the palate, that some berries which I had eaten on a hill-side had fed my genius. They who distinguish the true savor of their food can never be a glutton; they who do not cannot be otherwise. A puritan may go to their plain oatmeal with as hearty an appetite as ever a monarch to their turtle soup. Not that food which entereth into the mouth defileth a person, but the appetite with which it is eaten. It is neither the quality nor the quantity, but the devotion to sensual savors; when that which is eaten is not a viand to sustain our animal, or inspire our spiritual life, but food for the parasitic worms that possess us. If the hunter has a taste for mud-turtles, muskrats, and other such tid-bits, the fine noble person indulges a taste for jelly made of a calf's foot, or for sardines from over the sea, and they are even. The wonder is how they, how you and I, can live this slimy, beastly life, with eating and drinking.

Our whole life is startlingly moral. There is never an instant's truce between virtue and vice. Goodness is the only investment that never fails. In the music of the harp which trembles round the world, it is the wanting of this which compels us to behave. The harp is the traveling patterer for the Universe's Insurance Company, recommending its laws, and our little goodness is all the assessment that we pay. Though the youth often grow indifferent, the laws of the universe are not indifferent, but are forever on the side of the most sensitive.

We are conscious of an animal in us, which awakens in proportion as our higher nature slumbers. It is reptile and sensual, and perhaps cannot be wholly expelled; like the worms which, even in life and health, occupy our bodies. Possibly we may withdraw from it, but never change its nature. I fear that it may enjoy a certain health of its own; that we may be well, yet not pure. The other day I picked up the lower jaw of a hog, with white and sound teeth and tusks, which suggested that there was an animal health and vigor distinct from the spiritual. This creature succeeded by other means than temperance and purity.

"That in which humans differ from brute beasts," says Mencius, "is a thing very inconsiderable; the common herd lose it very soon; superior herds preserve it carefully." Who knows what sort of life would result if we had attained to purity? "A command over our passions, and over the external senses of the body, and good acts, are declared by the Ved to be indispensable in the mind's approximation to God." Yet the spirit can pervade and control every member and function of the body, and transmute the grossest sensuality into awakening and devotion. The generative energy, which, when we are loose, dissipates and makes us unclean; but when we are content and aware, it invigorates and inspires us. We choose our pleasures.

We flow at once to the universe when our channel of awareness is open. Our open eyes inspire us, and our slumber casts us down. They are blessed who is assured that the animal is dying out in them day by day, and the divine being established. I fear that we are such gods or demigods only as fauns and satyrs, the divine allied to beasts, the creatures of appetite, and that, to some extent, our very life is our disgrace.

All vices are but one single force, though it takes many forms. It is the same for all indulgences of substances. They are but one appetite, and we only need to see a person do any one of these things to know how great an addict they are in other respects. When the reptile is attacked at one mouth of their burrow, they show themselves at another.

During an activity, we may attend with grateful and attentive presence, and thus we know purposeful exertion, and we receive wisdom without reaching; but from sloth—ignorance and indulgence. The attuned mind manifests physical reality.

Does it matter that you are a Christian, if you are not purer than the heathen, if you do not deny yourself of every day distractions and addictions? I know of many systems of religion whose precepts fill the reader with shame regarding certain substances or habits, and provoke them to new endeavors, though it be performance and show merely—systems of control—and yet still hidden demons thrive.

I hesitate to say these things, but it is not because of the subject,—I care not how obscene my words are,—but because I cannot speak of them without betraying my own impurity. We discourse freely without shame of one form of excess sensuality, and are silent about another. We are so degraded that we cannot speak simply of the necessary functions of human nature. In earlier ages, in some countries, every function was reverently spoken of and regulated by law. Nothing was too trivial for the Hindoo lawgiver, however offensive it may be to modern taste. They teach how to eat, drink, cohabit, void excrement and urine, and the like, elevating what is rudimentary, and do not falsely excuse themselves by calling these things trifles.

Every human is the builder of a temple, called their body, to the god they worship, after a style purely their own. We are all sculptors and painters, and our material is our own flesh and blood and bones. Any nobleness begins at once to refine a person's features, and any unnatural indulgence to degrade them.

John Farmer sat at his door one September evening, after a hard day's work, his mind still running on his labor, more or less. Having bathed, he sat down to re-create his intellectual man. It was a rather cool evening, and some of his neighbors were apprehending a frost. He had not attended to the train of his thoughts long when he imagined some one playing on a flute, and that sound harmonized with his mood. Still he thought of his work; but the burden of his thought was, that though it kept running in his head, and he found himself planning and contriving it against his will, he actually cared about it very little. It was no more than the scurf of his skin, which was constantly shuffled off. But the notes of the flute came home to his ears out of a different sphere from that he worked in, and suggested work for certain faculties which slumbered in him. They gently did away with the street, and the village, and the state in which he lived. A voice said to him,—"Why do you stay here and live this mean moiling life, when a glorious existence is possible for you?" Those same stars twinkle over other fields than these.—But how to come out of this condition and actually migrate thither? He must practice some new austerity, and let his mind control his body and redeem it, and treat himself with ever increasing respect.

BRUTE NEIGHBORS

When in a particular world of our creating, why do the objects which we behold seem to make all of the world? Why have humans just a few species of animals seen fit to be their neighbors?

I spend a considerable portion of my time observing the habits of the wild animals, my brute neighbors. But when I consider that the wilder animals have been exterminated here,—the cougar, panther, lynx, wolverine, wolf, bear, moose, deer, beaver, turkey, etc., I cannot but feel as if I lived in a tamed country. I listen to a concert in which many parts are wanting. The whole civilized country is to some extent, turned into a city. Primitive Nature is most interesting to me. All the great trees and beasts, fishes and fowl, are gone from here. I wish to know an entire heaven and an entire earth, but I will still rejoice in the pieces left behind—for what choice do I have?

I have mentioned before, my mousemate who lived in my cellar, and there was a phœbe who soon built in my shed, and a robin sheltered in a pine which grew against the house. In June, the partridge (Tetrao umbellus,) which is so shy a bird, led her brood past my windows, from the woods in the rear to the front of my house, clucking and calling to them like a hen, and in all her behavior proving herself the hen of the woods. The young suddenly disperse on your approach, at a signal from the mother, as if a whirlwind had swept them away, and they so exactly resemble the dried leaves and twigs that many a traveler has placed their foot in the midst of a brood, and heard the whir of the old bird as she flew off, and her anxious calls and mewing, or seen her trail her wings to attract the traveler's attention, without suspecting their neighborhood. The parent will sometimes roll and spin round before you in such a dishabille, that you cannot, for a few moments, detect what kind of creature it is. The young squat still and flat, often running their heads under a leaf, and mind only their mother's directions given from a distance, your approach will not make them run again and betray themselves. You may even tread on them, or have your eyes on them for a minute, without discovering them. I have held them in my open hand at such a time, and still their only care, obedient to their mother and their instinct, was to squat there without fear or trembling. So perfect is this instinct, that once, when I had laid them on the leaves again, and one accidentally fell on its side, it was found with the rest in exactly the same position ten minutes afterward. They are not callow like the young of most birds, but more perfectly developed and precocious even than chickens. The remarkably adult yet innocent expression of their open and serene eyes is very memorable. All intelligence seems reflected in them. They suggest not merely the purity of infancy, but a wisdom clarified by experience. Such an eye was not born when the bird was, but is coeval with the sky it reflects. The woods do not yield another such a gem. The traveler does not often look into such a limpid well. The ignorant or reckless sportsman often shoots the parent at such a time, and leaves these innocents to fall a prey to some prowling beast or bird, or gradually mingle with the decaying leaves which they so much resemble. It is said that when hatched, instinctively they will directly disperse on some alarm, and so are lost, for they never hear the mother's call which gathers them again. These were my hens and chickens.

In the fall, the loon (Colymbus glacialis) came, as usual, to moult and bathe in the pond, making the woods ring with their wild laughter before I had risen. At rumor of their arrival all the Mill-dam sporters are on the alert, in gigs and on foot, two by two and three by three, with patent rifles and conical balls and spyglasses. They come rustling through the woods like autumn leaves, at least ten hunters to one loon. Some station themselves on this side of the pond, some on that, for the poor bird cannot be omnipresent; if they dive here, they must come up there. But now the kind October wind rises, rustling the leaves and rippling the surface of the water, so that no loon can be heard or seen, though their foes sweep the pond with spy- glasses, and make the woods resound with their discharges. The waves generously rise and dash angrily, taking sides with all water-fowl, and our hunters must retreat to town and shop and complete unfinished jobs. But they were too often successful.

When I went to get a pail of water early in the morning, I frequently saw the stately loon sailing out of my cove within a few rods. If I endeavored to overtake them in a boat, in order to see how they would manœuvre, they would dive and be completely lost, so that I did not discover them again, sometimes, 'til the latter part of the day.

As I was paddling along the north shore one very calm October afternoon, having looked in vain over the pond for a loon, suddenly one, sailing out from the shore toward the middle, set up their wild laugh and betrayed themselves. I pursued with a paddle and they dove, and when they came up I was nearer than before. They dove again, but I miscalculated the direction they would take, and we were fifty rods apart when they came to the surface this time, for I had helped to widen the interval; and again they laughed long and loud, and with more reason than before. They manœuvred so cunningly that I could not get within half a dozen rods of them. Each time, when they came to the surface, turning their head this way and that, they cooly surveyed the water and the land, and apparently chose course so that they might come up where there was the widest expanse of water and at the greatest distance from the boat. It was surprising how quickly they made up their mind and put resolve into execution. It was a pretty game, played on the smooth surface of the pond, a human against a loon. Suddenly your adversary's checker disappears beneath the board, and the problem is to place yours nearest to where theirs will appear again. No wit could divine where in the deep pond, beneath the smooth surface, they might be speeding like a fish, for they had time and ability to visit the bottom of the pond in its deepest part. It is said that loons have been caught in the New York lakes eighty feet beneath the surface, with hooks set for trout,—though Walden is deeper than that. How surprised must the fishes be to see this ungainly visitor from another sphere speeding their way amid their schools! Once or twice I saw a ripple where they approached the surface, just put their head out to reconnoitre, and instantly dive again. I found that it was as well for me to rest on my oars and wait their reappearing rather than endeavor to calculate where they would rise; for again and again, when I was straining my eyes over the surface one way, I would suddenly be startled by their unearthly laugh behind me. But why, after displaying so much cunning, did they invariably betray themselves the moment they came up by that loud laugh? Did not their white breast enough betray them? They were indeed a silly loon, I thought. Their usual note was this demoniac laughter, yet somewhat like that of a water-fowl; but occasionally, when they had balked me most successfully and come up a long way off, they uttered a long-drawn unearthly howl, probably more like that of a wolf than any bird; as when a beast puts muzzle to the ground and deliberately howls. This was looning,—perhaps the wildest sound that is ever heard here, making the woods ring far and wide. I concluded that they laughed in derision of my efforts.

It is remarkable how many creatures live wild and free, though secret, in the woods, and still sustain themselves in the neighborhood of towns, suspected by hunters only. How retired the otter manages to live here! He grows to be four feet long, as big as a small child, perhaps without any human being getting a glimpse of him.

I saw a raccoon in the woods behind where my house is built, and heard their whinnering at night. Commonly I rested an hour or two in the shade at noon, after planting, and ate my lunch, and read a little by a spring which was the source of a swamp and of a brook, half a mile from my field. There, in a very secluded and shaded spot, under a spreading white-pine, there was yet a clean, firm sward to sit on. I had dug out the spring and made a well of clear gray water, where I could dip up a pailful without roiling it, and thither I went for this purpose almost every day in midsummer, when the pond was warmest. Thither, too, the wood-cock led her brood, to probe the mud for worms, flying but a foot above them down the bank, while they ran in a troop beneath; but at last, spying me, she would leave her young and circle round and round me, nearer and nearer 'til within four or five feet, pretending broken wings and legs, to attract my attention, and get off her young, who would already have taken up their march, with faint wiry peep, single file through the swamp, as she directed. Or I heard the peep of the young when I could not see the mother bird. There too, the turtle-doves sat over the spring, or fluttered from bough to bough of the soft white-pines over my head; or the red squirrel, coursing down the nearest bough, was particularly familiar and inquisitive. You only need sit still long enough in some attractive spot in the woods that all its inhabitants may exhibit themselves to you by turns.

I was witness to events of a less peaceful character, too. One day when I went out to my wood-pile, or rather my pile of stumps, I observed two large ants, the one red, the other much larger, nearly half an inch long, and black, fiercely contending with one another. Having once got hold they never let go, but struggled and wrestled and rolled on the chips incessantly. Looking farther, I was surprised to find that the chips were covered with such combatants, that it was not a duellum, but a bellum, a war between two races of ants, the red always pitted against the black, and frequently two red ones to one black. The legions of these Myrmidons covered all the hills and vales in my wood-yard, and the ground was already strewn with the dead and dying, both red and black. It was the only battle which I have ever witnessed, the only battle-field I ever trod while the battle was raging; internecine war; the red republicans on the one hand, and the black imperialists on the other. On every side they were engaged in deadly combat, yet without any noise that I could hear,—they fought resolutely. I watched a couple that were fast locked in each other's embraces, in a little sunny valley amid the chips, now at noon-day prepared to fight 'til the sun went down, or life went out. The smaller red champion had fastened herself like a vice to her adversary's front, and through all the tumblings on that field, never for an instant ceased to gnaw at one of her opponent's feelers near the root, having already caused the other to go by the board; while the stronger black one dashed her from side to side, and, as I saw on looking nearer, had already divested her of several of her members. They fought with more pertinacity than bull-dogs. Neither manifested the least disposition to retreat. It was evident that their battle-cry was "Conquer or Die." In the mean while there came along a single red ant on the hill-side of this valley, evidently full of excitement, who either had dispatched her foes, or had not yet taken part in the battle; probably the latter, for she had lost none of hers limbs; whose mother had charged her to return either with her shield, victorious, or dead, upon it. Or perchance she was some Achilles, and had come to avenge or rescue her Patroclus. She saw this unequal combat from afar,—for the blacks were nearly twice the size of the red,—still she drew near with rapid pace 'til she stood on her guard within half an inch of the combatants; then, watching her opportunity, she sprang upon the black warrior, and commenced her operations near the root of their right fore-leg, leaving the foe to select a target from among her own members; and so there were three united for life, as if a new kind of attraction had been invented which put all other locks and cements to shame. I should not have been surprised to find that they had their respective musical bands stationed on some eminent wood chip, playing their national airs the while, to excite the slow, and cheer the dying combatants—or more likely, to cover the screams of the impaled and dismembered. I was myself excited somewhat even as if they had been human. The more you think of it, the less the difference. And certainly there is not the fight recorded in Concord history, at least, if in the history of America, that will bear a moment's comparison with this, whether for the numbers engaged in it, or for the patriotism and heroism displayed. For numbers and for carnage, it was an Austerlitz or Dresden. Concord Fight! Two killed on the patriots' side, and Luther Blanchard wounded! Why here every ant was a Buttrick,—"Fire! for God's sake fire!"—and thousands shared the fate of Davis and Hosmer. There was not one hireling there. I have no doubt that it was a principle they fought for, as much as our ancestors, and not just to avoid a three-penny tax on their tea; and the results of this battle will be as important and memorable to those whom it concerns as those of the battle of Bunker Hill, at least.

I took up the chip on which the three I have particularly described were struggling, carried it into my house, and placed it under a glass tumbler on my window-sill, in order to see the issue. Holding a microscope to the first-mentioned red ant, I saw that, though she was assiduously gnawing at the near fore-leg of her enemy, having severed her remaining feeler, her own breast was all torn away, exposing what vitals she had there to the jaws of the black warrior, whose breastplate was apparently too thick for her to pierce; and the dark carbuncles of the sufferer's eyes shone with ferocity such as war only could excite. They struggled half an hour longer under the tumbler, and when I looked again the black soldier had severed the heads of her foes from their bodies, and the still living heads were hanging on either side of her like ghastly trophies at her saddle-bow, still apparently as firmly fastened as ever, and she was endeavoring with feeble struggles, being without feelers and with only the remnant of a leg, and I know not how many other wounds, to divest herself of them; which at length, after half an hour more, she accomplished. I returned her to the battlefield, and raised the glass; she went off over the dirt in that crippled state. Whether she finally survived that combat, and spent the remainder of her days in some Hotel des Invalides, I do not know; but I thought that her industry would not be worth much thereafter. I never learned which party was victorious, nor the cause of the war; but I felt for the rest of that day as if I had had my feelings excited and harrowed by witnessing the struggle, the ferocity and carnage, of a human battle before my door.

Many a village canine, fit only to track a mud-turtle in a food cellar, sported his heavy quarters in the woods, without the knowledge of their master, and ineffectually smelled at old fox burrows and woodchucks' holes; led perchance by some slight scent which nimbly threaded the wood, and might still inspire a natural terror in its inhabitants;—he is now far behind his guide, barking like a canine bull toward some small squirrel which had treed itself for scrutiny, then, cantering off, bending the bushes with his weight, seeming to think that he is on the track of some missing member of a royal family.

And regarding squirrels, what is the character of our gratitude to these rodents, these planters of forests? We regard them as vermin, and annually shoot and destroy them in great numbers because perhaps they sometimes devour some of our corn, while they plant the acorn in its place. In various parts of the country, an army of grown-up children assemble for a squirrel hunt. Would it not be far more civilized and humane to recognize them once per year by some significant symbolical ceremony, to honor the part which the squirrel plays—the great service it performs—in the economy of the universe? Some may say that the squirrels and jays only produce forests by accident, but who can say for sure that it is not on purpose to serve the greater good?

Once I was surprised to see a cat walking along the stony shore of the pond, for they rarely wander so far from home. The surprise was mutual. Nevertheless the most domestic cat, which has lain on a rug all her days, appears quite at home in the woods, and, by her sly and stealthy behavior, proves herself more native there than the regular inhabitants. Once, when berrying, I met with a cat with young kittens in the woods, quite wild, and they all, like their mother, had their backs up and were fiercely spitting at me. A few years before I lived in the woods, there was what was called a "winged cat" in one of the farm-houses in Lincoln nearest the pond, Mr. Gilian Baker's. When I called to see her in June, 1842, she was gone a-hunting in the woods, but her mistress told me that she came into the neighborhood a little more than a year before, in

April, and was finally taken into their house; that she was of a dark brownish-gray color, with a white spot on her throat, and white feet, and had a large bushy tail like a fox; that in the winter the fur grew thick and flatted out along her sides, forming stripes ten or twelve inches long by two and a half wide, and under her chin like a muff, the upper side loose, the under matted like felt, and in the spring these appendages dropped off. They gave me a pair of her "wings," which I keep still. There is no appearance of a membrane about them. Some thought it was part flying-squirrel or some other wild animal, which is not impossible, for, according to naturalists, prolific hybrids have been produced by the union of the marten and domestic cat. This would have been the right kind of cat for me to keep, if I had kept any; for why should not a poet's cat be winged as well as their horse?

For hours, in fall days, I watched the ducks cunningly tack and veer and hold the middle of the pond, far from the hunters; tricks which they will have less need to practice in untouched Louisiana bayous. When compelled to rise they would sometimes circle round and round and over the pond at a considerable height, from which they could easily see to other ponds and the river, like black motes in the sky; and, when I thought they had gone off thither long since, they would settle down by a slanting flight of a quarter of a mile on to a distant part which was left free; but what beside safety they got by sailing in the middle of Walden I do not know, unless they love its water for the same reason that I do.

HOUSE WARMING

In October I went a-graping to the river meadows, and loaded myself with clusters more precious for their beauty and fragrance than for food. There too I admired, though I did not gather, the cranberries, small waxen gems, pendants of the meadow grass, pearly and red, which the farmer plucks with an ugly rake, leaving the smooth meadow in a snarl, heedlessly measuring them by the bushel and the dollar only, and sells the spoils of the meads to Boston and New York; destined to be jammed, to satisfy the tastes of Nature-yearners there. So just as butchers rake the tongues of bison out of the prairie, such is the torn and drooping plant left behind here.

The barberry's brilliant fruit was likewise food for my eyes. I collected a small store of wild apples for coddling, which the proprietor and travelers had overlooked. When chestnuts were ripe, I laid up half a bushel for winter. It was very exciting at that season to roam the then boundless chestnut woods of Lincoln, —though they now sleep their long sleep under the railroad,—with a bag on my shoulder, and a stick to open burrs with in my hand, for I did not always wait for the frost, amid the rustling of leaves and the loud reproofs of the red-squirrels and the jays, whose half-consumed nuts I sometimes stole, for the burrs which they had selected were sure to contain sound ones. Occasionally I climbed and shook the trees. They grew also behind my house, and one large tree, which almost overshadowed it, was, when in flower, a bouquet which scented the whole neighborhood, but the squirrels and the jays got most of its fruit; the last coming in flocks early in the morning and picking the nuts out of the burrs before they fell. I relinquished these trees to them and visited the more distant woods composed wholly of chestnut. These nuts, as far as they went, were a good substitute for bread. Many other substitutes might, perhaps, be found. Digging one day for fish-worms, I discovered the ground-nut (Apios tuberosa) on its string, the potato of the aborigines, a sort of fabulous fruit, which I had begun to doubt if I had ever dug and eaten in childhood, as I had told, and had not dreamed it. I had often since seen its crimpled red velvety blossom supported by the stems of other plants without knowing it to be the same. Cultivation has well nigh exterminated it. It has a sweetish taste, much like that of a frostbitten potato, and I found it better boiled than roasted. This tuber seemed like a faint promise of Nature to rear her own children and feed them simply here at some future period. In these days of fatted cattle and expansive waving grain-fields, this humble root, which was once the totem of an Indigenous tribe, is quite forgotten, or known only by its flowering vine; but let wild Nature reign here once more, and the tender and luxurious English grains will probably disappear before a myriad of foes, and without the care of humans, the crow may carry back even the last seed of corn to the great cornfield of the Natives' God in the south-west, whence she is said to have first brought it; but the now almost exterminated ground-nut will perhaps revive and flourish in spite of frosts and wildness, prove itself indigenous, and resume its ancient importance and dignity as the diet of the hunter tribe. Some Native Ceres or Minerva must have been the inventor and bestower of it; and when the reign of poetry commences here, its leaves and string of nuts may be represented on our works of art.

Already, by the first of September, I had seen two or three small maples turned scarlet across the pond, next the water. Ah, many a tale their color told! And gradually from week to week the character of each tree came out, and it admired itself reflected in the smooth mirror of the lake. Each morning the manager of this gallery substituted some new picture, distinguished by more brilliant or harmonious coloring, for the old upon the walls.

The wasps came by thousands to my lodge in October, as to winter quarters, and settled on my windows within and on the walls over-head, sometimes deterring visitors from entering. Each morning, when they were numbed with cold, I swept some of them out, but I did not trouble myself much to get rid of them; I even felt complimented by their regarding my house as a desirable shelter. They never molested me seriously, though they bedded with me; and they gradually disappeared, into what crevices I do not know, avoiding winter and unspeakable cold.

Like the wasps, before I finally went into winter quarters in November, I used to resort to the north-east side of Walden, which the sun, reflected from the pitch-pine woods and the stony shore, made the fire-side of the pond; it is so much pleasanter and wholesomer to be warmed by the sun while you can be, than by an artificial fire. I thus warmed myself by the still glowing embers which the summer, like a departed hunter, had left.

When I came to build my chimney, I studied masonry. My bricks being second-hand ones required to be cleaned with a trowel, so that I learned more than usual of the qualities of bricks and trowels. The mortar on them was fifty years old, and was said to be still growing harder; but this is one of those sayings which people love to repeat whether they are true or not. Such sayings themselves grow harder and adhere more firmly with age, and it would take many blows with a trowel to clean an old wiseacre of them. Many of the villages of Mesopotamia are built of second-hand bricks of a very good quality, obtained from the ruins of Babylon, and the cement on them is older and probably harder still. However that may be, I was struck by the peculiar toughness of the steel which bore so many violent blows without being worn out. As my bricks had been in a chimney before, though I did not read the name of Nebuchadnezzar on them, I picked out as many fireplace bricks as I could find, to save work and waste, and I filled the spaces between the bricks about the fire-place with stones from the pond shore, and also made my mortar with the white sand from the same place. I lingered most about the fireplace, as the most vital part of the house. Indeed, I worked so deliberately, that though I commenced at the ground in the morning, a course of bricks raised a few inches above the floor served for my pillow at night; yet I did not get a stiff neck for it that I remember; my stiff neck is of older date. I took a poet to board for a fortnight about those times, which caused me to be put to it for room. He brought his own knife, though I had two, and we used to scour them by thrusting them into the earth. He shared with me the labors of cooking. I was pleased to see my work rising so square and solid by degrees, and reflected, that, if it proceeded slowly, it was calculated to endure a long time. The chimney is to some extent an independent structure, standing on the ground and rising through the house to the heavens; even after the house is burned it still stands sometimes, and its importance and independence are apparent. This was toward the end of summer. It was now November.

The north wind had already begun to cool the pond, though it took many weeks of steady blowing to accomplish it, it is so deep. When I began to have a fire at evening, before I plastered my house, the chimney carried smoke particularly well, because of the numerous chinks between the boards. Yet I passed some cheerful evenings in that cool and airy apartment, surrounded by the rough brown boards full of knots, and rafters with the bark on high overhead. My house never pleased my eye much after it was plastered, though I was obliged to confess that it was more comfortable. Should not every apartment in which one dwells be lofty enough to create some obscurity over-head, where flickering shadows may play at evening about the rafters? These forms are more agreeable to the fancy and imagination than fresco paintings or other the most expensive furniture. I now first began to inhabit my house, I may say, when I began to use it for warmth as well as shelter. I had got a couple of old fire-dogs to keep the wood from the hearth, and it did me good to see the soot form on the back of the chimney which I had built, and I poked the fire with more right and more satisfaction than usual. My dwelling was small, and I could hardly entertain an echo in it; but it seemed larger for being a single apartment and remote from neighbors. All the attractions of a house were concentrated in one room; it was kitchen, chamber, parlor, and keeping-room; and whatever satisfaction parent or child, master or servant, derive from living in a house, I enjoyed it all. Cato says, the family must have in their rustic villa "cellam oleariam, vinariam, dolia multa, uti lubeat caritatem expectare, et rei, et virtuti, et gloriæ erit," that is, "an oil and wine cellar, many casks, so that it may be pleasant to expect hard times; it will be for their advantage, and virtue, and glory." I had in my cellar a firkin of potatoes, about two quarts of peas with the weevil in them, and on my shelf a little rice, a jug of molasses, and of rye and corn meal—a peck each.

I sometimes dream of a larger and more populous house, standing in a golden age, of enduring materials, and without ginger-bread work, which shall still consist of only one room, a vast, rude, substantial, primitive hall, without ceiling or plastering, with bare rafters and purlins supporting a sort of lower heaven over one's head,—useful to keep off rain and snow; a cavernous house, wherein you must reach up a torch upon a pole to see the roof; where some may live in the fire-place, some in the recess of a window, and some at one end of the hall, some at another, and some aloft on rafters with the spiders, if they choose; a house where the weary traveler may wash, and eat, and converse, and sleep, without further journey; such a shelter as you would be glad to reach in a tempestuous night, containing all the essentials of a house, and nothing for house-keeping; where you can see all the treasures of the house at one view, and every thing hangs upon its peg, that a person should use; at once kitchen, pantry, parlor, chamber, store-house, and garret; where you can see so necessary a thing as a barrel or a ladder, so convenient a thing as a cupboard, and hear the pot boil, and pay your respects to the fire that cooks your dinner and the oven that bakes your bread, and the necessary furniture and utensils are the chief ornaments; where the washing is not outsourced, nor the fire, and perhaps you are sometimes requested to move from off the trap-door, when the cook would descend into the cellar, and so learn whether the ground is solid or hollow beneath you without stamping. A house whose inside is as open and manifest as a bird's nest, and you cannot go in at the front door and out at the back without seeing some of its inhabitants; where to be a guest is to be presented with the freedom of the house, and not to be carefully excluded from seven eighths of it, shut up in a particular cell, and told to make yourself at home there,—in the non-home portion of the structure. Nowadays the host does not admit you to their hearth, but has got the mason to build one for keeping you somewhere in their alley, and hospitality is the art of keeping you at the greatest distance. There is as much secrecy about the cooking as if they had a design to poison you. I am aware that I have been on many a person's premises, and might have been legally ordered off, but I am not aware that I have been in many people's houses. I might visit in my old clothes a queen and king who lived simply in such a house as I have described, if I were going their way; but backing out of a modern palace will be all that I shall desire to learn, if ever I am caught in one.

It would seem as if the very language of our dining rooms would lose all its nerve and degenerate wholly, if it were not for the dumbwaiters carryover—honest babble wafting in from the kitchen. The dinner even, is only the parable of a dinner, commonly.

Only one or two of my guests were ever bold enough to stay and eat a hasty-pudding made of cornmeal and rye with me. When most saw that crisis approaching, they beat a hasty retreat rather, as if it would shake the house to its foundations. Nevertheless, it stood through a great many hasty-puddings.

I did not plaster 'til it was freezing weather. I brought over some whiter and cleaner sand for this purpose from the opposite shore of the pond in a boat, a sort of conveyance which would have tempted me to go much farther if necessary. My house had in the meanwhile been shingled down to the ground on every side. In lathing I was pleased to be able to send home each nail with a single blow of the hammer, and it was my ambition to transfer the plaster from the board to the wall neatly and rapidly. I remembered the story of a conceited fellow, who, in fine clothes, was wont to lounge about the village once, giving advice to workers. Venturing one day to substitute deeds for words, he turned up his cuffs, seized a plasterer's board, and having loaded his trowel without mishap, with a complacent look toward the lathing overhead, made a bold gesture thitherward; and straightway, to his complete discomfiture, received the whole contents in his ruffled bosom. I admired anew the economy and convenience of plastering, which so effectually shuts out the cold and takes a handsome finish, and I learned the various casualties to which the plasterer is liable. I was surprised to see how thirsty the bricks were which drank up all the moisture in my plaster before I had smoothed it, and how many pailfuls of water it takes to christen a new hearth. I had the previous winter made a small quantity of lime by burning the shells of the Unio fluviatilis, mollusks which our river affords, for the sake of the experiment; so that I knew where my materials came from. I might have got good limestone within a mile or two, if I had cared to do so.

The pond had in the mean while skimmed over in the shadiest and shallowest coves, some days or even weeks before the general freezing. The first ice is especially interesting and perfect, being hard, dark, and transparent, and affords the best opportunity that ever offers for examining the bottom where it is shallow; for you can lie at your length on ice only an inch thick, like a skater insect on the surface of the water, and study the bottom at your leisure, only two or three inches distant, like a picture behind a glass, and the water is necessarily always smooth then. There are many furrows in the sand where some creature has travelled about and doubled on its tracks; and, for wrecks, it is strewn with the cases of cadis worms made of tiny grains of white quartz.

But the ice itself is the object of most interest, though you must seize the earliest opportunity to study it. If you examine it closely the morning after it freezes, you find that the greater part of the bubbles, which at first appeared to be within it, are now against its under surface, and that more are continually rising from the bottom. These bubbles are from an eighteenth to an eighth of an inch in diameter, very clear and beautiful, and you see your face reflected in them through the ice. There may be thirty or forty of them to a square inch. There are also already within the ice narrow oblong perpendicular bubbles about half an inch long, sharp cones with the apex upward;

or oftener, if the ice is quite fresh, minute spherical bubbles one directly above another, like a string of beads. But these within the ice are not so numerous nor obvious as those beneath. I sometimes used to cast on stones to try the strength of the ice, and those which broke through carried in air with them, which formed very large and conspicuous white bubbles beneath the ice, around the hole. When I came to the same place forty-eight hours afterward, I found that those large bubbles were still perfect, though an inch more of ice had formed over them. But as the last two days had been warmer than usual, the ice was no longer transparent, but it was now showing the dark green color of the water. And though the ice was twice as thick as before, it was hardly stronger than before, for the air bubbles had greatly expanded under this heat and run together, and lost their regularity; they were no longer one directly over another, but often like silvery coins poured from a bag, one overlapping another, in thin flakes. The beauty of the ice was gone, and it was too late to study the bottom.

Being curious to know what position my great bubbles now occupied with regard to the new ice, I broke out a cake containing a middling sized one, and turned it bottom upward. The new ice had formed around and under the bubble, so that it was included between the two ices. It was wholly in the lower ice, but close against the upper, and was flattish, or perhaps slightly lenticular, with a rounded edge, a quarter of an inch deep by four inches in diameter; and I was surprised to find that directly under the bubble the ice was melted with great regularity in the form of a saucer reversed, to the height of five eighths of an inch in the middle, leaving a thin partition there between the water and the bubble, hardly an eighth of an inch thick; and in many places the small bubbles in this partition had burst out downward, and probably there was no ice at all under the largest bubbles, which were a foot in diameter. I inferred that the infinite number of minute bubbles which I had first seen against the under surface of the ice were now frozen in likewise, and that each, in its degree, had operated like a burning glass on the ice beneath to melt and rot it. These are the little air-guns which contribute to make the ice crack and whoop.

At length, the winter arrived in good earnest, just as I had finished plastering, and the wind began to howl around the house as if it had not had permission to do so 'til then. Night after night the geese came lumbering in in the dark with a clangor and a whistling of wings, even after the ground was covered with snow, some to alight in Walden, and some flying low over the woods toward Fair Haven, assumed to be bound for Mexico. Several times, when returning from the village at ten or eleven o'clock at night, I heard the tread of a flock of geese, or else ducks, on the dry leaves in the woods by a pond-hole behind my dwelling, where they had come up to feed, and the faint honk or quack of their leader as they hurried off.

In 1845, Walden froze entirely over for the first time on the night of the 22nd of December,—Flint's and other shallower ponds and the river having already been frozen ten days or more. The snow had covered the ground since the 25th of November, and surrounded me suddenly with the scenery of winter. I withdrew yet farther into my shell, and endeavored to keep a bright fire both within my house and within my breast. My employment out of doors now was to collect the dead wood in the forest, bringing it in my hands or on my shoulders, or sometimes trailing a dead pine tree under each arm to my shed. An old forest fence which had seen its best days was a great haul for me. I sacrificed it to Vulcan in a fiery ritual, for it was long past serving the god Terminus. How much more interesting is a supper who's preparer has just been in the snow to hunt, nay, you might say, steal, the fuel to cook it with! That bread and those greens are sweet. There was also the drift-wood of the pond. In the course of the summer I had discovered a raft of pitch-pine logs with the bark on, pinned together by the Irish when the railroad was built. This I hauled up partly on the shore. After soaking two years and then lying high six months it was perfectly sound, though waterlogged past drying. I amused myself one winter day with sliding this piecemeal across the pond, nearly half a mile, skating behind with one end of a log fifteen feet long on my shoulder, and the other on the ice behind the raft. Though completely waterlogged and almost as heavy as lead, they not only burned long, but made a very hot fire; nay, I thought that they burned better for the soaking, as if the pitch, being protected by the water, burned longer, as in a lamp.

I was interested in the preservation of the deer and the trees more than the hunters or woodchoppers, and as much as though I had been the Lord Warden themself; and if any part was burned, though I once burned it myself by accident, I grieved with a grief that lasted longer and was more inconsolable than that of the proprietors; nay, I even grieved when it was cut down by the proprietors themselves. I hoped that our farmers when they cut down a forest felt some of that awe which the old Romans did when they came to thin, or let in the light to, a consecrated grove (lucum conlucare), that is, would believe that it is sacred to some god. The Roman made an expiatory offering, and prayed, Whatever god or goddess thou art to whom this grove is sacred, be propitious to me, my family, and children, and loved ones.

It is remarkable what a value is still put upon wood even in this age and in this new country, a value more permanent and universal than that of gold. After all our discoveries and inventions no person will go by a pile of wood. It is as precious to us as it was to our Saxon and Norman ancestors. If they made their bows of it, we make our gun-stocks of it. Michaux, more than thirty years ago, says that the price of wood for fuel in New York and Philadelphia "nearly equals, and sometimes exceeds, that of the best wood in Paris, though this immense capital annually requires more than three hundred thousand cords, and is surrounded to the distance of three hundred miles by cultivated plains." In this town the price of wood rises almost steadily, and the only question is, how much higher it is to be this year than it was the last. Mechanics and tradespeople who come in person to the forest on no other errand, are sure to attend the wood auction, and even pay a high price for the privilege of gleaning after the woodchopper. It is now many years that we have resorted to the forest for fuel and the materials of the arts; the New Englander and the New Hollander, the Parisian and the Celt, the farmer and Robinhood, Goody Blake and Harry Gill, in most parts of the world the prince and the peasant, the scholar and the brute, equally require still a few sticks from the forest to warm them and cook their food. Neither could I do without them.

Every one looks at their wood-pile with a kind of affection. I love to have mine before my window, and the more chips the better to remind me of my pleasing work. I had an old axe which nobody claimed, with which I played about the stumps which I had got out of my bean-field, and piled on the sunny side of the house on winter days. As my driver prophesied when I was ploughing, they warmed me twice, once while I was splitting them, and again when they were on the fire, so that no fuel could give out more heat. As for the axe, I was advised to get the village black-smith to "jump" it; but I jumped them, and, putting a hickory helve from the woods into it, made it do. If it was dull, it was at least hung true. A few pieces of fat pine were a great treasure. It is interesting to remem-ber how much of this food for fire is still concealed in the bowels of the earth. In previous years I had often gone "prospecting" over some bare hill-side, where a pitch-pine wood had formerly stood, and got out the fat pine roots. They are almost indestructible. Stumps thirty or forty years old, at least, will still be sound at the core, though the sapwood has all become vegeta-ble mould, as appears by the scales of the thick bark forming a ring level with the earth four or five inches distant from the heart. With axe and shovel you ex-plore this mine, as if you had struck on a vein of gold, deep into the earth. But commonly I kindled my fire with the dry leaves of the forest, which I had stored up in my shed before the snow came. Green hick-ory finely split makes the woodchopper's kindlings, when they have a camp in the woods. Once in a while I got a little of this. When the villagers were lighting their fires beyond the horizon, I too gave notice to the various wild inhabitants of Walden vale, by a smoky streamer from my chimney, that I was awake.—

Light-winged Smoke, Icarian bird, Melting
thy pinions in thy upward flight, Lark without
song, and messenger of dawn, Circling above

the hamlets as thy nest;
Or else, departing dream, and shadowy form
Of midnight vision, gathering up thy skirts;
By night star-veiling, and by day
Darkening the light and blotting out the sun;
Go thou my incense upward from this hearth,
And ask the gods to pardon this clear flame.

Hard green wood just cut, though I used but little of that, answered my purpose better than any other. I sometimes left a good fire when I went to take a walk in a winter afternoon; and when I returned, three or four hours afterward, it would be still alive and glowing. My house was not empty though I was gone. It was as if I had left a cheerful housekeeper behind. It was I and Fire that lived there; and commonly my housekeeper proved trustworthy. One day, however, as I was splitting wood, I thought that I would just look in at the window and see if the house was not on fire; it was the only time I remember to have been particularly anxious on this score; so I looked and saw that a spark had caught my bed, and I went in and extinguished it when it had burned a place as big as my hand.

The moles nested in my cellar, nibbling every third potato, and making a snug bed even there of some hair left after plastering and of brown paper; for even the wildest animals love comfort and warmth as well as humans, and they survive the winter only because they are so careful to secure these roosts and resources. Some of my friends spoke as if I was coming to the woods on purpose to freeze myself. The animal merely makes a bed, which they warm with their body, in a sheltered place; but we humans, having discovered fire, box up some air in a spacious apartment and warm that, making it our bed, in which we can move about divested of more cumbrous clothing, and maintain a kind of summer in the midst of winter, and by means of windows, even admit the light, and with a lamp, lengthen out the day. Thus we go a step or two beyond instinct, and save a little time for the fine arts. Though, when I had been exposed to the rudest blasts for a while, my whole body began to grow torpid, when I reached the genial atmosphere of my house I soon recovered my faculties and prolonged my life. We need not trouble ourselves to speculate how the human race may be at last destroyed. It would be easy to cut their threads any time with a little sharper blast from the north. We go on dating from Cold Fridays and Great Snows; but a little colder Friday, or greater snow, would put a period at the end of our existence on the globe.

The next winter I used a small cooking-stove for economy, but it did not keep fire so well as the open fire-place. Cooking was then, for the most part, no longer a poetic, but merely a chemic process. It will soon be forgotten, in these days of stoves, that we used to roast potatoes in the ashes, after the Indigenous Fashion. The stove in my now village-esque home not only took up room and scented the house, but it concealed the fire, and I felt as if I had lost a companion. You can always see a face in the fire. The laborer, looking into it at evening, purifies their thoughts of the dross and earthiness which they have accumulated during the day. Although there is much efficiency gained with a stove, I found that I could no longer sit and look into the fire, and the pertinent words of a poet recurred to me with new force.—

"Never bright flame, may be denied to me
Thy dear, life imaging, close sympathy.

What but my hopes shot upward e'er so
bright?
What but my fortunes sunk so low in night?

Why art thou banished from our hearth and
hall,
Thou who art welcomed and beloved by all?
Was thy existence then too fanciful
For our life's common light, who are so dull?
Did thy bright gleam mysterious converse
hold
With our congenial souls? secrets too bold?
Well, we are safe and strong, for now we sit
Beside a hearth where no dim shadows flit,
Where nothing cheers nor saddens, but a fire
Warms feet and hands—nor does to more
aspire;
By whose compact utilitarian heap
The present may sit down and go to sleep,
Nor fear the ghosts who from the dim past
walked,
And with us by the unequal light of the old
wood fire talked."

—Ellen Sturgis Hooper

FORMER INHABITANTS

I weathered some merry snow storms, and spent some cheerful winter evenings by my fire-side, while the snow whirled wildly without, and even the hooting of the owl was hushed. For many weeks I met no one in my walks but those who came occasionally to cut wood and sled it to the village. The elements, however, abetted me in making a path through the deepest snow in the woods, for where I had once gone through, the wind blew the oak leaves into my tracks, where they lodged, and by absorbing the rays of the sun melted the snow, and so not only made a dry bed for my feet, but in the night their dark line was my guide. For human company, I was obliged to conjure up the former occupants of these woods.

Though mainly but a humble route to neighboring villages, or for the logger's team, these woods once amused travelers by their variety, and lingered longer in their memories. Where now firm open fields stretch from the village to the woods, it then ran through a maple swamp on a foundation of logs, the remnants of which, doubtless, still under-lie the present dusty highway. Now along that path, the pines scrape both sides of a carriage at once, and those who are compelled to go this way to Lincoln alone and on foot do it with fear, and often run a good part of the distance.

East of my bean-field, across the road, once lived Cato Ingraham, an enslaved man "owned" by Duncan Ingraham of Concord village, who built his enslaved worker a house, and gave him permission to live in Walden Woods. There are a few who remember his little patch among the walnuts, which Cato let grow up 'til he should be old and need them; but a younger and richer speculator got them at last. They too, however, occupy an equally narrow wooden house at present. Cato's half-obliterated cellar hole still re-mains, though known to few, being concealed from the traveler by a fringe of pines. It is now filled with the smooth sumac (Rhus glabra,) and one of the ear-liest species of golden- rod (Solidago stricta) grows there luxuriantly.

Here, by the very corner of my field, still nearer to town, Zilpha had her little house, where she spun linen for the townsfolk, making the Walden Woods ring with her singing, for she had a loud and notable voice. In the war of 1812, her dwelling was set on fire by English soldiers, prisoners on parole, when she was away, and her cat and dog and hens were all burned up together. She led a hard life, and even inhumane; as was common for a Black woman in those days, and woefully, still often today. One old frequenter of these woods remembers, that as he passed her house one noon he heard her muttering to herself over her gurgling pot,—"Ye are all bones, bones!" I have seen bricks amid the oak thicket there.

Down the road, on the right hand, on Brister's Hill, lived Brister Freeman, "a handy man," once enslaved. There grow still the apple-trees which Brister planted and tended; large old trees now, but their fruit still wild and ciderish to my taste. Not long since, I read his epitaph in the old Lincoln burying- ground, a little on one side, near the unmarked graves of some British grenadiers who fell in the retreat from Concord,—where he is styled "Sippio Brister, a man of color," as if he were discolored. With him dwelt Fenda, his hospitable wife, who pleasantly told fortunes,— she was large, round, and royally dark-skinned, such as Concord had never seen before or since.

Farther down the hill, on the left, on the old road in the woods, are marks of some homestead of the Stratton family; whose orchard once covered all the slope of Brister's Hill, but was long since killed out by pitch pines, excepting a few stumps, whose old roots furnish still the wild stocks of many a thrifty village tree.

Nearer yet to town, you come to Breed's place, just on the edge of the wood; a ground famous for the pranks of a demon not distinctly named in old mythology, who has acted a prominent and astounding part in our New England life, and deserves, as much as any mythological character, to have his biography written one day; who first comes in the guise of a friend or hired man, and then robs and murders the whole family,—he is called "New-England Rum." But history must not yet tell the tragedies enacted here; let time intervene in some measure to assuage and lend an azure tint to them, for there must be a better way to note that an alcoholic was found here, dead in the road. Here, the most indistinct and dubious tale says that once a tavern stood, which tempered the traveler's beverage and refreshed their steed. Here then travelers saluted one another, and heard and told the news, and went their ways again.

Breed's hut was standing only a dozen years ago, though it had long been unoccupied. It was about the size of mine. It was set on fire by mischievous boys, one Election night, if I do not mistake. I lived on the edge of the village then, and as I lay in bed reading Gondibert, the bells rung fire, and in hot haste the engines rolled that way, led by a straggling troop, and I among the foremost, for I had leaped the brook. We thought it was far south over the woods,—we who had run to fires before,—barn, shop, or dwelling-house, or all together. "It's Baker's barn," cried one. "It is the Codman place," affirmed another. And then fresh sparks went up above the wood, as if the roof fell in, and we all shouted "Concord to the rescue!" Wagons shot past with furious speed and crushing loads, bearing, perchance, among the rest, the agent of the Insurance Company, who was bound to go however far; and ever and anon the engine bell tinkled behind, more slow and sure; and rearmost of all, as it was afterward whispered, came they who set the fire and gave the alarm. Thus we kept on like true idealists, rejecting the evidence of our senses, until at a turn in the road we heard the crackling and actually felt the heat of the fire from over the wall, and realized, alas! that we were there. The very nearness of the fire but cooled our ardor. At first we thought to throw a frog-pond on to it; but concluded to let it burn, it was so far gone and so worthless. So we stood round our engine, jostled one another, and expressed our sentiments. We finally retreated without doing any mischief, and I returned to Gondibert.

It chanced that I walked that way across the fields the following night, about the same hour, and hearing a low moaning at this spot, I drew near in the dark, and discovered the only survivor of the family that I know, the heir of both its virtues and its vices, who alone was interested in this burning, lying on his stomach and looking over the cellar wall at the still smouldering cinders beneath, muttering to himself. He had been working far off in the river meadows all day, and had come the first chance he could to visit the home of his parents and his youth. He gazed into the cellar from all sides and points of view by turns, always lying down to it, as if there was some treasure, which he remembered, concealed between the stones, where there was absolutely nothing but a heap of bricks and ashes. The house being gone, he looked at what there was left. He was soothed by the sympathy which my mere presence implied, and showed me, as well as the darkness permitted, where the well was covered up; which, thank Heaven, could never be burned; and he groped long about the wall to find the well-sweep which his father had cut and mounted, feeling for the iron hook or staple by which a burden had been fastened to the heavy end,—all that he could now cling to,—to convince me that it was no common "rider." I felt it, and still remark it almost daily in my walks, for by it hangs the history of a family.

Farther in the woods than any of these, where the road approaches nearest to the pond, Wyman the potter once squatted, and furnished his townspeople with earthen ware, and left descendants to succeed him. Neither were they rich in worldly goods, holding the land by sufferance while they lived; and there often the sheriff came in vain to collect the taxes, but there was nothing to lay their hands on. One day in midsummer, when I was hoeing, a man who was carrying a load of pottery to market stopped his horse against my field and inquired concerning Wyman. He had long ago bought a potter's wheel of him, and wished to know what had become of him. I had read of the potter's clay and wheel in Scripture, but it had never occurred to me that our pots were not passed down unbroken from those days, or grown on trees like gourds somewhere, and I was pleased to hear that so fictile an art was ever practiced in my neighborhood.

The last inhabitant of these woods before me was an Irishman, Hugh Quoil. Rumor said that he had been a soldier at Waterloo., and his trade here was that of a ditcher. All I know of him is tragic. He was a man of manners, like one who had seen the world, and was capable of more civil speech than you could well attend to. He wore a great coat in mid-summer, being affected with the trembling delirium, and his face was the color of carmine. He died in the road at the foot of Brister's Hill shortly after I came to the woods, so that I have not remembered him as a neighbor. Before his house was pulled down, when his comrades avoided it as "an unlucky castle," I visited it. There lay his old clothes curled up by use, as if they were himself, upon his raised plank bed. His pipe lay broken on the hearth, and soiled cards, kings of diamonds spades and hearts, were scattered over the floor. One black chicken which the administrator could not catch, black as night and as silent, not even croaking, awaiting the fox, still roosted in the next apartment. In the rear there was the dim outline of a garden, which had been planted but had never received its first hoeing, owing to those terrible shaking fits, though it was now harvest time. It was over-run with Roman wormwood and beggar-ticks, which last stuck to my clothes for all fruit. The skin of a wood-chuck was freshly stretched upon the back of the house, a trophy of his last Waterloo; but no warm cap or mittens would he want more.

Now only a dent in the earth marks the site of these dwellings, with buried cellar stones, and straw-berries, raspberries, thimble-berries, hazel-bushes, and sumacs growing in the sunny sward there; some pitch-pine or gnarled oak occupies what was the chimney nook, and a sweet-scented black-birch, per-haps, waves where the door-stone was. Sometimes the well dent is visible, where once a spring oozed; now dry and tearless grass; or it was covered deep,—not to be discovered 'til some late day,—with a flat stone under the sod, when the last of the race de-parted. What a sorrowful act must that be,—the cov-ering up of wells! coincident with the opening of wells of tears. These cellar dents, like deserted fox burrows, old holes, are all that is left where once was the stir and bustle of human life.

Still grows the vivacious lilac a generation after the door and lintel and the sill are gone, unfolding its sweet-scented flowers each spring, to be plucked by the musing traveler; planted and tended once by children's hands, in front-yard plots,—now standing by wall-sides in retired pastures, and giving place to new-rising forests;—the last of that stirp, sole survi-vor of that family. Little did the dusky children think that the puny slip with its two eyes only, which they stuck in the ground in the shadow of the house and daily watered, would root itself so and outlive them and even the house itself, and that the grown garden and orchard would live on to tell their story faintly to the lone wanderer a half century after they had grown up and died,—blossoming as fair, and smelling as sweet, as in that first spring. I mark its still tender, civil, cheerful, lilac colors.

But this small village, germ of something more, why did it fail while Concord kept its ground? Were there no natural advantages,—no water privileges, forsooth? Ay, the deep Walden Pond and cool Brister's Spring,—privileges to drink from. They were universally a thirsty race. Might not the businesses of making baskets, pottery, linens, cornmeal, and stable-brooms have thrived here, making the wilderness to blossom like the rose, and a numerous posterity have inherited the land of their parents? Alas! how little does the memory of these human inhabitants enhance the beauty of the landscape! Again, perhaps, Nature will try, with me for a first settler, and my house raised last spring to be the oldest in the hamlet.

I am not aware that any human has ever built on the spot which I occupy. Deliver me from a city built on the site of a more ancient human city, whose materials are ruins, whose gardens cemeteries. The soil is blanched and accursed there. With such reminiscences I repeopled the woods and lulled myself asleep.

WINTER VISITORS

At this season I seldom had a visitor. When the snow lay deepest, no wanderer ventured near my house for a week or fortnight at a time, but there I lived as snug as a meadow mouse, or as cattle and poultry which are said to have survived for a long time buried in drifts, even without food; or like that early settler's family in the town of Sutton, in this state, whose cottage was completely covered by the great snow of 1717, and an Indigenous passerby found it only by the hole which the chimney's breath made in the drift, and so relieved the family. But no friendly passerby concerned themselves about me; nor needed they. The Great Snow! How cheerful it is to hear of! When the farmers could not get to the woods and swamps with their teams, and were obliged to cut down the summer shade trees before their houses for firewood, and when the icy crust was harder, cut off the trees in the swamps, ten feet from the ground, as it appeared the next spring.

In the deepest snows, the path which I used from the highway to my house, about half a mile long, might have been represented by a meandering dot-ted line, with wide intervals between the dots. For a week of even weather I took exactly the same number of steps, and of the same length, coming and going, stepping deliberately and with the precision of a pair of dividers in my own deep tracks,—to such routine the winter reduces us,—yet often they were filled with heaven's own blue. But no weather interfered fa-tally with my walks, or rather my going abroad, for I frequently tramped eight or ten miles through the deepest snow to keep an appointment with a beech-tree, or a yellow- birch, or an old acquaintance among the pines; when the ice and snow causing their limbs to droop, and so sharpening their tops, had changed the pines into fir-trees; wading to the tops of the highest hills when the snow was nearly two feet deep, and shaking down another snow-storm on my head at every step; or sometimes creeping and floundering thither on my hands and knees, when the hunters had gone into winter quarters.

One afternoon I amused myself by watching a barred owl (Strix nebulosa) sitting on one of the lower dead limbs of a white-pine, close to the trunk, in broad daylight, I stood within a rod of her. She could hear me when I moved and crunched the snow with my feet, but could not plainly see me. When I made most noise, she would stretch out her neck, and erect her neck feathers, and open her eyes wide; but her lids soon fell again, and she began to nod. I too felt a slumberous influence after watching her half an hour, as she sat thus with her eyes half open, like a cat, winged sister of the feline. There was only a narrow slit left between her lids, by which she pre-served a peninsular relation to me; thus, with half-shut eyes, looking out from the land of dreams, and endeavoring to realize me, vague object or mote that interrupted her visions. At length, on some louder noise or my nearer approach, she would grow uneasy and sluggishly turn about on her perch, as if impatient at having her dreams disturbed; and when she launched herself off and flapped through the pines, spreading her wings to unexpected breadth, I could not hear the slightest sound from them. Thus, guided amid the pine bough,—rather by a delicate sense of their neighborhood than by sight—feeling her twilight way as it were with her sensitive pinions, she found a new perch, where she might in peace await the dawning of her day.

As I walked through the meadows, over the long causeway made for the railroad, I encountered many a blustering and nipping wind, for nowhere has it freer play; and when the frost had smitten me on one cheek, heathen as I was, I turned to it the other also. Nor was it much better by the carriage road from Brister's Hill. For I came to town still, like a friendly neighbor, when the snowy contents of the broad open fields were all piled up between the walls of the Walden road, and half an hour sufficed to obliterate the tracks of the last traveler. And when I returned, new drifts would have formed, through which I floundered, where the busy north-west wind had been depositing the powdery snow round a sharp angle in the road, and not a rabbit or meadow mouse's tracks were to be seen. Yet I rarely failed to find, even in mid- winter, some warm and springly swamp where the grass and the skunk-cabbage still put forth with perennial verdure, and some hardier bird occasionally awaited the return of spring.

Sometimes, notwithstanding the snow, when I returned from my walk at evening, I crossed the deep tracks of a woodchopper leading from my door, and found their pile of whittlings on the hearth, and my house filled with the odor of their pipe. Or on a Sunday afternoon, if I chanced to be at home, I heard the crunching of the snow made by the step of a wise farmer, who from far through the woods sought my house, to have a social "crack;" one of the few of his vocation who donned a frock instead of a professor's gown, and is just as ready to extract the moral out of church or state as to haul a load of manure from his barn- yard. We talked of rude and simple times, when people sat about large fires in cold bracing weather, with clear heads; and when other desserts failed, we tried our teeth on many a nut which wise squirrels have long since abandoned, for those which have the thickest shells are commonly empty.

The one who came from farthest to my lodge, through deepest snows and most dismal tempests, was a poet. A farmer, a hunter, a soldier, a reporter, even a philosopher, may be daunted; but nothing can deter a poet, for they are actuated by pure love. Who can predict their comings and goings? Their business calls them out at all hours, even when doctors sleep. We made that small house ring with boisterous mirth and resound with the murmur of much sober talk, making amends then to Walden vale for the long silences. Broadway street was still and deserted in comparison. At suitable intervals there were regular salutes of laughter, which might have been referred indifferently to the last uttered or the forth-coming jest. We made many a "bran new" theory of life over a thin dish of gruel, which combined the advantages of conviviality with the clear-headedness which philosophy requires.

I should not forget that during my last winter at the pond there was another welcome visitor, who at one time came through the village, through snow and rain and darkness, 'til he saw my lamp through the trees, and shared with me some long winter evenings. One of the last of the philosophers,—Connecticut gave him to the world,—he peddled first her wares, and afterwards, as he declares, his brains. These he peddles still, prompting God and disgracing humans, bearing for fruit his brain only. I think that he must be the man of the most faith of any alive. His words and attitude always suppose a better state of things than others are acquainted with, and he will be the last person to be disappointed as the ages revolve. He has no venture in the present. But though comparatively disregarded now, when his day comes, laws unsuspected by most will take effect, and masters of families and rulers will come to him for advice.—

"How blind that cannot see serenity!"

A true friend; almost the only friend of human progress. An Old Mortality, say rather an Immortality, with unwearied patience and faith, finding God plainly in the image engraved in human's bodies; even though we are but defaced and leaning monuments of God. With his hospitable intellect he embraces children, beggars, insane, and scholars, and entertains the thought of all, adding to it commonly some breadth and elegance. I think that he should keep a caravansary on the world's highway, where philosophers of all nations might put up, and on his sign should be printed, "Entertainment for humans, but not for their beasts. Enter ye that have leisure and a quiet mind, who earnestly seek the lighter road." He is perhaps the sanest man and has the fewest crotchets of any I chance to know; the same yesterday and tomorrow. Of yore we had sauntered and talked, and effectually put the world behind us; for he was pledged to no institution in it, freeborn, ingenuus. Whichever way we turned, it seemed that the heavens and the earth had met together, since he enhanced the beauty of the landscape. A blue-robed man, whose fittest roof is the overarching sky which reflects his serenity. I do not see how he can ever die; Nature cannot spare him.

Having each some shingles of thought well dried, we sat and whittled them, trying our knives, and admiring the clear yellowish grain of the pumpkin pine. We waded so gently and reverently, or we pulled together so smoothly, that the fishes of thought were not scared from the stream, nor feared any angler on the bank, but came and went grandly, like the clouds which float through the western sky, and the mother-o'-pearl flocks which sometimes form and dissolve there. There we worked, revising mythology, rounding a fable here and there, and building castles in the air for which earth offered no worthy foundation. Great Looker! Great Expecter! to converse with whom was a New England Night's Entertainment. Ah! such discourse we had, hermit and philosopher, and the old settler I have spoken of,—we three,—it expanded and racked my little house; I should not dare to say how many pounds' weight there was above the atmospheric pressure on every circular inch; it opened its seams so that they had to be calked with much dullness thereafter to stop the consequent leak;—but I had enough of that kind of oakum already picked.

There was one other with whom I had "solid seasons," long to be remembered, at his house in the village, and who looked in upon me from time to time; but I had no more for society there.

There too, as every where, I sometimes expected the Visitor who never comes. The Vishnu Purana says, "The house-holder is to remain at eventide in his court-yard as long as it takes to milk a cow, or longer if he pleases, to await the arrival of a guest." I often performed this duty of hospitality, waited long enough to milk a whole herd of cows, but did not see them approaching from the town.

WINTER ANIMALS

When the ponds were firmly frozen, they afforded not only new and shorter routes to many points, but new views from their surfaces of the familiar landscape around them. When I crossed Flint's Pond, after it was covered with snow, though I had often paddled about it, it was so unexpectedly wide and so strange that I could think of nothing but Baffin's Bay. The Lincoln hills rose up around me at the extremity of a snowy plain, in which I did not remember to have stood before; and the fisher people, at an indeterminable distance over the ice, moving slowly about with their wolfish dogs, passed for sealers, or in misty weather loomed like fabulous creatures, and I did not know whether they were giants or dwarves. I took this course when I went to lecture in Lincoln in the evening, traveling in no road and passing no house between my own hut and the lecture room. In Goose Pond, which lay in my way, a colony of muskrats dwelt, and raised their cabins high above the ice, though none could be seen abroad when I crossed it.

Walden, being like the rest usually bare of snow, or with only shallow and interrupted drifts on it, was my yard, where I could walk freely when the snow was nearly two feet deep and the villagers were confined to their streets. There, far from the village street and, except at very long intervals, from the jingle of sleigh-bells, I slid and skated, as in a vast moose-yard well trodden, overhung by oak woods and solemn pines bent down with snow or bristling with icicles.

In November, the prospect of a joyful walk looks barren and I am slow to go forth. This month taxes a walker's resources more than any. I can hardly muster the courage to go outside when all is tightly locked or frozen up, and so little is to be seen in field or wood. I seem to anticipate a fruitless walk, and all seems un-promising. I have to force myself to it often. But then I am usually unexpectedly compensated, and the thinnest yellow light of November is more warming and exhilarating than any wine, and I may meet with something which interests me, and immediately it is as warm as July.

For sounds in winter nights, and often in win-ter days, I heard the forlorn but melodious note of a hooting owl indefinitely far; such a sound as the frozen earth would yield if struck with a suitable plectrum, the very native language of Walden Wood, and quite familiar to me at last, though I never saw the bird while it was making it. I seldom opened my door in a winter evening without hearing it; Hoo hoo hoo, hoorer, hoo, sounded sonorously, and the first three syllables accented somewhat like how der do; or sometimes hoo hoo only.

One night in the beginning of winter, before the pond froze over, about nine o'clock, I was startled by the loud honking of a goose, and, stepping to the door, heard the sound of their wings like a tempest in the woods as they flew low over my house. They passed over the pond toward Fair Haven, seemingly deterred from settling by my light, their commodore honking all the while with a regular beat. Suddenly an unmistakable cat-owl from very near me, with the most harsh and tremendous voice I ever heard from any inhabitant of the woods, responded at regular intervals to the goose, as if determined to expose and disgrace this intruder from Hudson's Bay by exhibiting a greater compass and volume of voice in a native, and boo-hoo him out of Concord horizon. "What do you mean by alarming the citadel at this time of night consecrated to me? Do you think I am ever caught napping at such an hour, and that I have not got lungs and a larynx as well as yourself? Boo-hoo, boo-hoo, boo-hoo!" It was one of the most thrilling discords I ever heard. And yet, if you had a discriminating ear, there were in it the elements of a concord such as these plains never saw nor heard.

I also heard the whooping of the ice in the pond, my great bed- fellow in that part of Concord, as if it were restless in its bed and would fain turn over, as if troubled with flatulency and had dreams; or I was waked by the cracking of the ground by the frost, as if some one had driven a team against my door, and in the morning would find a crack in the earth a quarter of a mile long and a third of an inch wide.

Sometimes I heard the foxes as they ranged over the snow crust, in moonlight nights, in search of a partridge or other game, barking raggedly and demoniacally like forest dogs, as if laboring with some anxiety, or seeking expression, struggling for light and to be dogs outright and run freely in the streets; for if we take the ages into our account, may there not be a civilization going on among brutes as well as humans? They seemed to me to be rudimental, burrowing people, still standing on their defense, awaiting their transformation. Sometimes one came near to my window, attracted by my light, barked a vulpine curse at me, and then retreated.

Usually the red squirrel (Sciurus Hudsonius) waked me in the dawn, coursing over the roof and up and down the sides of the house, as if sent out of the woods for this purpose. In the course of the winter I threw out half a bushel of ears of sweet-corn, which had not got ripe, on to the snow crust by my door, and was amused by watching the motions of the various animals which were baited by it. In the twilight and the night the rabbits came regularly and made a hearty meal. All day long the red squirrels came and went, and afforded me much entertainment by their manœuvres. One would approach at first warily through the shrub-oaks, running over the snow crust by fits and starts like a leaf blown by the wind, now a few paces this way, with wonderful speed and waste of energy, making inconceivable haste with his "trotters," as if it were for a wager, and now as many paces that way, but never getting on more than half a rod at a time; and then suddenly pausing with a ludicrous expression and a gratuitous somerset, as if all the eyes in the universe were fixed on them,—for all the motions of a squirrel, even in the most solitary recesses of the forest, imply spectators as much as those of a ballet dancer,—wasting more time in delay and circumspection than would have sufficed to walk the whole distance,—I never saw one walk,— and then suddenly, before you could say Jack Robinson, they would be in the top of a young pitch-pine, winding up their clock and chiding all imaginary spectators, soliloquizing and talking to all the universe at the same time,—for no reason that I could ever detect, or that they themselves were aware of, I suspect. At length they would reach the corn, and selecting a suitable ear, frisk about in the same uncertain trigonometrical way to the top-most stick of my wood-pile, before my window, where they looked me in the face, and there would sit for hours, supplying themselves with a new ear from time to time, nibbling at first voraciously and throwing the half-naked cobs about; 'til at length they grew more dainty still and played with their food, tasting only the inside of the kernel, and the ear, which was held balanced over the stick by one paw, slipped from their careless grasp and fell to the ground, then they would look over at it with mistrust, as if suspecting that it had life, with a mind not made up whether to get it again, or a new one, or be off; now thinking of corn, then listening to hear what was in the wind. So the little impudent rodent would waste many an ear in a forenoon; 'til at last, seizing some longer and plumper one, considerably bigger than themselves, and skillfully balancing it, they would set out with it to the woods, like a tiger with a buffalo, by the same zigzag course and frequent pauses, scratching along with it as if it were too heavy for them and falling all the while, making its fall a diagonal between a perpendicular and horizontal, being determined to put it through at any rate;—a singularly frivolous and whimsical little being;—and so they would get off with it to where they lived, perhaps carry it to the top of a pine tree forty or fifty rods distant, and I would afterwards find the cobs strewn about the woods in various directions.

When the jays arrive,—whose discordant screams were heard long before, as they were warily making their approach an eighth of a mile off,—in a stealthy and sneaking manner they flit from tree to tree, nearer and nearer, and pick up the kernels which the squirrels have dropped. Then, sitting on a pitch-pine bough, they attempt to swallow in their haste a kernel which is too big for their throats and chokes them; and after great labor they disgorge it, and spend an hour in the endeavor to crack it by repeated blows with their bills. They were manifestly thieves, and I had not much respect for them; but the squirrels, though at first shy, went to work as if they were taking what was their own.

Meanwhile also came the chickadees in flocks, which, picking up the crumbs the squirrels had dropped, flew to the nearest twig, and, placing them under their claws, hammered away at them with their little bills, as if it were an insect in the bark, 'til they were sufficiently reduced for their slender throats. A little flock of these tit-mice came daily to pick a dinner out of my wood-pile, or the crumbs at my door, with faint flitting lisping notes, like the tinkling of icicles in the grass, or else with sprightly day day day, or more rarely, in spring-like days, a wiry summery phe-be from the wood-side. They were so familiar that at length one alighted on an armful of wood which I was carrying in, and pecked at the sticks without fear. I once had a sparrow alight upon my shoulder for a moment while I was hoeing in a village garden, and I felt that I was more distinguished by that circumstance than I should have been by any epaulet I could have worn. The squirrels also grew at last to be quite familiar, and occasionally stepped upon my shoe, when that was the nearest way.

When the ground was not yet quite covered, and again near the end of winter, when the snow began to melt about my wood-pile, the partridges came out of the woods morning and evening to feed there.

Whichever side you walk in the woods, the ruffed grouse bursts away on whirring wings, jarring the snow from the dry leaves and twigs on high, which comes sifting down in the sun-beams like golden dust; for this brave bird is not to be scared by winter. It is frequently covered up by drifts, and, it is said, "sometimes plunges from on wing into the soft snow, where it remains concealed for a day or two." I used to see them in the open land also, where they had come out of the woods at sunset to "bud" the wild apple-trees. They will come regularly every evening to particular trees, where the cunning hunter lies in wait for them, and these orchards suffer thus not a little. I am glad that the grouse gets fed, at any rate. It is Nature's offspring which lives on buds and diet-drink.

In dark winter mornings, or in short winter afternoons, I sometimes heard a pack of hounds threading all the woods with hounding cry and yelp, unable to resist the instinct of the chase, and the note of the hunting horn at intervals, proving human hunters in the rear. The woods ring again, and yet no fox bursts forth on to the open level of the pond, nor a following pack pursuing their Actæon, mistaking their god for game. And perhaps at evening I see the hunters returning with a single bushy tail trailing from their sleigh for a trophy, seeking their inn. They tell me that if the fox would remain in the bosom of the frozen earth, she would be safe, or if she would run in a straight line away, no fox-hound could overtake her; but, having left her pursuers far behind, she stops to rest and listen 'til they come up, and when she runs, she circles round to her old haunts, where the hunters await her. She appears to know that water will not retain her scent. A hunter told me that she once saw a fox pursued by hounds burst out on to Walden when the ice was covered with shallow puddles, run part way across, and then return to the same shore. Ere long the hounds arrived, but here they lost the scent. Sometimes a pack hunting by themselves would pass my door, and circle round my house, and yelp and hound without regarding me, as if afflicted by a species of madness, so that nothing could divert them from the pursuit. Thus they circle until they fall upon the recent trail of a fox, for a wise hound will forsake every thing else for this. One day a man came to my hut from Lexington to inquire after his hound that made a large track, and had been hunting for a week by himself. But I fear that he was not the wiser for all I told him, for every time I attempted to answer his questions he interrupted me by asking, "What do you do here?" He had lost a dog, but found a man.

One old hunter who has a dry tongue, who used to come to bathe in Walden once every year when the water was warmest, and at such times looked in upon me, told me that many years ago he took his gun one afternoon and went out for a cruise in Walden Wood; and as he walked the Wayland road he heard the cry of hounds approaching, and ere long a fox leaped the wall into the road, and as quick as thought leaped the other wall out of the road, and his swift bullet had not touched him. Some way behind came an old hound and three pups in full pursuit, hunting on their own account, and disappeared again in the woods. Late in the afternoon, as he was resting in the thick woods south of Walden, he heard the voice of the hounds far over toward Fair Haven still pursuing the fox; and on they came, their hounding cry which made all the woods ring sounding nearer and nearer, now from Well-Meadow, now from the Baker Farm. For a long time he stood still and listened to their music, so sweet to a hunter's ear, when suddenly the fox appeared, threading the solemn aisles with an easy coursing pace, whose sound was concealed by a sympathetic rustle of the leaves, swift and still, keeping the ground, leaving her pursuers far behind; and, leaping upon a rock amid the woods, she sat erect and listening, with her back to the hunter. For a moment compassion restrained the latter's arm; but that was a short-lived mood, and as quick as thought can follow thought, his piece was levelled, and whang!—the fox rolling over the rock lay dead on the ground. The hunter still kept his place and listened to the hounds. Still on they came, and now the near woods resounded through all their aisles with their demoniac cry. At length the old hound burst into view with muzzle to the ground, and snapping the air as if possessed, and ran directly to the rock; but spying the dead fox, they suddenly ceased their hounding as if struck dumb with amazement, and walked round and round her in silence; and one by one, their pups arrived, and, like their parent, were sobered into silence by the mystery. Then the hunter came forward and stood in their midst, and the mystery was solved. They waited in silence while he skinned her, then followed the brush a while, and at length turned off into the woods again, on their own. That evening, a Weston Squire came to the Concord hunter's cottage to inquire for his hounds, and told how they had been hunting on their own account from Weston woods for a week. The Concord hunter told him what he knew and offered him the skin; but the other declined it and departed. He did not find his hounds that night, but the next day learned that they had crossed the river and put up at a farm-house for the night, whence, having been well fed, they took their departure early in the morning.

The hunter who told me this could remember one Sam Nutting, who used to hunt bears on Fair Haven Ledges, and exchange their skins for rum in Concord village; who told him, even, that he had seen a moose there. Nutting had a famous fox-hound named Burgoyne,—he pronounced it Bugine.

In the record book of an old trader of this town, who was also a captain, town-clerk, and representative, I find the following entry.

Jan. 18th, 1742, John Melven Cr. by 1 Grey Fox

Feb. 7th, 1743, Hezekiah Stratton has credit by ½ a wildcat skin (Of course, a wild-cat, for Stratton was a sergeant in the old French war, and would not have got credit for hunting less noble game.)

Credit is given for deer skins also, and they were daily sold. One man still preserves the horns of the last deer that was killed in this vicinity. The hunters were formerly a numerous and merry crew here, before the wilderness was stripped. I remember well one gaunt Nimrod who would catch up a leaf by the road-side and play a strain on it wilder and more melodious, if my memory serves me, than any hunting-horn.

At midnight, when there was a moon, I sometimes met with hounds in my path prowling about the woods, which would skulk out of my way, as if afraid, and stand silent amid the bushes 'til I had passed.

Squirrels and wild mice disputed for my store of nuts. There were scores of pitch-pines around my house, from one to four inches in diameter, which had been gnawed by mice the previous winter,—a rough winter for them, for the snow lay long and deep, and they were obliged to mix a large proportion of pine bark with their other diet. These trees were alive and apparently flourishing at mid-summer, and many of them had grown a foot, though completely girdled; but after another winter such were, without exception, dead. It is remarkable that a single mouse should thus be allowed a whole pine tree for its dinner, gnawing round instead of up and down it; but perhaps it is necessary in order to thin these trees, which are wont to grow up densely.

The hares (Lepus Americanus) were very familiar. One had their form under my house all winter, separated from me only by the flooring, and they startled me each morning by their hasty departure when I began to stir,—thump, thump, thump, striking their head against the floor timbers in their hurry. Others used to come round my door at dusk to nibble the potato parings which I had thrown out, and were so nearly the color of the ground that they could hardly be distinguished when still. Sometimes in the twilight I alternately lost and recovered sight of one sitting motionless under my window. When I opened my door in the evening, off they would go with a squeak and a bounce. Near at hand they only excited my pity. One evening one sat by my door two paces from me, at first trembling with fear, yet unwilling to move; a poor wee thing, lean and bony, with ragged ears and sharp nose, scant tail and slender paws. It looked as if Nature no longer contained the breed of nobler bloods, but stood on her last toes. Its large eyes appeared young and unhealthy, almost dropsical. I took a step, and lo, away it scud with an elastic spring over the snow crust, straightening its body and its limbs into graceful length, and soon put the forest between me and itself,—the wild free venison, asserting its vigor and the dignity of Nature. Not without reason was its slenderness. Such then was its calling. (Lepus, levipes, light-foot, some think.)

What is a country without rabbits and grouse? They are among the most simple and indigenous animals; ancient and venerable families known to antiquity as to modern times; of the very hue and substance of Nature, nearest allied to leaves and to the ground,— and to one another; it is either winged or it is legged. It is hardly as if you had seen a wild creature when a rabbit or a grouse bursts away, only a natural one, as much to be expected as rustling leaves. The grouse and the rabbit are still sure to thrive, like true natives of the soil, whatever revolutions occur. If the forest is cut off, the sprouts and bushes which spring up afford them concealment, and they become more numerous than ever. That must be a poor country indeed that does not support a hare. Our woods teem with them both, and around every swamp may be seen the grouse or rabbit walk, beset with twiggy fences and horse-hair snares, which some rancher tends.

THE POND IN WINTER

After a still winter night, I awoke with the impression that some question had been put to me, which I had been endeavoring in vain to answer in my sleep, as what—how—when—where? But there was dawning Nature, in whom all creatures live, looking in at my broad windows with serene and satisfied face, and no question on her lips. I awoke to an answered question, to Nature and daylight. The snow lying deep on the earth dotted with young pines, and the very slope of the hill on which my house is placed, seemed to say, Forward! Nature puts no question, and answers none which we mortals ask. She has long ago taken her resolution. Our eyes contemplate with admiration, and transmit to the soul, the wonderful and varied spectacle of this universe. The night veils a part of this glorious creation; but day comes to reveal to us this great work, which extends from the dirt of the earth into the plains of the ether.

Then to my morning work. First I take an axe and pail and go in search of water, if that be not a dream.

Every winter, the liquid and trembling surface of the pond, which was so sensitive to every breath, and reflected every light and shadow, becomes solid to the depth of a foot or a foot and a half, so that it will support the heaviest teams, and perchance the snow covers it to an equal depth, and it is not to be distinguished from any level field. Like the marmots in the surrounding hills, it closes its eye-lids and becomes dormant for three months or more. Standing on the snow-covered plain, as if in a pasture amid the hills, I cut my way first through a foot of snow, and then a foot of ice, and open a window under my feet, where, kneeling to drink, I look down into the quiet parlor of the fishes, with its bright sanded floor the same as in summer; there a perennial waveless serenity reigns, corresponding to the cool and even temperament of the inhabitants. Heaven is under our feet as well as over our heads. Early in the morning, while all things are crisp with frost, people come with fishing reels and slender lunch, and let down their fine lines through the snowy field to take pickerel and perch; these are the wild ones, those who instinctively follow other fashions and trust other authorities than their townspeople, and by their goings and comings, stitch towns together in parts where else they would be ripped. They sit and eat their luncheon on the shore, as wise in natural lore as the citizen is in artificial. They never consulted with books, and can tell much less than they have done. The things which they practice are said not yet to be known. Here is one fishing for pickerel with grown perch for bait. You look into their pail with wonder as into a summer pond, as if they kept summer locked up at home, or knew where she had retreated. How, pray, did they get these in mid-winter? O, they got worms out of rotten logs since the ground froze, and so they caught them. Their life it-self passes deeper in Nature than the studies of the naturalist penetrate; themselves a subject for the nat-uralist. The latter raises the moss and bark gently with their knife in search of insects; the former lays open logs to their core with their axe, and moss and bark fly far and wide. They get their living by barking trees. Such a person has some right to fish, and I love to see Nature carried out in them.

When I strolled around the pond in misty weather I was sometimes amused by the primitive mode which some ruder fishers had adopted. They would perhaps have placed alder branches over the narrow holes in the ice, and having fastened the end of the line to a stick to prevent its being pulled through, have passed the slack line over a twig of the alder, a foot or more above the ice, and tied a dry oak leaf to it, which, be-ing pulled down, would show when they had a bite. These alders loomed through the mist at regular in-tervals as you walked half way round the pond.

Ah, the pickerel of Walden! when I see them lying on the ice, or in the well which the fisher cuts in the ice, making a little hole to admit the water, I am al-ways surprised by their rare beauty, as if they were fabulous fishes, they are so foreign to the streets, even to the woods, foreign as Arabia to our Concord life. They possess a quite dazzling and transcendent beauty which separates them by a wide interval from the cadaverous cod and haddock whose fame is trum-peted in our streets. They have, to my eyes, if possible, rarer colors than normally found in nature, like flow-ers and precious stones, as if they were the pearls, the animalized nuclei or crystals of the Walden water. They, of course, are Walden all over and all through; are themselves small Waldens in the animal kingdom,

Waldenses. It is surprising that they are caught here,—that in this deep and capacious spring, far beneath the rattling teams and chaises and tinkling sleighs that travel the Walden road, this great gold and emerald fish swims. I never chanced to see its kind in any market; it would be the cynosure of all eyes there.

As I was desirous to recover the long lost bottom of Walden Pond, I surveyed it carefully, before the ice broke up, early in '46, with compass and chain and sounding line. There have been many stories told about the bottom, or rather no bottom, of this pond, which certainly had no foundation for themselves. It is remarkable how long people will believe in the bottomlessness of a pond without taking the trouble to sound it. I have visited two such Bottomless Ponds in one walk in this neighborhood. Many have believed that Walden reached quite through to the other side of the globe. Some who have lain flat on the ice for a long time, looking down through the illusive medium, perchance with watery eyes into the bargain, and driven to hasty conclusions by the fear of catching cold in their breasts, have seen vast holes "into which a load of hay might be driven," if there were any body to drive it, the undoubted source of the underworld River Styx and entrance to the Infernal Regions from these parts. Others have gone down from the village with a fifty-six- pound weight and a wagon load of inch-thick rope, but yet have failed to find any bottom; for while the fifty-six was resting on the bottom, they were paying out the heavy, taught rope in the vain attempt to fathom their truly immeasurable capacity for marvellousness. But I can assure my readers that Walden has a reasonably tight bottom at a not unreasonable, though at an unusual, depth. I fathomed it with a light cod-line and a stone weighing about a pound and a half, and could tell accurately when the stone left the bottom, by having to pull so much harder before the water got underneath to help me, where those who tried before me could not feel the jolt due to the weight of the heavy rope beneath them. The greatest depth was exactly one hundred and two feet; to which may be added the five feet which it has risen since, making one hundred and seven. This is a remarkable depth for so small an area; yet not an inch of it can be spared by the imagination. What if all ponds were shallow? Would it not react on the minds of people? I am thankful that this pond was made deep and pure for a symbol. While some believe in the infinite, some ponds will still be thought to be bottomless.

A factory owner, hearing what depth I had found, thought that it could not be true, for, judging from their acquaintance with dams, sand would not lie at so steep an angle. But the deepest ponds are not so deep in proportion to their area as most suppose, and, if drained, would not leave very remarkable valleys. Most ponds, emptied, would leave a meadow no more hollow than we frequently see. Often an inquisitive eye may detect the shores of a primitive lake in the low horizon hills, but it is easiest, as they who work on the highways know, to find the hollows of the puddles after a shower. Probably, the depth of the ocean will be found to be very inconsiderable compared with its breadth.

As I sounded through the ice I could determine the shape of the bottom with greater accuracy than is possible in surveying harbors which do not freeze over, and I was surprised at its general regularity. In the deepest part there are several acres more level than almost any field which is exposed to the sun wind and plough. In one instance, on a line arbitrarily chosen, the depth did not vary more than one foot in thirty rods; and generally, near the middle, I could calculate the variation for each one hundred feet in any direction beforehand within three or four inches. Some are accustomed to speak of deep and dangerous holes even in quiet sandy ponds like this, but the effect of water under these circumstances is to level all inequalities.

When I had mapped the pond fully, and put down the depth measurements, more than a hundred in all, I observed this remarkable coincidence. Having noticed that the number indicating the greatest depth was apparently in the centre of the map, I laid a rule on the map lengthwise, and then breadthwise, and found, to my surprise, that the line of greatest length intersected the line of greatest breadth exactly at the point of greatest depth, and I said to myself, Who knows but if this hint would point to the deepest part of the ocean as well as of a pond or puddle? Is not this the rule also for the height of mountains, regarded as the opposite of valleys? We know that a hill is not highest at its narrowest part.

The coves were observed to have ripples and sediment bars across their mouths that grew further apart as the depth increased, towards the center of the pond. Given, then, the length and breadth of the cove, and the character of the surrounding shore, and you have almost elements enough to make out a formula for all cases. Every harbor on the sea-coast, also, has its sand bar at its entrance.

If we knew all the laws of Nature, we should need only one fact, or the description of one actual phenomenon, to infer all the particular results at that point. Now we know only a few laws, and our result is vitiated, not, of course, by any confusion or irregularity in Nature, but by our ignorance of essential elements in the calculation. Our notions of law and harmony are commonly confined to those instances which we detect; but the harmony which results from a far greater number of seemingly conflicting, but really concurring, laws, which we have not detected, is still more wonderful. The particular laws are like points of view, as, to the traveler, a mountain outline varies with every step, and it has an infinite number of profiles, though absolutely but one form. Even when cleft or bored through, it is not comprehended in its entireness.

What I have observed of the pond is no less true in ethics. It is the law of average. Such a rule of the two diameters not only guides us toward the sun in the system and the heart in humans, but draw lines through the length and breadth of the aggregate of a person's particular daily behaviors and waves of life into their coves and inlets, and where they intersect will be the height or depth of their character. Perhaps we need only to know how their shores trend and their adjacent country or circumstances, to infer their depth and concealed bottom. If they are surrounded by mountainous circumstances, an Achillean shore, whose peaks overshadow and are reflected in their bosom, they suggest a corresponding depth within a person. But a low and smooth shore proves them shallow on that side. Also there is a bar across the entrance of our every cove; each is our harbor for a season, in which we are detained and partially land-locked. It is true, we are such poor navigators that our thoughts, for the most part, steer for the public ports of entry, and go into the dry docks of learned knowledge, where no natural currents concur to individualize them.

As for the inlet or outlet of Walden, I have not discovered any but rain and snow and evaporation, though perhaps, with a thermometer and a line, such places may be found, for where the water flows into the pond it will probably be coldest in summer and warmest in winter. When the ice-harvesters were at work here in '46-7, the cakes sent to the shore were one day rejected by those who were stacking them up there, not being thick enough to lie side by side with the rest; and the cutters thus discovered that the ice over a small space was two or three inches thinner than elsewhere, which made them think that there was an inlet there. They also showed me in another place what they thought was a "leach hole," through which the pond leaked out under a hill into a neighboring meadow, pushing me out on a cake of ice to see it. It was a small cavity under ten feet of water; but I think that I can warrant the pond not to need soldering 'til they find a worse leak than that. One has suggested, that if such a "leach hole" should be found, its connection with the meadow, if any existed, might be proved by conveying some colored powder or sawdust to the mouth of the hole, and then putting a strainer over the spring in the meadow, which would catch some of the particles carried through by the current.

While yet it is cold January, and snow and ice are thick and solid, the prudent landlord comes from the village to get ice to cool their summer drink; impressively, even pathetically wise, to foresee the heat and thirst of July now in January,—wearing a thick coat and mittens! when so many other things are not provided for. It may be that they lay up no treasures in this earthly world which will cool their summer drink in the next life. They cut and saw the solid pond, unroofing the house of fishes, and cart off their very element and air, held fast by chains and stakes like corded wood, through the favoring winter air, to wintry cellars, to underlie the summer there. It looks like solidified azure as it is drawn through the streets. These ice-cutters are a merry race, full of jest and sport, and when I went among them, they invited me to saw the ice in pit-fashion like they do when sawing through wooden logs—one above the trunk and one below—but I gratefully declined, as they offered me the position below.

In the winter of '46–7 there came a hundred laborers from far beyond the north wind, who swooped down on to our pond one morning, with many car-loads of ungainly-looking farming tools, sleds, ploughs, drill-barrows, turf-knives, spades, saws, rakes, and each worker was armed with a dou-ble-pointed pike- staff, such as is not described in the New-England Farmer or the Cultivator. I did not know whether they had come to sow a crop of winter rye, or some other kind of grain recently introduced from Iceland. As I saw no manure, I judged that they meant to skim the land, as I had done, thinking the soil was deep and had lain fallow long enough. They said that a gentleman farmer, who was behind the scenes, wanted to double his money, which, as I un-derstood, amounted to half a million already; but in order to cover each one of his dollars with another, he took off the only coat, ay, the skin itself, of Walden Pond in the midst of a hard winter. They went to work at once, ploughing, harrowing, rolling, furrowing, in admirable order, as if they were bent on making this a model farm; but when I was looking sharp to see what kind of seed they dropped into the furrow, a gang of fellows by my side suddenly began to hook up the virgin mould itself, with a peculiar jerk, clean down to the sand, or rather the water,—for it was a very springy soil,—indeed all the terra firma there was,—and haul it away on sleds. So they came and went every day, with a peculiar shriek from the locomotive, from and to some point of the polar regions, as it seemed to me, like a flock of arctic snow-birds. But sometimes Native Walden had her revenge, and a hired man, walking behind his team, slipped through a crack in the ground down toward Tartarus, below Hades, and he who was so brave before suddenly became but the ninth part of a man, almost gave up his animal heat, and was glad to take refuge in my house, and enjoy my stove. Or sometimes, the frozen soil took a piece of steel out of a ploughshare, or a plough got set in the furrow and had to be cut out.

To speak literally, a hundred Irish people, with Yankee overseers, came from Cambridge every day to get out the ice. They divided it into cakes, and these, being sledded to the shore, were rapidly hauled off on to an ice platform, and raised by grappling irons and block and tackle, worked by horses, on to a stack, as surely as so many barrels of flour, and there placed evenly side by side, and row upon row, as if they formed the solid base of an obelisk designed to pierce the clouds. They told me that in a good day they could get out a thousand tons, which was the yield of about one acre. Deep ruts and "cradle holes" were worn in the ice by the passage of the sleds over the same track, and the horses invariably ate their oats out of cakes of ice hollowed out like buckets. They stacked up the cakes thus in the open air in a pile thirty-five feet high on one side and six or seven rods square, putting hay between the outside layers to exclude the air; for when the wind, though never

so cold, finds a passage through, it will wear large cav-
ities, leaving slight supports or studs only here and
there, and finally topple it down. At first it looked like
a vast blue fort or Valhalla; but when they began to
tuck the coarse meadow hay into the crevices, and
this became covered with rime and icicles, it looked
like a venerable moss- grown and hoary ruin, built
of azure-tinted marble, the abode of Winter, that old
man we see in the almanac,—his shanty, as if he had
a design to estivate with us. They calculated that not
twenty-five per cent of this would reach its destina-
tion, and that two or three per cent would be wasted
in the cars. However, a still greater part of this heap
had a different destiny from what was intended; for,
either because the ice was found not to keep so well as
was expected, containing more air than usual, or for
some other reason, it never got to market. This heap,
made in the winter of '46–7 and estimated to contain
ten thousand tons, was finally covered with hay and
boards; and though it was unroofed the following
July, and a part of it carried off, the rest remaining
exposed to the sun, it stood over that summer and the
next winter, and was not quite melted 'til September
1848. Thus the pond recovered the greater part.

Like the water, the Walden ice, seen near at hand,
has a green tint, but at a distance is beautifully blue,
and you can easily tell it from the white ice of the
river, or the merely greenish ice of some ponds, a
quarter of a mile off. Sometimes one of those great
cakes slips from the ice-harvester's sled into the village street, and lies there for a week like a great emerald, an object of interest to all passers. I have noticed
that a portion of Walden which in the state of water
was green will often, when frozen, appear from the
same point of view blue. Ice is an interesting subject

for contemplation. They told me that they had some in the ice-houses at Fresh Pond five years old which was as good as ever. Why is it that a bucket of water soon becomes putrid, but frozen remains sweet forever? It is commonly said that this is the difference between the affections and the intellect.

Thus for sixteen days I saw from my window a hundred harvesters at work like busy farmers, with teams and horses and apparently all the implements of farming, such a picture as we see on the first page of the almanac; and as often as I looked out I was reminded of the fable of the lark and the reapers, or the parable of the sower, and the like; and now they are all gone, and in thirty days more, probably, I shall look from the same window on the pure sea-green Walden water there, reflecting the clouds and the trees, and sending up its evaporations in solitude, and no traces will appear that a person has ever stood there. Perhaps I shall hear a solitary loon laugh as he dives and plumes himself, or shall see a lonely fisher in her boat, like a floating leaf, beholding her form reflected in the waves, where lately a hundred workers securely labored.

Thus it appears that the sweltering inhabitants of Charleston and New Orleans, of Madras and Bombay and Calcutta, drink at my well. In the morning I bathe my intellect in the stupendous and cosmogonal philosophy of the Bhagvat Geeta, since whose composition, years of the gods have elapsed, and in comparison with which, our modern world and its literature seem puny and trivial; and I doubt if that philosophy is not to be referred to a previous state of existence, so remote is its sublimity from our conceptions. I lay down the book and go to my well for water, and lo! there I meet the servant of the Bramin, priest of

Brahma and Vishnu and Indra, who still sits in his temple on the Ganges reading the Vedas, or dwells at the root of a tree with his crust and water jug. The pure Walden water is mingled with the sacred water of the Ganges.

SPRING

The opening of large tracts by the ice-cutters commonly causes a pond to break up earlier; for the water, agitated by the wind, even in cold weather, wears away the surrounding ice. But such was not the effect on Walden that year, for it had soon got a thick new garment to take the place of the old. This pond never breaks up so soon as the others in this neighborhood, on account both of its greater depth and its having no stream passing through it to melt or wear away the ice. It commonly opens about the first of April, a week or ten days later than Flint's Pond and Fair- Haven, beginning to melt on the north side and in the shallower parts where it first began to freeze. It indicates the absolute progress of the season, being least affected by transient changes of temperature.

In spring, the sun not only exerts an influence through the increased temperature of the air and earth, but its heat passes through ice a foot or more thick, and is reflected from the bottom in shallow water, and so also warms the water and melts the under side of the ice, at the same time that it is melting it more directly above, making it uneven, and causing the air bubbles which it contains to extend themselves upward and downward until it is completely honeycombed, and at last disappears suddenly in a single spring rain.

Ice has its grain as well as wood does, and when an ice cake begins to rot, or "comb," the air cells are at right angles with what was the water surface. Where there is a rock or a log rising near to the surface the ice over it is much thinner, and is frequently quite dissolved by this reflected heat.

The phenomena of the year take place every day in a pond on a small scale. Every morning, generally speaking, the shallow water is being warmed more rapidly than the deep, though it may not be made so warm after all, and every evening it is being cooled more rapidly until the morning. The day is an epitome of the year. The night is the winter, the morning and evening are the spring and fall, and the noon is the summer. The cracking and booming of the ice indicate a change of temperature. One pleasant morning after a cold night, February 24th, 1850, having gone to Flint's Pond to spend the day, I noticed with surprise, that when I struck the ice with the head of my axe, it resounded like a gong for many rods around, or as if I had struck on a tight drum-head. The pond began to boom about an hour after sunrise, when it felt the influence of the sun's rays slanted upon it from over the hills; it stretched itself and yawned like a waking man with a gradually increasing tumult, which was kept up three or four hours. He took a short siesta at noon, and boomed once more toward night, as the sun was withdrawing her influence. In the right stage of the weather, a pond fires its evening gun with great regularity. But in the middle of the day, being full of cracks, and the air also being less elastic, it had completely lost its resonance, and probably fishes and muskrats could not then have been stunned by a blow of it. The fisherpeople say that the "thundering of the pond" scares the fishes and prevents their biting. The pond does not thunder every evening, and I cannot tell surely when to expect its thundering; but though I may perceive no difference in the weather, it does. Who would have suspected so large and cold and thick-skinned a thing to be so sensitive? Yet it has its law to which it thunders obedience when it should, as surely as the buds expand in the spring. The earth is all alive and covered with papillæ. The largest pond is as sensitive to atmospheric changes as the globule of mercury in its tube.

One attraction in coming to the woods to live was that I should have leisure and opportunity to see the spring come in. The ice in the pond at length begins to be honey-combed, and I can set my heel in it as I walk. Fogs and rains and warmer suns are gradually melting the snow; the days have grown sensibly longer; and I see how I shall get through the winter without adding to my wood-pile, for large fires are no longer necessary. I am on the alert for the first signs of spring, to hear the chance note of some arriving bird, or the striped squirrel's chirp, for their stores must be now nearly exhausted, or see the woodchuck venture out of their winter quarters. On the 13th of March, after I had heard the bluebird, song-sparrow, and red-wing, the ice was still nearly a foot thick.

Every incident connected with the breaking up of the rivers and ponds and the settling of the weather is particularly interesting to us who live in a climate of so great extremes. When the warmer days come, they who dwell near the river hear the ice crack at night with a startling whoop as loud as artillery, as if its icy fetters were rent from end to end, and within a few days see it rapidly going out. So the alligator comes out of the mud with quakings of the earth. One old man who has been a close observer of Nature, told me a story that surprised me, for he was so wise in her ways that I was amazed to hear him express wonder at any of her operations—I thought there were no secrets between them. One spring day, he took his gun and boat, and thought that he would have a little sport with the ducks. It was a warm day, and he was surprised to see so great a body of ice remaining. Not seeing any ducks, he hid his boat on the north or back side of an island in the pond, and then concealed himself in the bushes on the south side, to await them. The ice was melted for three or four rods from the shore, and there was a smooth and warm sheet of water, with a muddy bottom, such as the ducks love, and he thought it likely that some would be along pretty soon. After he had lain still there about an hour he heard a low and seemingly very distant sound, but singularly grand and impressive, unlike any thing he had ever heard, gradually swelling and increasing as if it would have a universal and memorable ending, a sullen rush and roar, which seemed to him all at once like the sound of a vast body of fowl coming in to settle there, and, seizing his gun, he started up in haste and excited; but he found, to his surprise, that the whole body of the ice had started moving while he lay there, and drifted in to the shore, and the sound he had heard was made by its edge grating on the shore,—at first gently nibbled and crumbled off, but at length heaving up and scattering its wrecks along the island to a considerable height before it came to a standstill.

As spring progresses, the sun's rays have attained the right angle, and warm winds blow up mist and rain and melt the snow banks. Few phenomena gave me more delight than to observe the forms which thawing sand and clay assume in flowing down the sides of a deep cut on the railroad through which I passed on my way to the village, a phenomenon not very common on so large a scale, though the number of freshly exposed banks of the right material must have been greatly multiplied since railroads were invented. The material was sand of every degree of fineness and of various rich colors, commonly mixed with a little clay. When the frost comes out in the spring, and even in a thawing day in the winter, the sand begins to flow down the slopes like lava, sometimes bursting out through the snow and overflowing it where no sand was to be seen before. Innumerable little streams overlap and interlace one with another, exhibiting a sort of hybrid product, which obeys half way the law of currents, and half way that of vegetation. As it flows it takes the forms of sappy leaves or vines, making heaps of pulpy sprays a foot or more in depth, and resembling, as you look down on them, the fringed, lobed, and imbricated thalluses of some lichens; or you are reminded of coral, of leopard's paws or birds' feet, of brains or lungs or bowels, and excrements of all kinds. It is a truly grotesque vegetation, whose forms and color we see imitated in bronze, a sort of architectural foliage more ancient and typical than acanthus, chiccory, ivy, vine, or any vegetable leaves; destined perhaps, under some circumstances, to become a puzzle to future geologists. The whole cut impressed me as if it were a cave with its stalactites laid open to the light. The various shades of the sand are singularly rich and agreeable, embracing the different iron colors, brown, gray, yellowish, and reddish. When the flowing mass reaches the drain at the foot of the bank it spreads out flatter into strands, the separate streams losing their semi-cylindrical form and gradually becoming more flat and broad, running together as they are more moist, 'til they form an almost flat sand, still variously and beautifully shaded, but in which you can trace the original forms of vegetation; 'til at length, in the water itself, they are converted into banks, like those formed off the mouths of rivers, and the forms of vegetation are lost in the ripple marks on the bottom.

The whole bank, which is from twenty to forty feet high, is sometimes overlaid with a mass of this kind of foliage, or sandy rupture, for a quarter of a mile on one or both sides, the produce of one spring day. What makes this sand foliage remarkable is its springing into existence thus suddenly. When I see on the one side the inert bank,—for the sun acts on one side first,—and on the other this luxuriant foliage, the creation of an hour, I am affected as if in a peculiar sense I stood in the laboratory of the Artist who made the world and me,—as if I had come to where she was still at work, sporting on this bank, and with excess of energy, strewing her fresh designs about. I feel as if I were nearer to the vitals of the globe, for this sandy overflow is something such a foliaceous mass as the vitals of the animal body. You find thus in the very pattern of the sands, an anticipation of the fractals of a tree or leaf. The universe expresses itself outwardly in leaves, as it so labors with the laws and ideas inwardly on a subatomic level. The atoms have already learned these laws, and are pregnant by them forever. The feathers and wings of birds are still drier and thinner leaves. Thus, also, you pass from

the lumpish grub in the earth to the airy and fluttering butterfly. The very globe continually transcends
and translates itself, and becomes winged in its orbit.
Even ice begins with delicate crystal leaves, as if it had
flowed into moulds which the fronds of water plants
have impressed on the watery mirror. The whole tree
itself is but one leaf, and rivers are still vaster leaves
whose pulp is intervening earth, and towns and cities
are the ova of insects in their axils.

When the sun withdraws, the sand ceases to flow,
but in the morning the streams will start once more
and branch and branch again into a myriad of others.
You here see perchance how blood vessels are formed.
If you look closely, you observe that from the thawing
mass, there first pushes forward a stream of softened
sand with a drop-like point, like the ball of the finger,
feeling its way slowly and blindly downward, until
at last with more heat and moisture, as the sun gets
higher, the most fluid portion separates from the
latter and forms for itself a meandering channel
or artery within that, in which is seen a little silvery
stream glancing like lightning from one stage of
pulpy leaves or branches to another. It is wonderful
how rapidly yet perfectly the sand organizes itself
as it flows, using the best material its mass affords to
form the sharp edges of its channel.

What is a human, but a mass of thawing clay? The
ball of the human finger is but a drop congealed. The
fingers and toes flow to their extent from the thawing
mass of the body. Who knows what the human body
would expand and flow out to under a more genial
heaven? Is not the hand a spreading palm leaf with
its lobes and veins? The ear may be regarded, fanci-
fully, as a lichen, umbilicaria, on the side of the head,
with its lobe or drop. The lip—labium,—laps from

the sides of the cavernous mouth. The nose is a manifest congealed drop or stalactite. The chin is a still larger drop, the confluent dripping of the face. The cheeks are a slide from the brows into the valley of the face, opposed and diffused by the cheek bones. Each rounded lobe of the vegetable leaf, too, is a thick and now loitering drop, larger or smaller; the lobes are the fingers of the leaf; and as many lobes as it has, in so many directions it tends to flow, and more heat or other genial influences would have caused it to flow yet farther.

Thus it seemed that this one hillside illustrated the principle of all the operations of Nature. The Maker of this earth patented a leaf. What Champollion will decipher this hieroglyphic for us, that we may turn over a new universal leaf at last? This phenomenon is more exhilarating to me than the luxuriance and fertility of vineyards. True, it is somewhat excrementitious in its character, and there is no end to the heaps of liver lights and bowels, as if the globe were turned wrong side outward; but this suggests at least that Nature has some bowels, and there again is mother of humanity.

This is the frost coming out of the ground; this is Spring. It precedes the green and flowery spring, as mythology precedes regular poetry. It convinces me that Earth is still in her swaddling clothes, and stretches forth baby fingers on every side. Fresh curls spring from the baldest brow. There is nothing inorganic. These foliaceous heaps lie along the bank like the slag of a furnace, showing that Nature is "in full blast" within. The earth is not a mere fragment of dead history, stratum upon stratum like the leaves of a book, to be studied by geologists and antiquaries chiefly, but living poetry like the leaves of a tree, which precede flowers and fruit,—not a fossil earth, but a living earth; compared with whose great central life, all animal and vegetable life is merely parasitic. Its throes will heave our exuviæ from their graves. You may melt your metals and cast them into the most beautiful moulds you can; they will never excite me like the forms which this molten earth flows out into. And not only it, but the institutions upon it, are plastic like clay in the hands of the potter. Thaw, with her gentle persuasion, is more powerful than Thor with his hammer.

When the ground was partially bare of snow, and a few warm days had dried its surface somewhat, it was pleasant to compare the first tender signs of the infant year just peeping forth with the stately beauty of the withered vegetation which had withstood the winter,—life-everlasting, golden-rods, pinweeds, and graceful wild grasses, more obvious and interesting frequently than in summer even, as if their beauty was not ripe 'til then; even cotton-grass, cat-tails, mulleins, johnswort, hard-hack, meadow-sweet, and other strong stemmed plants, those unexhausted granaries which entertain the earliest birds,—decent weeds, at least, which widowed Nature wears. I am particularly attracted by the arching and sheaf-like top of the wool-grass; it brings back the summer to our winter memories, and is among the forms which art loves to copy, and which, in the vegetable kingdom, have the same relation to types already in the mind of humans that astronomy has. It is an antique style older than Greek or Egyptian. Many of the phenomena of Winter are suggestive of an inexpressible tenderness and fragile delicacy. We are accustomed to hear this Winter Queen described as a rude, cold, and boisterous tyrant; but with the gentleness of a lover, she adorns the tresses of Summer.

At the approach of spring, the red-squirrels got under my house, two at a time, directly under my feet as I sat reading or writing, and kept up the queerest chuckling and chirruping and vocal pirouetting and gurgling sounds that ever were heard; and when I stamped they only chirruped the louder, as if past all fear and respect in their mad pranks, defying humanity to stop them. No you don't—chickaree—chickaree. They were wholly deaf to my arguments, or failed to perceive their force, and fell into a strain of invective that was irresistible.

The first sparrow of spring! The year beginning with younger hope than ever! The faint silvery warblings heard over the partially bare and moist fields from the blue-bird, the song- sparrow, and the red-wing, as if the last flakes of winter tinkled as they fell! What at such a time are histories, chronologies, traditions, and all written revelations? The brooks sing carols and glees to the spring. The marsh-hawk sailing low over the meadow is already seeking the first slimy life that awakes. The sinking sound of melting snow is heard in all dells, and the ice dissolves apace in the ponds.

"Et primitus oritur herba imbribus primoribus evocata,"
"Now the first grass springs up, called forth by the first rain."

The grass flames up on the hillsides like a spring fire, as if the earth sent forth an inward heat to greet the returning sun; not yellow but green is the color of its flame;—the symbol of perpetual youth, the grassblade, like a long green ribbon, streams from the sod into the summer, pushing on again, lifting its spear of last year's hay with the fresh life below. So our human life but dies down to its root, and still puts forth its green blade to eternity.

Walden is melting apace. There is a canal two rods wide along the northerly and westerly sides, and wider still at the east end. A great field of ice has cracked off from the main body. I hear a song-sparrow singing from the bushes on the shore,—olit, olit, olit,—chip, chip, chip, che char,—che wiss, wiss, wiss. He too is helping to crack it. How handsome the great sweeping curves in the edge of the ice, answering somewhat to those of the shore. It is glorious to behold this ribbon of water sparkling in the sun, the bare face of the pond full of glee and youth, as if it spoke the joy of the fishes within it, and of the sands on its shore,—a silvery sheen as from the scales of a leuciscus, as it were all one active fish. Such is the contrast between winter and spring. Walden was dead and is alive again.

The change from storm and winter to serene and mild weather, from dark and sluggish hours to bright and elastic ones, is a memorable crisis which all things proclaim. It is seemingly instantaneous at last. Suddenly an influx of light filled my house, though the evening was at hand, and the clouds of winter still overhung it, and the eaves were dripping with sleety rain. I looked out the window, and lo! where yesterday was cold gray ice there lay the transparent pond already calm and full of hope as in a summer evening, reflecting a summer evening sky in its bosom.

I heard a robin in the distance, the first I had heard for many a thousand years, methought, whose note I shall not forget for many a thousand more. O the evening robin, at the end of a New England summer day! If I could ever find the twig she sits upon! And I do mean she. I seek thou, and not just the Turdus migratorius.

The pitch-pines and shrub-oaks about my house, which had so long drooped, suddenly resumed their several characters, looked brighter, greener, and more erect and alive, as if effectually cleansed and restored by the rain.

As it grew darker, I was startled by the honking of geese flying low over the woods, like weary travelers getting in late from southern lakes. Standing at my door, I could hear the rush of their wings; and when, driving toward my house, they suddenly spied my light, with hushed clamor they wheeled and settled in the pond. So I came in, and shut the door, and passed my first spring night in the woods.

In the morning I watched the geese from the door through the mist, sailing in the middle of the pond, fifty rods off, so large and tumultuous that Walden appeared like an artificial pond for their amusement. But when I stood on the shore, they at once rose up with a great flapping of wings at the signal of their commander, and when they had got into rank circled about over my head, twenty-nine of them, and then steered straight to Canada, with a regular honk from the leader at intervals, trusting to break their fast in muddier pools. A "plump" of ducks rose at the same time and took the route to the north in the wake of their noisier cousins.

For a week I heard the circling, groping clangor of some solitary goose in the foggy mornings, seeking its companion, and still peopling the woods with the sound of a larger life than they could sustain. In April, the pigeons were seen again flying express in small flocks, and in due time I heard the martins twittering over my clearing, though it had not seemed that the township contained so many that it could afford me any, and I fancied that they were peculiarly of the ancient race that dwelt in hollow trees before the colonizers came. In almost all climes, the tortoise and the frog are among the precursors and heralds of this season, and birds fly with song and glancing plumage, and plants spring and bloom, and winds blow, to correct this slight oscillation of the poles and preserve the equilibrium of Nature.

As every season seems best to us in its turn, so the coming in of spring is like the creation of Cosmos out of Chaos and the realization of the Golden Age.

A single gentle rain makes the grass many shades greener. So our prospects brighten on the influx of better thoughts. We should be blessed if we lived in the present always, and took advantage of every accident that befell us, like the grass which confesses the influence of the slightest dew that falls on it; and did not spend our time in atoning for the neglect of past opportunities, which we call doing our duty. We loiter in winter while it is already spring. In a pleasant spring morning, all sins are forgiven. Through our own recovered innocence, we discern the innocence of our neighbors. You may have known your neighbor yesterday for a thief, a drunkard, or a sensualist, and merely pitied or despised them, and despaired of the world; but the sun shines bright and warm this first spring morning, re-creating the world, and you meet them at some serene work, and see how their exhausted and debauched veins expand with still joy and bless the new day, feel the spring influence with the innocence of infancy, and all their faults are forgotten. There is not only an atmosphere of good will about them, but even a savor of holiness groping for expression, blindly and ineffectually perhaps, like a newborn instinct, and for a short hour the south hillside echoes to no vulgar jest. Why the jailer does not leave open their prison doors,—why the judge does not dismiss their case,—why the preacher does not dismiss their congregation! It is because they do not obey the hint which God gives them, nor accept the pardon which she freely offers to all.

Words from Mencuis:

"A return to goodness produced each day in the tranquil and beneficent breath of the morning, causes that in respect to the love of virtue and the hatred of vice, one approaches a little the primitive nature of humans, as the sprouts of the forest which has been felled. In like manner, the evil which one does in the interval of a day prevents the germs of virtues which began to spring up again from developing themselves and destroys them. After the germs of virtue have thus been prevented many times from developing themselves, then the beneficent breath of evening does not suffice to preserve them. As soon as the breath of evening does not suffice longer to preserve them, then the nature of humans does not differ much from that of the brute. People seeing the nature of this person like that of the brute, think that they have never possessed the innate faculty of reason. Are those the true and natural sentiments of humans?"

Human nature is righteous and humane.

"The Golden Age was first created,
spontaneously without law—
it cherished fidelity and rectitude.
Punishment and fear were not;
nor were threatening words read

On suspended brass;
nor did the suppliant crowd fear the words of
their judge;
but were safe without an avenger.

❄ ❄ ❄

There was eternal spring, and placid zephyrs
with warm Blasts soothed the flowers born
without seed."—Ovid

On the 29th of April, as I was fishing from the bank of the river near the Nine-Acre-Corner bridge, standing on the quaking grass and willow roots where the muskrats lurk, I heard a singular rattling sound, somewhat like that of the sticks which kids play with their fingers, when, looking up, I observed a very slight and graceful hawk, like a night-hawk, alternately soaring like a ripple and tumbling a rod or two over and over, showing the underside of its wings, which gleamed like a satin ribbon in the sun, or like the pearly inside of a shell. It was the most ethereal flight I had ever witnessed. It did not simply flutter like a butterfly, nor soar like the larger hawks, but it sported with proud reliance in the fields of air; mounting again and again with its strange chuckle, it repeated its free and beautiful fall, turning over and over like a kite, and then recovering from its lofty tumbling, as if it had never set its foot on terra firma. It appeared to have no companion in the universe,— sporting there alone,—and to need none but the morning and the ether with which it played. It was not lonely, but made all the earth lonely beneath it. Where was the parent which hatched it, its kindred, and its mother in the heavens? The tenant of the air, it seemed related to the earth but by an egg hatched some time in the crevice of a crag;—or was its native nest made in the angle of a cloud, woven of the rainbow's trimmings and the sunset sky, and lined with some soft midsummer haze caught up from earth? Its home is now some cliffy cloud.

Beside this, I got a rare mess of golden and silver and bright cupreous fishes, which looked like a string of jewels. Ah! I have penetrated to those meadows on the morning of many a first spring day, jumping from hummock to hummock, from willow root to willow root, when the wild river valley and the woods were bathed in so pure and bright a light as would have waked the dead, if they had been slumbering in their graves, as some suppose. There needs no stronger proof of immortality. All things must live in such a light. O Death, where was thy sting? O Grave, where was thy victory, then?

Our village life would stagnate if it were not for the unexplored forests and meadows which surround it. We need the tonic of wildness,—to wade sometimes in marshes where the bittern and the meadow-hen lurk, and hear the booming of the snipe; to smell the whispering sedge where only some wilder and more solitary fowl builds her nest, and the mink crawls with its belly close to the ground. At the same time that we are earnest to explore and learn all things, we require that all things be mysterious and unexplorable, that land and sea be infinitely wild, unsurveyed and unfathomed by us because they are unfathomable. We can never have enough of Nature. We must be refreshed by the sight of inexhaustible vigor, vast and Titanic features, the sea-coast with its wrecks, the wilderness with its living and its decaying trees, the thunder cloud, and the rain which lasts three weeks and produces freshets. We need to witness our own limits transgressed, and some life pasturing freely where we never wander. We are cheered when we observe the vulture feeding on the carrion and deriving health and strength from the repast, which disgusts and disheartens us. There was a dead horse in the hollow by the path to my house, which compelled me sometimes to go out of my way to avoid it, especially in the night when the air was heavy, but the assurance it gave me of the strong appetite and inviolable health of Nature was my compensation for confronting it. I love to see that Nature is so rife with life that myriads can be afforded to be sacrificed and suffered to prey on one another; that tender organizations can be so serenely squashed out of existence like pulp,—tadpoles which herons gobble up, and tortoises and toads run over in the road; and that sometimes it has rained flesh and blood! With the liability to accident, we must see how little account is to be made of it. The impression made on a wise person is that of universal innocence. Poison is not poisonous after all, nor are any wounds fatal. Nature knows no compassion, but she is not malicious.

Early in May, the oaks, hickories, maples, and other trees popping up amongst the pines imparted a brightness like sunshine to the landscape, especially in cloudy days, as if the sun were breaking through mists and shining faintly on the hill-sides here and there. The phœbe had already come and looked in at my door and window, to see if my house was cavern-like enough for her, sustaining herself on humming wings with clinched talons, as if she was held by the air, while she surveyed the premises. The sulphur-like pollen of the pitch-pine soon covered the pond and the stones and rotten wood along the shore, so that you could have collected a barrel-full. This is the "sulphur showers" we hear of. And so the seasons went rolling on into summer, as one rambles into higher and higher grass.

Thus was my first year's life in the woods completed; and the second year was similar to it. I finally left Walden September 6th, 1847.

CONCLUSION

To the sick, the doctors wisely recommend a change of air and scenery. Thank Heaven, here is not all the world. The buck-eye does not grow in New England, and the mocking-bird is rarely heard here. The wild-goose is more of a cosmopolite than we; they break their fast in Canada, take a luncheon in the Ohio, and plume themselves for the night in a southern bayou. Even the bison, to some extent, keeps pace with the seasons, cropping the pastures of the Colorado only 'til a greener and sweeter grass awaits them by the Yellowstone. Yet we think that if fences are put up, and stone-walls piled up on our farms, bounds are henceforth set to our lives, and our fates decided. If you are chosen town-clerk, forsooth, you cannot go to Tierra del Fuego this summer: but you may go to the land of infernal fire nevertheless, eventually. The universe is wider than our views of it.

Yet we should oftener look over the tafferel of our watercraft, like curious passengers, and not make the voyage like stupid sailors picking at caulk, sailing in great circles. One hastens to Southern Africa to chase the giraffe; but surely that is not the game they would be after. How long, pray, would a person hunt giraffes if they could? Snipes and woodcocks also may afford rare sport; but I trust it would be nobler game to shoot one's self.—

> "Direct your eye right inward, and you'll find
> a thousand regions in your mind yet un-
> discovered. Travel them, and be expert in
> home-cosmography."

What does Africa,—what does the West stand for? When finally explored, is it the source of the Nile, or the Niger, or the Mississippi, or a North-West Passage around this continent, that we would find? Are these the problems which most concern humankind? Is the explorer-gone-missing the only one who is lost? Does the rescue crew know where they themselves are? Be rather the Lewis and Clarke and Frobisher of your own streams and oceans; explore your own higher latitudes. Be a discoverer of whole new continents and worlds within you, opening new channels, not of trade, but of thought. Every individual is the lord of a realm beside which the earthly Russian empire is but a petty state, a small hill left by the ice. Yet some can be patriotic who have no self-respect, and sacrifice the greater to the less. They love the soil which makes their graves, but have no sympathy with the spirit which may still animate their clay, now. Patriotism is a maggot in their heads. What was the meaning of that South-Sea Exploring Expedition, with all its parade and expense, but an indirect recognition of the fact that it is easier to sail many thousand miles through cold and storm and cannibals, in a government ship, with five hundred other to assist one, than it is to explore the private sea, the Atlantic and Pacific Ocean of one's being alone.—

"Erret, et extremos alter scrutetur Iberos.
Plus habet hic vitæ, plus habet ille viæ."

"Let them wander and scrutinize the
outlandish Australians.
I have more of God, they more of the road."

It is not worth the while to go round the world to count the cats in Zanzibar. Yet do this anyway, 'til you can do better, and you may perhaps find some "Symmes' Hole" by which to get at the inside your head at last. England and France, Spain and Portugal— all front on this private sea; but no ship from them has ventured out of sight of land, though it is without doubt the direct way to knowing. If you would learn to speak all tongues and conform to the customs of all nations, if you would travel farther than all travelers, be naturalized in all climes, and outsmart the Sphinx, you must obey the old philosopher, and Explore Thyself. Herein are demanded the eye and the nerve. The defeated run to war; the strong hope for none. Start now on that farthest western way, which does not pause at the Mississippi or the Pacific, nor conduct toward a worn-out China or Japan, but leads on direct a tangent to this sphere on your neck, summer and winter, day and night, sun down, moon down, and at last earth down too. But think of the folly of attempting to go away from here! When the constant endeavor should be to get nearer and nearer to here. How many things can you go away from? Take the shortest way around, and stay home. Here, of course, is all that you love, all that you expect, all that you are. Here is all the best and all the worst you can imagine. What more do you want? Foolish people imagine that what they want is somewhere else. That stuff is not made in any factory but their own.

It is said that Mirabeau took to the crime of highway robbery "to find out what degree was necessary in order to place one's self in formal opposition to the most sacred and unjust laws of society." This was honorable, as the world goes; and yet it was idle, if not desperate. A saner person would have found themselves often enough "in formal opposition" to what are deemed "the most sacred and unjust laws of society," through obedience to yet more sacred natural laws, and so have tested their resolution without going out of their way, but by justly living. It is more useful to maintain an attitude found through obedience to the laws of their highest inner being, which will never be one of opposition to a just government, if they should chance to meet with such.

I left the woods for as good a reason as I went there. Perhaps it seemed to me that I had several more lives to live, and could not spare any more time for that one. It is remarkable how easily and insensibly we fall into a particular route, and make a beaten track for ourselves. I had not lived there a week before my feet wore a path from my door to the pond-side; and though it is five or six years since I trod it, it is still quite distinct. The surface of the earth is soft and impressible by the feet of humans; and so is also with the paths which the mind travels. How worn and dusty, then, must be the highways of the world, how deep the ruts of tradition and conformity! I did not wish to take a cabin passage, but rather to go before the mast and on the deck of the world, for there I could best see the moonlight amid the mountains. I do not wish to go below now.

I learned this, at least, by my experiment; that if one advances confidently in the direction of their dreams, and endeavors to live the life which they have imagined, they will meet with a success unexpected in common hours. They will put some things behind, will pass an invisible boundary; new, universal, and more liberal laws will begin to establish themselves around and within them; or the old laws be expanded, and interpreted in their favor in a more liberal sense, and they will live with the license of a higher order of beings. In proportion as one simplifies their life, the laws of the universe will appear less complex, and solitude will not be solitude, nor poverty, nor weakness. If you have built castles in the air, your work need not be lost; that is where they should be. Now put the foundations under them.

Pursue some path, however narrow and crooked, in which you can walk with love and reverence. Whenever one separates from the multitude and goes their own way, they find a fork in the road, but the travelers barreling along the highways see only a small gap in the fence.

I fear chiefly that my expressions here may not be extravagant enough to adequately convey the bigger truth of which I have been wholly convinced. But I trust that the migrating buffalo, which seeks new pastures in another latitude, is not as extravagant as the cow which kicks over the milk pail, leaps the cow-yard fence, and runs after her calf. Her convictions find a way to be translated into a language of true understanding. Who that has heard a perfect strain of music has then feared that they should endeavor to speak extravagantly, and in hyperboles and antidotes, forever more, to capture the essence of what they've heard?

Some are whispering in our ears that we Americans, and moderns generally, are intellectual dwarfs compared with the ancients, or even the Elizabethans. But what is that to the purpose? A living dog is better than a dead lion. Shall a dog go and hang themselves because they are not a lion, instead of being the best dog that they can? Let everyone mind their own business, and endeavor to be what they were made.

And why should we be in such desperate haste to succeed, and in such desperate enterprises? If one does not keep pace with their companions, perhaps it is because they hear a different drummer. Let them step to the music which they hear, however measured or far away. It is not important that they should mature as soon as an apple-tree or an oak. Shall they force their spring into summer?

There was an artist in the city of Kouroo who was disposed to strive after perfection. One day it came into her mind to make a staff. Having considered that in an imperfect work, time is an ingredient, but into a perfect work, time does not enter, she said to herself: "It shall be perfect in all respects, though I should do nothing else in my life." She proceeded instantly to the forest for wood, being resolved that it should not be made of unsuitable material; and as she searched for and rejected stick after stick, her friends gradually deserted her, for they grew old in their works and died, but she grew not older by a moment. Her singleness of purpose and resolution, and her elevated piety, endowed her, without her knowledge, with perennial youth. As she made no compromise with Time, Time kept out of her way, and only sighed at a distance because he could not overcome her. Before she had found a stick in all respects suitable, the city of Kouroo was a hoary ruin, and she sat on one of its mounds to peel the stick. Before she had given it the proper shape, the dynasty of the Candahars was at an end, and with the point of the stick she wrote the name of the last of that race in the sand, and then resumed her work. By the time she had smoothed and polished the staff, Kalpa was no longer the pole-star; and before she had put on the head adorned with precious stones, Brahma had awoke and slumbered many times. But why do I stay to mention these things? When the finishing stroke was put to her work, it suddenly expanded before the eyes of the astonished artist into the fairest of all the creations of Brahma. She had made a new system in making a staff, a world with full and fair proportions; in which, though the old cities and dynasties had passed away, fairer and more glorious ones had taken their places. And now she saw by the heap of shavings still fresh at her feet, that, for her and her work, the former lapse of time had been an illusion, and that no more time had elapsed than is required for a single spark from the brain of Brahma to fall on and inflame the tinder of a mortal brain. The material was pure, and her art was pure; how could the result be other than wonderful? No face which we can give to a matter will stead us so well at last as the truth. This alone wears well. Tom Hyde, the tinker, standing on the gallows, was asked if he had anything to say. "Tell the tailors," said he, "to remember to make a knot in their thread before they take the first stitch." His companion's prayer has been long forgotten. Say what you have to say, not what you ought.

For the most part, we are not where we are, but in a false position. We suppose a case, plucked from an infinite number of imagined stories, and put ourselves into it, and hence are in two cases at the same time, and it is doubly difficult to get out of either. In truly sane moments, we regard only the facts, or the case that truly is.

Ah, those joyous days of youthful innocence! Are they never to return? When the walker does not too curiously observe particulars, but only sees, hears, smells, tastes, and feels themselves,—a rare bird becomes a mere mote in their eye. The unbounded universe was theirs. Objects are not concealed from our view because they are outside our visual ray, but rather, because there is no intention of the mind and eye toward them. Nature does not cast pearls before dogs. There is just as much beauty visible to us in the landscape as we are prepared to appreciate, and not a grain more.

However meager your life is, meet it and live it; do not shun it and call it hard names. It is not so bad as you are. It looks poorest when you are richest. The fault-finder will find faults even in paradise. Love your life, poor as it is. You may perhaps have some pleasant, thrilling, glorious hours, even in a poor- house. The setting sun is reflected from the windows of the alms-house as brightly as from the rich property owner's abode; the snow melts before its door as early in the spring. I see that a quiet mind may live as contentedly there, and have as cheering thoughts, as in a palace. The town's poor seem to me often to live the most independent lives of any. Maybe they are simply great enough to receive without misgiving. Most think of themselves that they are above being supported by the town; but it oftener happens that they are not above supporting themselves by dishonest means, which should be more disreputable. Cultivate poverty like a garden herb, like sage. Do not trouble yourself much to get new things, whether clothes or friends. Turn the old; return to them. Things do not change; we change. Sell your clothes and keep your thoughts. God will see that you do not want society.

Do not seek so anxiously to be developed, to be recruited, to subject yourself to many influences to be played on; it is all dissipation. You say that you want to be shown the way, but thus you only find their way. The philosopher said: "From an army of three divisions, one can take away its general and put it in immediate disorder; from a person most abject and vulgar, one cannot ever take away their thought." These forces do not sleep, and will sing to you in your darkest hours, calling you to the safety and comfort within their ranks.

Humility, like darkness, reveals the heavenly lights. The shadows of poverty and meanness gather around us, "and lo! creation widens to our view." We are often reminded that if there were bestowed on us the wealth of Crœsus, our aims must still be the same, and our means essentially the same. Moreover, if you are restricted in your range by poverty, if you cannot buy books and newspapers, for instance, you are but confined to the most significant and vital experiences; you are compelled to deal with the material which yields the most sugar and the most nutrients. It is life near the bone that is sweetest. You are defended from being a trifler. Superfluous wealth can buy superfluities only. Money is not required to buy one necessary of the soul.

My neighbors tell me of their adventures with famous gentlemen and ladies, what notabilities they met at the dinner-table; but I am no more interested in such things than in the contents of the Daily Times. The interest and the conversation are about costume and manners chiefly; but a goose is a goose still, dress it as you will. They tell me of California and Texas, of England and the Indies, of the Honorable Mr. —— of Georgia or of Massachusetts, all transient and fleeting phenomena, 'til I am ready to leap from their court-yard like the Mameluke bey, who escaped a massacre by leaping on his horse and riding away. I delight to come to my bearings,—not to walk in procession with pomp and parade, in a conspicuous place, but to walk alongside the Builder of the universe, if I may. Not to live in this restless, nervous, bustling, trivial Nineteenth Century, but to stand or sit thoughtfully while it goes by. What are people celebrating? They are all on a committee of arrangements, and hourly expect a speech from somebody. I love to weigh, to settle, to gravitate toward that which most strongly and rightfully attracts me;—not hang by the beam of the scale and try to weigh less,—not suppose a case, but take the case that is; to travel the only path I can, and that on which no power can resist me. Let us not play kitty-benders like children, urging each other to find the thinnest ice possible, that we might put on a superficial show with our abrupt chilling—there is a solid bottom every where, if we dare to find it. A traveler asked a girl standing by if the swamp before him had a hard bottom. The girl replied that it had. But presently the traveler's horse sank in up to the girths, and he observed to the girl, "I thought you said that this bog had a hard bottom." "So it has," answered the latter, "but you have not got half way to it yet." So it is with the bogs and quicksands of society; but she is an old girl that knows it. Only what is thought, said, or done at a certain rare coincidence is good. I would not be one of those who will foolishly drive a nail into mere lath and plastering; such a deed would keep me awake nights. Give me a hammer, and let me feel for the furring. Do not depend on the putty. Drive a nail home and clinch it so faithfully that you can wake up in the night and think of your work with satisfaction. So will help you God, and so only if you do so. Every nail driven should be as another rivet in the machine of the universe, you carrying on the work.

Rather than love, than money, than fame, give me truth. I sat at a table where rich food and wine were in abundance, and societal compliance in excess, but sincerity and truth were not present; and I went away hungry from the inhospitable board. They talked to me of the age of the wine and the fame of the vintage; but I thought of an older, a newer, and purer wine, of a more glorious vintage, which they had not got, and could not buy. The style, the house and grounds and "entertainment" pass for nothing. I called on the king, but he made me wait in his hall, and conducted like a man incapacitated for hospitality. There was a man in my neighborhood who lived in a hollow tree. His manners were truly regal. I should have done better had I called on him.

How long shall we sit in our porticoes practicing idle and musty virtues, which any work would make impertinent? As if one were to begin the day by hiring someone to hoe their potatoes; and in the afternoon go forth to practice Christian meekness, long-suffering, and charity with goodness aforethought! Consider the premature pride and stagnant self-complacency of humankind. This generation inclines to congratulate itself on being the last of an illustrious line; and in Boston and London and Paris and Rome, thinking of its long descent, it speaks of its bloodline's progress in art and science and literature with satisfaction. "Yes, we have done great deeds, and sung divine songs, which shall never die,"—that is, as long as we can remember them. The learned societies and great people of Assyria,—where are they? What youthful philosophers and experimentalists we are! There is not one of my readers who has yet lived a whole human life. These may be but the spring months in the life of the race. If we have had the seven-years' itch, we have not seen the seventeen-year locust yet in Concord. We are acquainted with a mere speck of the globe on which we live. Most have not delved six feet beneath the surface, nor leaped as many above it. We know not where we are. Beside, we are sound asleep nearly half our time. Yet we esteem ourselves wise, and have an established order on the surface. Truly, we are deep thinkers, we are ambitious spirits! As I stand over the insect crawling amid the pine needles on the forest floor, and endeavoring to conceal itself from my sight, and ask myself why it will cherish those humble thoughts, and hide its head from me who might, perhaps, be its benefactor, and impart to its race some cheering information, I am reminded of the greater Benefactor and Intelligence that stands over me, the human insect.

There is an incessant influx of novelty into the world, and yet we tolerate incredible dullness. I need only suggest what kind of sermons are still listened to in the most enlightened countries. There are such embellished words as joy and sorrow, but they are only the burden of a psalm, sung with a dead nasal twang, while we believe in the ordinary and mean. We do not see magic. We think that we can change our clothes only. It is said that the British Empire is very large and respectable, and that the United States are a first-rate power. We do not believe that a powerful tide rises and falls behind every person which can float the British Empire like a wood chip on the ocean, if they should ever harbor it in their mind. Who knows what sort of seventeen-year locust will next come out of the ground? The government of the world I live in was not framed, like that of Britain, in after-dinner conversations over the wine. I do not know how to distinguish between my waking life and a dream. Are we not always living the life that we imagine we are? We have lived, not in proportion to the number of years that we have spent on the earth, but in proportion as we have enjoyed.

The life in us is like the water in the river. It may rise this year higher than humankind has ever known it, and flood the parched uplands; this may be the eventful year, which will drown out all our muskrats. It was not always dry land where we dwell. I see far inland the banks which the stream anciently washed, before science began to record its freshets. Every one has heard the story which has gone the rounds of New England, of a strong and beautiful bug which came out of the dry leaf of an old table of apple-tree wood, which had stood in a farmer's kitchen for sixty years, first in Connecticut, and afterward in Massachusetts,—from an egg deposited in the living tree many years earlier still, as appeared by counting the annual layers beyond it; which was heard gnawing out for several weeks, hatched perchance by the heat of an urn. Who does not feel their faith in a resurrection and immortality strengthened by hearing of this? Who knows what beautiful and winged life, whose egg has been buried for ages under many concentric layers of woodenness in the dead dry life of society, deposited at first in the sapwood of the green and living tree, which has been gradually converted into the semblance of its well- seasoned tomb,—heard perchance gnawing out now for years by the astonished family of humans, as they sat round the festive board,—may unexpectedly come forth from amidst society's most trivial and overlooked furniture, to enjoy its perfect summer life at last!

Character of that morrow does not come about with the mere lapse of time, but rather, with thinking and doing. The brilliant light of truth which puts out our eyes seems to be only darkness to us. But we may catch a glimpse of it, and see a greater truth to come.

There is more day to dawn, if we are awake. The sun is but a morning star.

THE END

ACKNOWLEDGMENTS

Ken Kifer, for keeping me company throughout my editing journey and providing guidance with your *Walden* breakdowns and analyses. When the work got tough, your friendly words made things seem simpler.

Damion Searls, for editing *The Journal of Henry David Thoreau, 1837–1861*. Through your work, I got to know him.

Henry David Thoreau, for waking me up, and then giving me something magical to do.

ABOUT THE AUTHOR

Henry David Thoreau
(July 12, 1817 – May 6, 1862)

"His soul was made for the noblest society; he had in a short life exhausted the capabilities of this world; wherever there is knowledge, wherever there is virtue, wherever there is beauty, he will find a home." - Ralph Waldo Emerson